THE FATHERS
OF THE CHURCH

MEDIAEVAL CONTINUATION

VOLUME 4

THE FATHERS
OF THE CHURCH

MEDIAEVAL CONTINUATION

BL. HENRY SUSO
WISDOM'S WATCH UPON THE HOURS

Translated by

EDMUND COLLEDGE, O.S.A.

THE CATHOLIC UNIVERSITY OF AMERICA PRESS
Washington, D.C.

Copyright 1994
THE CATHOLIC UNIVERSITY OF AMERICA PRESS
All rights reserved

Printed in the United States of America

The paper used in this publication meets the minimum
requirements of the American National Standards for
Information Science—Permanence of Paper for Printed Library
materials,
ANSI Z39.48-1984
∞

LIBRARY OF CONGRESS CATALOGING-IN-PUBLICATION DATA
Seuse, Heinrich, 1295-1366.

   [Horologium sapientiae. English]
   Wisdom's watch upon the hours / an English translation by Edmund
Colledge of the critical Latin edition of Henry Suso's Horologium
Sapientiae by Pius Künzle and Dominikus Planzer.
     p.   cm.—(The Fathers of the church, mediaeval continuation ; v. 4)
   Includes bibliographical references and indexes.
   1. Mysticism—Early works to 1800. I. Colledge, Edmund.
   II. Künzle, Pius. III. Planzer, Dominikus. IV. Title. V.
Series.
BV5080.S4814   1994   93-23232
248.2'2—dc20
ISBN 0-8132-0792-4

In Loving Memory of
Ursula Fleming

CONTENTS

PREFACE

It was an occasion of great satisfaction to the learned world that in 1977 the long-awaited critical edition of the *Horologium Sapientiae*, on which Dominikus Planzer, O.P., had worked for many years, but which remained incomplete at his death, was successfully concluded and issued by his Swiss confrere, Pius Künzle; but soon thereafter, scholars were saddened at the news that he, too, had died. It is good to remember that he did see the publication of his masterly edition, and the beginnings at least of the critical acclaim that it has since received.

The translator recalls with happiness his only meeting, many years ago, in Lucerne, with Fr. Dominikus, and the friendly correspondence that was exchanged with Fr. Pius when this translation was first being considered.

He wishes to record his own great indebtedness to two younger scholars who have helped him in this work, Frank Mantello, now of the Catholic University of America, who has examined his translations with an expert and searching eye, and J. C. Marler, of the Department of Philosophy in the University of St. Louis, Missouri, who has given him much advice and encouragement. That they took time from their own much more pressing needs to befriend him is a mark of their generosity.

He would also express his gratitude to the Augustinian community of Marylake in Ontario, whose kind hospitality made possible the continuation of this work.

ABBREVIATIONS

AFP	*Archivum Fratrum Praedicatorum*
CCL	*Corpus Christianorum, Series Latina*
CG	St. Thomas Aquinas, *Summa Contra Gentiles*
Conf.	St. Augustine, *Confessiones*
CSEL	*Corpus Scriptorum Ecclesiasticorum Latinorum*
DS	*Dictionnaire de Spiritualité*
MS	*Mediaeval Studies*
RAM	*Revue d'Ascétique et Mystique*
S	*Scriptorium*
ST	St. Thomas Aquinas, *Summa Theologiae*

SELECT BIBLIOGRAPHY

Texts

Anicii Manlii Severini Boethii Philosophiae Consolatio. Ed. L. Bieler. CCL 94. Turnhout, 1957.

Heinrich Seuse: Deutsche Schriften. Ed. K. Bihlmeyer. Stuttgart, 1907. Reprint. Frankfurt, 1961.

Kraus, Carl von. Cf. Lachmann.

Künzle, P., ed. *Heinrich Seuses Horologium Sapientiae. Erste kritische Ausgabe unter Benützung der Vorarbeiten von Dominikus Planzer, O.P.* Fribourg, 1977.

Lachmann, E., ed. *Die Gedichte Walthers von der Vogelweide.* Revised by Carl von Kraus. Darmstadt, 1926.

Marigo, A. ed. *Dante Alighieri: De vulgari eloquentia.* Florence, 1938.

Notermans, J., ed. *Hendrijk van Veldeke. 25 Minneliederen.* Gorinchem, 1966.

Petschenig, M., ed. *Conlationes.* CSEL 2. Vienna, 1886.

Reichert, B., ed. *Acta capitulorum generalium ordinis praedicatorum.* Rome, 1899.

Secondary Sources

Ancelet-Hustache, Jeanne. "Elisabeth Stagel." DS 4 (1960): 588–89.

———. "Le problème de l'authenticité de la Vie de Suso." In *Colloque de Strasbourg.* Paris, 1963, 193–205.

Baier, Walter. *Untersuchungen zu den Passionsbetrachtungen in der Vita Christi von Ludolf von Sachsen.* 3 vols. Salzburg, 1977.

Baldwin, Mary. "Some Difficult Words in *Ancrene Riwle.*" MS 38 (1976): 268–90.

Bizet, Jean-A. "Henri Suso." DS 7 (1969): 234–57.

Clark, James M. *The Great German Mystics: Eckhart, Tauler and Suso.* Oxford, 1949.

———. *Suso: The Life of the Servant.* London, 1952.

———. *The Little Book of Eternal Wisdom and Little Book of Truth.* London, 1953.

Colledge, Edmund. "South Netherlands Book of Hours Made for England." S 32 (1978): 55–57.

———. "Meister Eckhart: His Times and His Writings." *The Thomist* 42 (1978): 240–58.

———. "If All the World Were Paper: Henry Suso's Use of a Much-travelled Commonplace." AFP 50 (1980): 113–16.

——— and J. C. Marler. "'Mystical' Pictures in the Suso 'Exemplar'—MS Strasbourg 2929." AFP 54 (1984): 293–354.

——— and J. C. Marler. "'Poverty of the Will': Ruusbroec, Eckhart and *The Mirror of Simple Souls.*" In *Jan van Ruusbroec: the Sources, Content and Sequels of His Mysticism.* Louvain, 1984, 14–47.

——— and J. C. Marler. "*Tractatus Magistri Johannis Gerson De Mistica Theologia.* St. Pölten, Diözesanarchiv MS 25." MS 41 (1979): 354–80.

——— and Bernard McGinn. *Meister Eckhart. Selections from His Latin and German Works.* New York, 1981.

_____ and James Walsh. *A Book of Showings to the Anchoress Julian of Norwich.* Toronto, 1978.

Courcelle, Pierre. "Étude critique sur les commentaires de la *Consolation* de Boèce (ixe–xve siècles)." *Archives d'histoire doctrinale et littéraire du moyen âge* 14 (1939): 5–140.

_____. *La Consolation de Philosophie dans le tradition littéraire.* Paris, 1967.

Deböngnie, Pierre. "Henri Suso et *l'Imitation de Jésus-Christ*." RAM 21 (1940): 242–68.

dell'Acqua, Gian A. *Arte Lombarde dai Visconti agli Sforza.* Milan, 1959.

Fleming, John V. *The "Roman de la Rose": A Study in Allegory and Iconography.* Princeton, 1969.

Hussey, Stanley S. "Latin and English in The Scale of Perfection." MS 35 (1973): 456–76.

Kaeppeli, Thomas. *Scriptores ordinis praedicatorum medii aevi* 1. Rome, 1970.

Kärcher, Ludwig. "Heinrich Suso aus dem Predigerorden. Abhandlung über Ort und Zeit seiner Geburt." *Freiburger Diözesan-Archiv* 3 (1868): 202–5.

Mommaers, P., and N. De Paepe. *Jan van Ruusbroec: The Sources, Content and Sequels of His Mysticism.* Louvain, 1984.

Perkins, Justin. "The Revelation of the Blessed Apostle Paul." *Journal of the American Oriental Society* 8 (1866): 183–212.

Ragusa, Isa, and Rosalie B. Green. *Meditations on the Life of Christ.* Princeton, 1961.

Rodriguez, Otilio. *Leyenda Aurea Teresiana.* Madrid, 1970.

Rowland, Beryl. *Animals with Human Faces: A Guide to Animal Symbolism.* Knoxville, 1973.

Sargent, Michael G. "The Transmission by the English Carthusians of Some Late Mediaeval Spiritual Writings." *Journal of Ecclesiastical History* 27 (1976): 225–40.

_____. *James Grenehalgh as Textual Critic. Analecta Cartusiana.* 2 vols. Salzburg, 1984.

Spencer, Eleanor P. "L'Horloge de Sapience: Bruxelles Bib. Royale MS IV.111." S 17 (1963): 277–99.

Stahl, William. *Macrobius: Commentary on the Dream of Scipio.* New York, 1952.

INTRODUCTION

WISDOM'S WATCH UPON THE HOURS

Introduction

1. Suso's Birth, Parentage, and Life

The earliest statement concerning the date of Suso's birth is in an anonymous edition of his works, A.D. 1518, where it is claimed that when he died in 1366, he was eighty-six years of age. But the year 1280 seems too early by far; of the numerous other suggestions later made, much the most probable is that he was born in 1300.[1]

(2) It was once commonly accepted that he was born in Constance, but the early chroniclers, including the Dominicans, do not state that this was so. They express themselves in general terms, calling him *"Suevus* by nation"; and Kärcher observes that when, towards the end of the seventeenth century, the magistrates at Ulm, where he had died and was buried, were asked to permit his remains to be transferred to Constance, it was never stated that this was his birthplace. Kärcher makes out what seems to be a good case for his belief that he was in fact born in nearby Ueberlingen,[2] though not all of his arguments are equally convincing.

(3) His father was a knight, born of a landowning family, the von Bergs. He had done as many of his equals were doing, and had turned to commerce to augment his dwindling fortunes. In Constance, he had married the daughter of a patrician family, named Süs or Süse ("Suso" is a Latinization of this name, first given currency by Denifle, the Austrian Domini-

---

1. For various theories, cf. P. Künzle, ed., *Heinrich Seuses Horologium Sapientiae. Erste kritische Ausgabe unter Benützung der Vorarbeiten von Dominikus Planzer, O.P* (Fribourg, 1977) 2–3.
2. Ludwig Kärcher, "Heinrich Suso aus dem Predigerorden. Abhandlung über Ort und Zeit seiner Geburt," *Freiburger Diözesan-Archiv* 3 (1868): 202–5.

can, who took "Heinrich Seuse" as his own religious name, and who was the nineteenth-century pioneer in the study of late medieval German spirituality). It seems to have been out of devotion to his mother, whose piety evidently influenced him strongly, that when Suso entered religion, he chose to be known by her name rather than by his father's.[3]

(4) The story goes that he joined the Dominican order at the age of thirteen, two years younger than the stipulated age, in return for a gift of money from the von Bergs, and that he was for long tormented by scruples over the legality of his admission and profession, scruples which were at length quieted by Eckhart, after he had been sent for higher studies to Cologne. But we shall be wise to treat all the stories about intimate relations between the two men with much caution, for they are based on mere conjecture.

(5) Controversy will probably never cease over the disputed authenticity of the *Vita* (despite its title, a biography written in German, often called in English *The Life of the Servant*), which claims to have been written partly by him, partly by a spiritual daughter, Elisabeth Stagel, a nun at Töss near Winterthur. Bihlmeyer considered the work genuine, Preger was convinced that it was fraudulent, Clark adopted a somewhat vacillating attitude, but inclined, for what may seem not very strong reasons, to treat it as a true record of Suso's life.[4] The present editor is disposed to accept it as genuine, but it would be idle to use this work to supplement what we can learn of his inner life and his thought, since the details that we find in the *Vita* could easily have been borrowed by some pious fabricator from what are unquestionably his authentic works.

(6) These are, in German, *The Little Book of Truth* and *The Little Book of Eternal Wisdom*, the second of which he later treated as a preliminary sketch for his only Latin work, his masterpiece, *Wisdom's Watch upon the Hours*. Soon we shall dis-

---

3. Künzle, 2.

4. For a recent statement of the "inauthentic" viewpoint, cf. Jeanne Ancel-et-Hustache, "Le problème de l'authenticité de la Vie de Suso," in *Colloque de Strasbourg* (Paris, 1963) 193–205; for arguments against this, J.-A.Bizet, "Henri Suso," DS 7 (1969): 234–57.

cuss the important differences between *Eternal Wisdom* and the *Watch*. There will now be few to defend the authenticity of *The Little Book of Love*. Preger discovered the manuscript of this work and was zealous in promoting his discovery, but he did not convince Denifle or many of their contemporaries. And Denifle was even less persuaded by Preger's presentation of a Munich manuscript which, he considered, contained the best tradition of Elisabeth Stagel's edition of Suso's letters. In 1907 Bihlmeyer produced a much superior edition, from many more manuscripts than were known either to Preger or to Denifle; but the letters are characterized by a mild and diffuse piety, highly edifying, but of little help towards elucidating the problems presented by Suso's mature treatises.

(7) There is much discrepancy between what the data will tell us of Suso's external life, which, after the early years, when he was troubled by the repercussions of the great Eckhart scandal, would appear to have been passed in tranquillity and happiness, so that he attracted the attention of none of the chroniclers of those unquiet times, and what his own writings reveal to us about his personal history. One must, of course, always allow for the literary extravagances of a gifted writer, of a temperament both poetic and romantic, as the *Watch* shows Suso to have been. Then, too, some of the turbulent unhappiness that the *Watch* records may be his own compensations for what must have seemed, even to him, the humdrum life that he passed, as Tauler and others of his confreres did, in the "care for women," the spiritual direction, by letters, sermons and retreats, of convents of nuns. And his many allusions in the *Watch* to the envy and betrayal that he had encountered may be his oblique manner of testifying that as an academic teacher he did not score the success of the young Eckhart; in the pulpit he did not attract the same attention as did Eckhart as an older man (for which he would hardly have wished) or even the genial, equable Tauler. We may think that the *Watch* dwells too long on the disappointments and frustrations of one who had retreated from uncongenial society into a solitude of his own making, but "it is the pardonable vanity of lonely people everywhere to assume that they have no counterpart."

(8) Yet the *Watch* is very much more than "a history of tears." It gained its great success in Suso's own lifetime because readers found in it a celebration of the joys and rewards of divine Wisdom's love that can scarcely be matched in all the history of Christian letters.

(9) One of the benefits that Wisdom conferred upon Suso was a commendable prudence. Early in his career as a writer he had come to the defense of Eckhart, who had died condemned for heresy, not so wholly repentant as he has usually been shown;[5] and Tauler and Suso had, since then, found their own methods of dissenting from the adverse verdict of the Holy See. This, the *Vita* tells us, had landed Suso in hot water.

(10) Perhaps he comes closest in his writings to examining the teaching that is central to all of Eckhart's thought, "the birth of the Word in the soul," in chapter 5 of *The Little Book of Truth*, when the Disciple asks his interlocutor, who has already been identified as Truth and soon will be called "the pure Word": "What do you call the manner in which man attains to his blessedness?"[6] He receives the reply: "One can accept it as a kind of birth, as it is written in St. John's Gospel that God has given power and ability to become his sons to all those who have been born of nothing else than God. And that happens in the same way as one commonly understands of birth. For whoever gives birth to something else forms it in his likeness and in him, and endows it with being and action like to his own. And therefore, in a man who has abandoned himself and whose only Father is God. . . ." But this is so carefully qualified—"a *kind* of birth"—and our dual identity, as children of God and of human parents, is so stressed that all Eckhart's extravagance and hyperbole is avoided, and the passage becomes an implicit rebuke to such hyperbole. We can see the same process at work elsewhere: in chapter 3, Suso writes: "In this issuing forth, all creatures have attained their God, for

5. Cf. Edmund Colledge, "Meister Eckhart: His Times and His Writings," *The Thomist* 42 (1978): 240–58.

6. *Heinrich Seuse: Deutsche Schriften*, ed. K. Bihlmeyer (Stuttgart, 1907; reprint, Frankfurt, 1961) 340.

when the creature finds itself to be a creature, it acknowledges its Creator and God";[7] and in chapter 4 he tells us that God's all-ness should bring the self to "knowledge of its own nothingness."[8]

(11) Throughout *The Little Book of Truth,* Suso supports what we may consider as his "moderate Eckhartism" by adducing the Fathers, especially what he knows of pseudo-Dionysius, Augustine and Bernard; but he is at pains to insist that truth, and the answers to the problems posed by our disordered feelings and thinking, are to be found only in the Person and the life of the incarnate Christ. "The cross signifies that a man who has truly abandoned himself, outwardly and inwardly, must at all times be resigned to everything that God wants him to suffer, wherever it may come from, and that he must be disposed to die to himself and to accept it to the glory of his heavenly Father. Such men have an interior nobility and an outward guard. . . . However much they suffer, their own resignation teaches them to despise it. Whichever way their heads might turn, the body followed the head; and that signified how wholeheartedly and faithfully they imitated Christ's life, which was their pure mirror."[9]

(12) In *The Little Book of Truth,* Suso can be seen taking his leave of "Eckhartism," dissociating himself from the problems with which it had beset him, insisting on the answers that he had found, moving towards the simplicity that informs all of the *Watch*; and it is in the light of this that his famous defense of Eckhart against the "nameless Wild One"[10] must be read. But there were those who did not read it so, as he tells us in the *Vita.*

(13) If we assume this work to be in part his, as the present writer believes, Suso recounts that on one occasion he traveled to a chapter of his order in the Netherlands, where on arrival he was attacked by two prominent friars. "He was made to answer with a quaking heart, and many things were said of

7. Ibid., 332   8. Ibid., 336.
9. Ibid., 339
10. Cf. Edmund Colledge: "Meister Eckhart: His Times and His Writings," 254.

him. One was, they said, that he had made books in which false doctrine was contained, through which the whole land was being defouled with heretical filth. For this he was very ill-used, with harsh and threatening words, which promised him great troubles; yet God and the world knew him to be innocent."[11] Although he writes of "books," it is probably *The Book of Truth*, generally regarded as his first work, which is concerned, and his defense in it of Eckhart. Kärcher thought that the Dominican chapter in the Low Countries must have been that of 1337 at Valenciennes,[12] but information on this matter was then inadequate. It was much more probably at the Maastricht chapter of 1330,[13] (less than two years after the promulgation of *In agro dominico*, be it recalled) that this took place. Of Eckhart and his condemnation, and of this attack on Suso—evidently, as he had to some extent shown himself to be, as Eckhart's supporter—there is no mention; but the acts show that the chapter was in an uproar over the heretical and schismatic activities of the former minister-general of the Franciscans, Michael of Cesena; and the acts conclude: "The following is a list of the errors or heresies of Friar Michael of Cesena,"[14] very much in the manner of *In agro dominico*. One suspects that the Dominicans may have welcomed this opportunity to divert attention from the aberrations of their own brother to those of a friar of a different rule. But this affair, so far as it concerned Eckhart, seems to have blown over; and Suso was careful never again to take such risks.

(14) Yet, though he remained thereafter untouched by suspicions of his orthodoxy, the minor schism provoked by Michael of Cesena's protector, the emperor Louis of Bavaria, brought further troubles to Suso. The civic authorities of Constance incurred the penalties of the papal interdict, since a show of loyalty to the emperor was essential for their safety; and they obliged the city's Dominicans, who did not weaken in their allegiance to the Holy See, to leave. It may be, as Bihl-

11. Ed. Bihlmeyer, 68.
12. Cf. B. Reichert, ed., *Acta capitulorum generalium ordinis praedicatorum* (Rome, 1899) 2:293–95.
13. Ibid., 2:194–205.   14. Ibid., 2:204–5.

meyer suggests,[15] that for a time Suso continued his preaching tours, after he went away from Constance. That would account for the story, in chapter 25 of the *Vita*, of how during the Black Death (which was at its most virulent in Germany in 1348, the year in which his community went into exile), Suso was almost murdered in a village on the Rhine by those who suspected him of poisoning the wells. But he made his way to Ulm, entered the community there, and died, peacefully, it seems, on 25 January 1365. There are no documents to support the stories that he was prior of Ulm, and that at the general chapter of 1363 he was once again accused of heresy. There is, however, evidence that he was already widely venerated for his sanctity, and that his fame as a writer of great piety spread. He was held in special esteem by the Brethren of the Common Life, and when John Vos, the prior of Windesheim, was in Constance for the Council, he and his party went to the Dominican church and visited with great devotion the cell once inhabited by Suso, "who by the inspiration of the Holy Spirit wrote the *Watch*."[16] In 1831 Pope Gregory XVI confirmed his veneration *per viam cultus*—that is, because of evidence of continued popular devotion—and permitted his feast to be celebrated in the Dominican Order on March 11.

2. Wisdom's Watch upon the Hours: *Chronology*

(15) Suso is thought to have completed his vernacular works, with the one exception of his German autobiography, the *Vita*, before the publication of the *Watch*. There has been much argument about the date of its composition, but Künzle was satisfied with Bihlmeyer's solution, which he was able to reinforce with further supporting evidence.

(16) The prologues to the *Watch* and to the German *Little Book of Eternal Wisdom* make it equally clear that both works originated in the *Hundred Meditations*. The *Watch*'s prologue concludes its account: "For the sake of brevity I have not here written these meditations in full, but I did faithfully record them in our own German vernacular for the benefit of devout

15. Ed. Bihlmeyer, 130*–31*.   16. Ibid., 138*.

men, both learned and simple." In *Eternal Wisdom* we are told
that the meditations on the sufferings of Christ came to him,
the last ten, dealing with the Passion and the death on the
Cross, through supernatural grace, and how for the benefit
of others he recorded them ". . . in German, because they had
so come . . . from God."[17]

(17) The clearest evidence that we possess for dating *Eternal
Wisdom* is in chapter 23 of the *Vita*. This was Suso's last work,
rewritten by him, as he recounts, from the material furtively
prepared by his "spiritual daughter," Elisabeth Stagel, a Dominican nun enclosed at Töss near Winterthur. The probable
date of her death was c. 1360,[18] and Suso is known to have died
in 1366.[19] Writing thus in the 1360s, he tells of a happening
evidently still vividly recollected: how once, at a Dominican
chapter in the Low Countries, he was arraigned to appear
before a commission, which treated him very harshly, "for he
had been accused of many things, one of which (already recounted) was that, according to them, he had written books
(*bücher*) containing false doctrine, through which a whole region had been polluted with filthy heresy."[20]

(18) Künzle argues, convincingly, that this must have occurred in 1330, when a chapter of Suso's own province and another of the entire Dominican order were held at Maastricht.
He considers that the books in which Suso's brethren suspected heresy were two in number, and that the handling that
they received is described allegorically in Book I, chapter 13
of the *Watch*, when we are told how "the Disciple" had the
misfortune to choose for a wife a woman whom he loved
dearly, but who "out of a lover, turned into an enemy." Plainly,
this was inspired by Osee's mournful story. Suso goes on:
"After this, 'adding sorrow to sorrow,' and inflicting a wound
where I was already wounded, she took away from me my
dearest kinsman,"[21] which may, as Künzle and others have considered, or may not refer to Eckhart's condemnation. Then

17. Ibid., 197.
18. Jeanne Ancelet-Hustache, "Elisabeth Stagel," DS 4 (1960): 588–89.
19. Ed. Bihlmeyer, 136*.   20. Ibid., 68.
21. *Watch*, 186.

"my most cruel bride intensified her anger against me . . . in this way. For I had only two sheep left to me, eating with me from my platter and drinking with me, and working to help me in every way; and then, when I least expected it, there came 'evening wolves,' carrying off my lambs and tearing them to pieces, rending them miserably with all kinds of bodily death."

(19) Beyond doubt, Künzle is right in asserting that the *Watch* is here telling us in allegory what the *Vita* was to relate as historical narrative, that the "two sheep," so dear to Suso, which had helped him in his work, are two books of his that his brethren held as suspect. One of these must have been the German *Book of Truth*, in chapter 6 of which the "Disciple," Suso, enters into a Boethian dialogue with "the nameless Wild One."[22] The present editor has elsewhere written: "In the 'Wild One,' Suso has drawn a vivid and skilled portrait of the anonymous masses who had gone astray, listening too readily to 'liberty of the spirit' and such other perversions of the Christian faith, identifying Eckhart too easily with the other heresiarchs whom they had followed."[23]

(20) In *The Book of Truth*, Suso was saying, as openly as he dared, that among the "Wild One's" other errors, it had been mistaken in reading its own false beliefs into what Eckhart had written. In appealing to him, the "Wild One" says: "I have heard it said that there was a great teacher . . ." (*daz ein hoher meister si gewesen*); and the tense that Suso uses indicates that the "teacher" was by this time dead. It follows therefore that *The Book of Truth* must have been written between 30 April 1328, when John XXII, writing to the archbishop of Cologne, referred to Eckhart as already deceased,[24] and the convening of the Maastricht chapters in 1330; and this must also be the date *ante quem* for the composition of *Eternal Wisdom*.

(21) Another matter should be briefly mentioned. Bihlmeyer and others have claimed that in his last years Suso recorded, in chapter 6 of the *Vita*, that the dead Eckhart had

22. Ed. Bihlmeyer, 352–57.
23. Edmund Colledge and Bernard McGinn, *Meister Eckhart. Selections from His Latin and German Works* (New York, 1981) 16.
24. Ibid., 14.

appeared to him to describe the wonders of the Beatific Vision, which he now enjoyed;[25] but it has recently been shown[26] that it is far more probable that Suso is here referring to a second German Dominican "Meister Eckhart," who had served as *diffinitor* at the general chapter held at Valenciennes in 1337, and who died on his return journey. That it was he who had been shown to "Henry, the Disciple of Everlasting Wisdom," is recorded in the sixteenth century by their Tuscan confrere Leander Alberti; and in Suso's own lifetime his critics, however anxious they may have been to find occasion for scandal, can hardly have been guilty of this particular mistake.

(22) So far, we have seen that *Eternal Wisdom* must have been written and published before 1330, if it was attacked at Maastricht, and that, if the second of the "two sheep" was *The Book of Truth*, it must have been composed in the brief period *ante* 30 April 1328, and the convening in 1330 of the Maastricht chapters. Künzle's examination of the content and style of *Eternal Wisdom* and the *Watch* was adequate demonstration that the German *Eternal Wisdom*, itself in part a reworking of the *Hundred Meditations*, served Suso as the material that, in the Latin *Watch*, he extensively revised and augmented. But it would seem that no unduly long interval passed before the *Watch* was issued.

(23) This work is, in its prologue, presented to Hugh of Vaucemain, who became Dominican Master General at Pentecost, 1333. Suso writes that Hugh's spiritual gifts and zeal are attested "by your letters, in which as a father you exhort your dear sons to seek peace and fraternal love";[27] and although we know that Hugh during his years in office sent out in all seven "exhortatory letters," Bihlmeyer was able to establish that Suso's prologue alludes only to the first, written as soon as he was elected. Thus, the prologue cannot have been written before that event.

(24) Yet it is evident that the prologue was composed after

25. Ed. Bihlmeyer, 22–23.
26. Edmund Colledge and Bernard McGinn, 18.
27. *Watch*, 56.

the rest of the work was finished. What Suso writes of its plan and subject matter, its style and the circumstances under which it was written show this. How long the writing of the book itself occupied we do not know, but there is in it no sign of haste or incompleteness. Perhaps we can assign a period of time after which the *Watch*'s composition was undertaken through Suso's different treatment of two separate historical events.

(25) About the first, Eckhart's condemnation of 27 March 1329, by *In agro dominico*, we can only deduce from Suso's silence. In the *Watch* there are not even the discreet allusions to it that we find in *The Little Book of Truth*. As we have seen, Künzle thought that Suso's "dearest kinsman, only solace in this world of my heart" was Eckhart, but we have no other evidence to support the suggestion that the two friars ever did establish this close relationship—chapter 6 of the *Vita* probably does not—and the rest of the *Watch* may make us think that Suso preferred to regard this distressing episode as now over and done with, and to allow his readers to forget about it. What is more, as the present writer hopes soon to show in his forthcoming examination of Suso's autobiography (for he follows J.-A. Bizet and dissents from Jeanne Ancelet-Hustache in accepting the *Vita* as genuine), Suso remained critical, not of Eckhart's orthodoxy, but of the dangers that his writings contained for the uncritically devout.

(26) The second event that Suso reports is given detailed and elaborate treatment in Book I, chapter 5, the "allegory of the ram." Preger, followed by Bihlmeyer and others, identified the scene of this narrative as Constance (which has never been questioned), but believed that it described the impact upon the city of the strife between Avignon and the Holy Roman Empire. Künzle, however, was able to show that a different key, fitting what Suso narrated down to very small details, is possible: that it is a disguised story of how Constance was divided, during the year 1334, between the supporters of rival candidates for the episcopal see. Suso's allegory tells of the outcome, to him most satisfactory, of this dispute as achieved and now of common report, which suggests that by the time

that he had reached his fifth chapter, the events of the summer of 1334 were already past. This argues against Bihlmeyer's interpretation of the allegory, but in favor of the date of composition that for other reasons he had postulated.

3. The Watch and the Little Book of Eternal Wisdom.

(27) Although Suso's Latin was translated, early in the text's history, into a variety of European vernacular languages, there is no version in his own tongue, German. There are at least two different good reasons why this should be so. In the first place, there was already in circulation his own German treatise, *The Little Book of Eternal Wisdom,* which contained some of the *Watch*'s matter; but, more important than this, there would have been no object in Suso or anyone else attempting to produce a German version of the *Watch,* since the reading public to which it was directed had no need of any medium other than Latin.

(28) Künzle himself suggested that no scholar in Germany in Suso's own times would have considered it worth his while to undertake a translation of the *Watch* because there already existed what is in effect Suso's own preliminary draft for it, and Jeanne Ancelet-Hustache, in the 1977 re-edition of her French translations, which she calls Suso's *Oeuvres complètes,* excuses the absence from them of any version of the *Watch* on the grounds that there still was no satisfactory edition of the Latin (Künzle's work was to appear in the same year as her reprint), that she wished to avoid repetition (which would have been inevitable), and that "the text of Suso's only Latin work repeats for the most part that of the *Little Book.*" This is so wide of the mark that it cannot have been based upon any serious attention to the Latin, available to her in Strange's edition, by Künzle's own showing far from unreliable.

(29) The *Watch* omits entirely the *Book*'s third part, the "Hundred Meditations." The *Book* contains none of the *Watch*'s new prologue, Book I, chapters 1, 2, 5, 12 or 16; parts only of Book I, chapters 6, 7, 9, 13 and 15; and none of Book II, chapters 1, 3, 6, 7 and 8. When the *Watch* does use material from the *Book*, this has been re-ordered and rephrased with

such care that it would seem as if Suso had to hand the original notes and first drafts for his German work. This is especially evident in the pains he takes to restore the exact Latin wording of all his quotations from the Vulgate and the liturgy, the sources of which are often obscured in the vernacular renderings. But, more important than any of this, we can see his anxiety, in writing his Latin versions, to avoid both topics and terminology that might suggest that his thinking derived from that of Eckhart.

4. Reception and Circulation.

(30) That the *Watch* was, in the fourteenth century and thereafter, one of the three most popular devotional treatises in Western Europe, we have much evidence. Its only two rivals in general esteem were the pseudo-Bonaventure's *Meditations on the Life of Christ*[28] and Ludolph of Saxony's *Life of Christ.*[29] Pseudo-Bonaventure's *Meditations* is an older work; internal evidence points to its composition in the earliest years of the century. Walter Baier, the modern authority on Ludolph, has shown how, after his early years as a Dominican, which ended in Strasburg in 1339 (where he cannot have been unaffected by knowledge of Suso's personality and writings) he joined the Carthusians, but continued to practice "the apostolate of the pen," which found its finest expression in the *Life*, written, in Baier's opinion, after he had finished his term of office as prior of Coblence, and had retired, during the 1350s, to Mainz.

(31) One estimates the *Watch*'s appeal as one does that of the other two works: by the number of manuscripts that have survived, by those known to have existed which are now lost, by the vernacular translations made from them, by excerpts from it and allusions to it in other men's works, and by its early printed editions.

(32) Künzle knew of two hundred and thirty-three surviving

28. Cf. Isa Ragusa and Rosalie B. Green, *Meditations on the Life of Christ* (Princeton, 1961).

29. Cf. Walter Baier, *Untersuchungen zu den Passionsbetrachtungen in der Vita Christi von Ludolf von Sachsen*, 3 vols. (Salzburg, 1977).

manuscripts of the *Watch*, and of records of another eighty-eight that now seem to be lost. Early translations appeared in French, Dutch, Italian, English, Czech, Swedish, Danish, Hungarian and perhaps Polish. The French version ends with a dated poem of 28 April 1389. Jeanne Ancelet-Hustache knew of forty-eight complete or partial manuscripts of French translations, to which Künzle was able to add another fifteen. This *Orloge* was printed or reprinted five times. The Dutch version was even more popular: Stephanus Axters knew of three hundred and fifty-four extant manuscripts and of twenty-two now lost. Less so were the Italian and English translations, but the Italian was published by Simon de Luere at Venice in 1511, the English by William Caxton at Westminster, c. 1490. This English treatment, *Seven Points of True Love and Everlasting Wisdom*, has more the nature of a series of excerpts; and now that there is a critical Latin text available, and Michael Sargent is occupying himself with Carthusian editorial and scribal activity[30] —James Greenhalgh of Sheen showed concern with both the English and Latin texts[31]—it is to be hoped that there may be further study of it.

(33) Another, separate undertaking would be the examination of the use made by different writers of the *Watch*'s Latin in their devotional writings. Such a study would have value as showing which elements in Suso's work proved most telling to those drawing on him to make their own points, devotional, admonitory or moralizing.

(34) The first printed Latin edition seems to have appeared in Cologne, c. 1480, and in the years before 1540 nine others are known, two from Paris, four more from Cologne, one from Aals and two from Venice. All this points to the work's extravagant success in its first years after publication, a success that did not diminish until Europe was split into contending camps, in one of which Catholic teaching and devotion were no longer acceptable.

---

30. Cf. Michael G. Sargent, "The Transmission by the English Carthusians of Some Late Mediaeval Spiritual Writings," *Journal of Ecclesiastical History* 27 (1976): 225–40.

31. Cf. Michael G. Sargent, *James Grenehalgh as Textual Critic*, *Analecta Cartusiana*, 2 vols. (Salzburg, 1984).

(35) It is easy to see how Suso obtained this success. The doctrine of the *Watch* is sound; it is conveyed with a wealth of literary art, but it remains traditional and unexceptionable. The Dominicans' enemies (and they had many), if they hoped for any repetitions of the scandals of the 1320s, would have been disappointed. It has already been suggested that Suso, in this portrait of a Black Friar at his prayers, was seeking to obliterate recent, unhappy impressions. Yet his account of his own spiritual growth has allure. It is a dazzling treatment of the themes of romantic, Christian love, of a purified *Minne*, looking back to the courtly, chivalric past, the disappearance of which so many were lamenting. But the *Watch* is by no means blind to the world around, as Suso saw it. He has sharply critical things to say about trends in lay society and in religious life. We have written of the esteem that he and his book enjoyed among the Brethren of the Common Life, and it is a tribute to the shrewdness of his observation, his firm grasp upon the essentials of ascetic theology, and to his prescience, that he could, in Book II, chapter 2, in his use of that well-worn theme, the "art of dying," castigate the increase of secular hedonism and materialism in a fashion which remarkably anticipates the *Imitation* and the literature of the "Devotio Moderna."

(36) Even so, Suso was a man of his own times, his thought deeply rooted—as Eckhart's had been, and more so than in Tauler's case—in classical expositions by the Fathers, and in the method and content of modern scholastic philosophers and their works, even if he had taken warning from the troubles with his peers that Eckhart had experienced. In the Prologue, he confesses that before the *Horologium* was published, he had been gripped "by a certain human fear of jealous men." How this had modified what he might have written we can observe in the *Watch*'s Book I, chapter 11, where Suso's Latin is expounding, as his German had, the scholastics' distinction between the "two rewards," the essential reward and the accidental, which Suso has symbolized in the faithful spouse's golden crown and her second, the little coronet (or "halo") of Exodus 25.25. In *The Book of Wisdom,* Suso had written:

But essential reward lies in the contemplative union of the soul with the naked godhead, for it will never rest until it is led above all its powers and strength, and brought into the essential nature of the Persons, and into the simplest purity of the Being. And it is in this object that it finds satisfaction and eternal bliss. The more detached the going out, the more free the ascension; and the more free the ascension, the deeper the penetration into the wild desert and the profound abyss of the pathless godhead, into which it sinks, is swept away, and united in such a way that it cannot will anything but what God wills; and that is to be the same as God is, that is, that they are blessed by grace, as he is blessed by nature.[32]

(37) If we compare this with the version of the Latin now offered, with the paragraph beginning "But the essential reward consists indeed in the perfect conjunction of the soul with God . . .," we can see how drastically Suso has rewritten his first presentation of the topic, substituting harmless synonyms for the markedly Dionysian vocabulary which he had used in the German. "Naked godhead" becomes "God," his "essential nature" is now called "depths," the "wild desert" and the "profound abyss" are rechristened "spiritual things," and the soul, instead of "sinking," being "swept away" and "united," merely "surrenders itself." Most significant of all, the dangerous continuation of this, ". . . in such a way that it cannot will anything but what God wills, and that is to be the same as God is . . ." has been omitted altogether. Suso must have known well that Eckhart's teaching on "poverty of the will" had been condemned by the Church; he may also have known how more than suspect were the sources in which Eckhart had found some of this teaching.[33]

(38) Towards the end of Book I, chapter 13, we can see the same principles at work. Where in *The Book of Wisdom*, Suso had written: "Now hear the sweet music of the lute of a God-suffering man,"[34] Clark's expert eye had detected the equation God=suffering, suffering=God, so dear to Eckhart, as when,

32. Ed. Bihlmeyer, 245.
33. Cf. Edmund Colledge and J. C. Marler, "'Poverty of the Will': Ruusbroec, Eckhart and *The Mirror of Simple Souls*," in *Jan van Ruusbroec: the Sources, Content and Sequels of His Mysticism* (Louvain, 1984) 14–47.
34. Ed. Bihlmeyer, 250.

in *The Book of Divine Consolation*, one of his most masterly and extended treatments of the topic, he wrote:

> But if my suffering is in God, and God is suffering with me, how then can suffering be sorrow to me, if suffering loses its sorrow, and my sorrow is in God, and my sorrow is God? Truly, as God is truth and as I find the truth, I find my God, the Truth, there; and too, neither less nor more, as I find pure suffering for the love of God and in God, I find God my suffering. If anyone does not recognize this, let him blame his blindness, not me.[35]

But in the *Watch*, Suso is wary of such blind readers, and this passage has become: "if you wish to hear the harping of this spiritual man resounding sweetly. . . ."[36] Early in Book II, chapter 3, "A Concise Form for Spiritual Living," Wisdom directs the Disciple that

> If you want to obtain that perfection of all spiritual life, which everyone desires, if you want to work hard to acquire it, you must withdraw yourself from all harmful company and friendships, from all the people who frustrate your intention, in a word, from all mortal men, so far as that is compatible with the vows of your religious profession, always preserving the humble and prompt obedience which you owe to your superiors; and you must seize every opportunity of place and time to seek out somewhere to be at peace and gather contemplation's silent secrets, shunning this life's shipwrecks and fleeing from the uproars of this noisy world. . . . You should turn inward to yourself, and you should keep the doors of your heart carefully bolted, so far as you can, against sensory forms and earthly imaginings.[37]

Contrast this with the terseness of the corresponding passage in the *Book of Wisdom*:

> 1. Keep thyself detached from all men.
> 2. Keep thyself pure from all images introduced from outside.
> 3. Keep thyself from everything that might bring hindrance, attachment, and care.
> 4. Devote thy mind at all times to a secret divine contemplation. . . .[38]

35. Edmund Colledge and Bernard McGinn, 235.
36. *Watch*, 195.   37. Ibid., 259.
38. Ed. Bihlmeyer, 288.

(39) This shows well how clearly Suso had come to see that some of Eckhart's difficult concepts, his teaching on "abandonment," for example, and that the soul must attain "freedom from images," could not be presented so baldly as he had done in the *Book*, if readers of the *Watch* (even though, as the additions here make plain, the Latin is intended specifically for a learned and religious public) were not to attribute to him some of the tendencies which Eckhart's opponents held that his writings showed. "Sensory forms and earthly imaginings" is no kind of dilution, but it does represent a care—and an ability—for caution and moderation, which one may wish that Eckhart too had always possessed and used.

(40) If we examine the *Watch*'s Latin closely, comparing it with the German of the *Book*, we must be impressed by the pains and the attention to detail that Suso employed in his work of revision. We find the account of the beginnings of the dialogue with Wisdom, "One day, after matins, the same Disciple did as he was accustomed . . ." as in the *Book*,[39] but there, we have Suso's apology for having written his earlier treatise in his native tongue:

The words which are conceived in pure grace, and which flow from a living heart through a living mouth are different from when they are written down on dead parchment, and especially in the German language, for then they are somehow withered and faded, like roses that have been picked, for the lovely melody, moving men's hearts above all else, has fallen silent, and is dried up as it is received in dried-up hearts.[40]

(41) Justly, Clark observes that "Suso was one of the greatest exponents of the vernacular he criticized."[41] Yet we must remember that in what he was achieving, he was not helped by any tradition. Although there had been in Germany, as everywhere else in Europe, many previous attempts to transform the vernacular languages into media capable of treating Dante's "great themes of literature"—love and warfare and

---

39. *Watch*, 57; ed. Bihlmeyer, 196.   40. Ibid., 199.
41. James M. Clark, *The Little Book of Eternal Wisdom and Little Book of Truth* (London, 1953) 46, note 1.

men's commerce with God[42]—with the flexibility and eleva-
tion that writers of Latin could command, it was only in Suso's
own age, and through new masters such as Suso himself, that
such traditions were being established. He was seeking to do
with German what he had been schooled to achieve in Latin;
what he writes in *The Book of Wisdom* defines the total literary
effect at which he will aim in the *Watch*. His Latin too is to be
mellifluous, emotional, hortatory.

(42) In both versions, there is a general commendation of
the exercise of the "Hundred Meditations." In the German
prologue, there is the same justification as we find in the *Watch*
of the use of the dialogue form, and also Suso's warning
against overliteral interpretation of his allegories,[43] though
without the *Watch*'s specific scriptural examples, which, it
seems, he thought would be of profit only to the Latin's more
learned readers. There is no such submission of the German
for his superiors' approval as we find in the address to the
master general. Recent events, culminating in the 1329 condemnation of Eckhart, must have made it desirable for Suso
to show that he had nothing to fear, and every reason to expect
the approbation for which he was asking; and when he goes
on in his Latin prologue to write of his "human fear of jealous
men,"[44] and to defend the acceptability of private revelations
prudently scrutinized, one suspects that he is afraid that other
Dominicans nearer home may read the *Watch* with less than
the benevolence for which he hopes from the master general.
"Men who have never tasted the fruits of the Holy Spirit . . .
have faith in nothing but their own commonplace inventions
and their dubious propositions," seems to be aimed at the
professional philosophers in his own province who had enjoyed the academic promotion for which he had hoped and
of which, he says elsewhere, he had been defrauded.

(43) The first chapter of Book I of the *Watch* is a much more
extended literary treatment of the theme proposed in the cor-

42. *Dante Alighieri: De vulgari eloquentia*, ed. A. Marigo (Florence, 1938)
II.2:176.
43. *Watch*, 55; ed. Bihlmeyer, 197–98.   44. *Watch*, 58.

responding chapter 1 of *The Book of Wisdom*. Both begin with a somewhat vague account of how the Disciple was turned away from the world's seductions to a renewal of his espousals with Eternal Wisdom.[45] Most spiritual autobiographies of the Middle Ages seem to consider that such reminiscences of Augustine's *Confessions* are obligatory, but Suso's childhood and youth seem in fact to have been uncommonly circumspect. We may guess that what he knew of young men's folly and depravity he had learned from pastoral experience and from romantic literature. He sees no harm, in this first chapter, in quoting from the standard treatment of such topics, *The Art of Love*,[46] just as later, in Book I, chapter 10, writing, "Farewell, earth, farewell, companions whom I have cherished with a kind love,"[47] he finds it not incongruous to use the very words of one of the *Carmina Burana*. Then, in the Latin he introduces, with a quotation from Ecclesiastes, "I have found a woman more bitter than death, who is the hunter's snare,"[48] what is to become a recurring topic; and he skillfully contrasts the evil temptress's lineaments with those of the "divine spouse," Wisdom.

(44) He has opened chapter 1 with words from the Book of Wisdom: "Her have I loved and have sought out from my youth, and I have desired to take her for my spouse." This reverence for Wisdom, expressed as veneration for women, is as ancient as the sapiential books themselves. "Say to Wisdom: 'You are my sister.'"[49] "Wisdom has built her house; she has set up her seven pillars."[50] "All good things have come to me together with her, and countless honors from her hands, and I have found delight in everything, because she, Wisdom, went before me."[51] This tradition, of her affective celebration as the bestower and means of all creation's good things, was continued by Augustine, and so was commended to all scholars of the West. "O sweetest light of a mind purged of dross! Wisdom, you never cease to show us who you are, how great you are;

45. Ibid., 66.
47. Ibid., 160.
49. Prv 7.4.
51. Wis 7.11.

46. Ibid., 68.
48. Ibid., 70.
50. Prv 9.1.

and the performance of your will is the whole glory of God's creatures."[52] This being so, it is surprising that Suso seems to have been the first to do for Wisdom what Boethius did for Philosophy, Alan of Lille and Jean de Meun for Nature: to endow her with the character and attributes of a queen, a Queen of the Universe. The influence of Boethius, as Suso first presents Wisdom to us, is very evident. As he writes:

When the Disciple wished to speak familiarly to her, since she seemed near enough for this, she was soon seen to move very far off. First her height would extend beyond the arch of the highest heaven, then she seemed to be very small, and though she remained motionless, she looked to be "more active than all active things." She was present, yet she was not descried; she let herself be apprehended, and yet she was not comprehended. She "reached from end to end mightily, and ordered all things sweetly,"[53]

it is plain that Suso is remembering the description in the *Consolation* of Lady Philosophy's first appearance; but then he contributes a detail of his own: "First one thought that here one had a delicate young girl, then suddenly a most handsome youth was found."[54] Here we have a very clear allusion to one of the topics of medieval romantic literature, the notion of the beloved one as the master-mistress of the lover's heart; and none of this do we find in the corresponding German.

(45) Book I, chapter 2 is almost wholly original to the Latin, and it examines a paradox that would be familiar to any connoisseur of contemporary Passion-iconography such as Suso; in the Disciple's words: "This lover is misshapen by the sorrow of death, and how he could appear lovable I do not understand, he whose disposition seems all opposed to loving, since his outward appearance is all hideous with bruises, and inwardly he shrivels up for sorrow, so that he could show 'no beauty whatever in him or comeliness' to lovers' eyes, but he is all full of sorrow and miseries. So how can you call him lovable whom plain fact shows to be wretched?"[55]

52. *De libero arbitrio* II.16 (PL 32.1264).
53. *Watch*, 71.   54. Ibid.
55. Ibid., 77.

(46) The *Book of Wisdom*'s second chapter elucidates this problem by showing that contemplation of the Passion should lead to perception of the divine essence: "No one can attain to the heights of the divinity or to any unaccustomed sweetness without being drawn by the image of my bitter human sufferings. The higher anyone mounts by evading my humanity, the deeper he will fall. My humanity is the way on which men go, my Passion is the gate through which they must enter, if they want to attain to what you are seeking."[56] As if in emphasis, the *Book* elaborates this: "When I was hanged high upon the Cross for you and all mankind out of my unbounded love, my whole aspect was most pitifully transformed. My bright eyes were dimmed and clouded . . . and in all the earth I had not one spot where I could rest, for my divine head was brought low by anguish and torment."[57] Yet in the *Watch*, Suso diverts his imagery and his thought so as to present such contemplation as matter for the soul's consolation: ". . . how could this way be made easier except in this manner, that he who told us of it should go along it before us making that toilsome path lighter by his own most bitter suffering, and so easing for the creature the road that its Creator had first trodden?"[58]

(47) Then the *Book of Wisdom* breaks into a lamentation for the soul's loss of the love of God: "Woe is me, the heavenly Father adorned me more richly than any other earthly creature, and chose me for his delicate and adorable bride; and now I have strayed from him! Alas, I have lost him, the one love whom I longed for is gone! Sorrow, sorrow, never-ending sorrow for my aching heart, what have I done, what have I lost?"[59] This is very much in the tradition of the Old Testament, and it develops into another favorite theme, a railing, first against sin, the "unhappy fault,"[60] and then, by a kaleidoscopic shift of persons in which the speaker changes into the Disciple, against the "deceiving woman," who has ensnared him so that he compares himself with the hapless Samson. An elegiac

56. Ed. Bihlmeyer., 205.
58. *Watch*, 84.
60. Cf. *Watch*, 93, note 20.
57. Ibid., 208.
59. Ed. Bihlmeyer, 211.

change of mood introduces the meditation, "Therefore happy is the soul, and deserving to be called queen of great possessions, whom dangers from without have made wary . . .";[61] and then a passage of dialogue with Wisdom warns the Disciple of the folly, the sinfulness of despair, and leads him to a joyful contemplation of divine mercy, of the trust in that mercy which he should have, and of the unwearying service which he should pay to it. This conclusion, with its introductory hyperbole about the inflammability of the handful of flax placed within the great globe of fire, comes from chapter 5 of the *Book.*

(48) Chapter 6 of the German begins with a consideration of the folly of worldlings, and Wisdom interposes with an allusion to Matthew 20.16: many are called to the divine espousals, but few are chosen for them. To illustrate this, she bids the servant look on an allegorical vision, that of the exiled and unhappy pilgrim who is Christ, standing forlorn and rejected in a ruined city. This becomes the subject matter of the *Watch*'s chapter 5, in which the allegory is much elaborated into that of the ram. Here only are we reminded of *The Divine Comedy*; and we may think that Suso and Dante alike show a deficient sense of proportion, in turning aside from the perennial, epic contest between good and evil for the possession of man's soul to record with such zestful minuteness the fighting that had gone on around their own parish pumps. But, in the end, Suso adroitly brings us back to his matter in his prayer: "Pour into them, I beg, a good spirit, so that they may turn back from their errors and return to unity and peace, so that we may all serve you in the bosom of our holy Mother, the Catholic Church, and that we may be valiant to attain to the glorious city of our heavenly native land."[62]

(49) There are certain details in chapter 7 of the *Book*, such as Wisdom's aristocratic lineage, which makes her so eligible a spouse, that have been taken over in chapter 6 of the *Watch*, and their basic themes are the same: the Old Testament symbolism of earthly marriage to signify the love between God

61. Ibid., 94.   62. Ibid., 114.

and the soul, and the praises of the divine nature, symbolized as Wisdom's beauty and splendid adornments. But the treatment in the *Watch* is more consciously literary, and filled with allusions to secular letters. Suso's description of the boys and girls dancing and singing in the vernal meadows—"The time that we have to live is short and full of cares, and in man's end there is no solace; and no one has been known to have returned from hell, for we are born of nothing, and after this we shall be as if we had never been"[63]—evokes for us the world of the *Carmina Burana*, with their artful presentation of black cynicism masquerading as blithe innocence. Then Wisdom reappears, queenly, glorious, quelling this riot, "the mother of fair love, and of fear, and of knowledge and of holy hope."[64] She proclaims her royal descent and invokes to her praises "the sound of the trumpet, the flute and the harp . . . the harmonious notes of the nightingale," and to compliment the Disciple, she reminds him that "your love is seeking for the heights and is not content to love as do cooks and bakers and perfume-makers and others like them, and unlike us."[65] Then, with much skill, the Disciple's inquiries about her ancestry are made to lead to the demonstration of her unknowability and her ineffability, "the most joyful vision of my most simple essence, the longed-for enjoyment of my supersubstantial divinity 'the possession, complete and also perfect, of a life that cannot end.'"[66] Whatever the depths of his learning may have been, Suso is here able to marshal a wide variety of quotations and allusions, using Augustine, pseudo-Dionysius and others, to support his thesis that the analogies between human and divine love are feeble and misleading, and that those who wish to vow themselves to Wisdom's service must learn a wisdom that is not of this world. A comparison of this chapter 6 of the Latin with the German chapter 7 shows the mastery of literary arts that Suso could now command.

(50) Chapter 7 of the *Watch* and chapter 8 of the *Book* have essentially the same subject matter, the mystery of the divine

63. Ibid., 116.   64. Ibid., 117.
65. Ibid., 118.   66. Ibid., 121.

Being manifested in God's appearance, now as a terrible judge, now as a lovable redeemer. Both versions make use of the "pathetic fallacy": a raging storm presages the terrors of the last judgment. But otherwise their treatment is quite different. The Latin makes less than does the German of the alternations between the terrifying and the benign portents of the divine presence (perhaps because that was an effect that Suso now was holding in reserve for the next chapter of the *Watch*), and in the Disciple's version of himself, dragged before the judgment throne to answer for his sins, Christ the Judge is portrayed with attributes borrowed from the Book of Daniel and the Apocalypse which are not found in the *Book*.

(51) In the *Book* and the *Watch*, chapter 14 turns to the spiritual benefits of a constant contemplation of Christ's own sufferings, and offers Paul and Bernard as the supreme Christian examples of lives transformed by and in the Passion. The words that Wisdom who is Christ uses to enjoin a careful and heartfelt recollection of that Passion are almost literally translated from the German into Latin, but the Latin chapter concludes with considerable amplifications of this teaching.

(52) Chapter 15, in either version, contains Wisdom-Christ's own account of his sufferings on the cross, and of how his mother stood by it; and then there is a demonstration of how the Disciple can, by willing acceptance of his afflictions, among which the ingratitude and hostility of others are specifically mentioned, share in that Passion. This will be the spiritual death for which he asks. Both versions end with Christ giving the Disciple leave to ask Mary herself about her sorrows.

(53) The Latin chapter 16, with which Book I of the *Watch* ends, combines the subject matter of the German chapters 16 and 17, traditional praises of the Virgin, and her own narrative of her share in the Passion, strongly influenced, as Bihlmeyer pointed out, by *The Book of the Passion of Christ*, in Suso's time still spuriously attributed to Bernard.

(54) Book II, chapter 1, of the Latin, "Of the Marvelous Variety of Teachings and of Disciples" deals very briefly with a few matters touched on in the German chapter 22; but it then proceeds to the circumstantial allegory of the schools

and their disputatious residents, probably first suggested to Suso by Hugh of St. Victor in his *Pursuit of Learning*, but used by Suso for his most trenchant criticisms of those higher studies from which, he claimed, he had been excluded; and the *Watch*'s Book II, chapter 2, "Of the Knowledge Most Profitable to a Mortal Man, Which is to Know How to Die," is a much revised and expanded version of the *Book*'s chapter 21. It will be seen that the matter of the German chapters 18, 19 and 20, describing the anguish of Wisdom-Christ at the moment of death, and Mary's account of the descent from the cross and the entombment, have been largely omitted.

(55) Book II, chapter 3, of the *Watch*, "A Concise Form for Spiritual Living," corresponds with the *Book*'s chapter 22; but when Clark states that the *Book*'s pronouncement that "not one man among a thousand understands" the way of unbroken contemplation, he is quoting from Eckhart's work, he is less than exact. The *Watch* and the *Book* both contain the statement that aspirations to this have been suggested to the soul only as a counsel of perfection, to attain which it must overcome many weaknesses and distractions.[67] This certainly is taken from Eckhart (in the alternative ending, both the "Alpha" and the "Beta" versions, found by Kurt Ruh and printed by Quint): "All this has been said to you only for you to know what is the very highest. . . ." Then the *Book* and the *Watch* repeat Eckhart's question: "Who in this frail body can always be applying himself to this science of the spirit?"[68] which is Germanus's observation in Cassian's *Conversations*: "Can our mind always remain in one place and ever persist in the same quality?"[69] The *Watch* praises purity of heart as man's first object, and it teaches, as do the *Book* and Eckhart, that this purity is attained by freedom from "sensory forms and earthly imaginings," "all images introduced from outside," "all created things."[70] This, and little more, is borrowed by the *Book* and the *Watch* from Eckhart; but then, as Book II, chapter 3, proceeds, we find a narrative developing that has no counterpart,

67. Ibid., 259.
68. Ibid., 260.
69. Ibid., 260, note 9.
70. Ibid., 259 et seq.

the story of how the Disciple is shown the "very ancient tome" containing the teachings of Arsenius. This reference presents problems that have not yet been solved. General resemblances to some of the aphorisms in Cassian's *Conversations* can be seen, but it would appear that Suso was using a different collections of sayings attributed to Arsenius that has not yet been identified.

(56) Book II, chapter 4, deals, as does the German chapter 23, with the soul's dispositions when receiving Holy Communion; but the Latin is a much longer and more theological treatment, and reflects, as the German does not, an atmosphere of inquiry that must be answered, of doubts that must be resolved. The prayers to the Blessed Sacrament with which the Latin and German chapters end are not identical.

(57) The Latin Book II, chapter 5, and the German chapter 24 deal with the same topic, the possibility for finite human minds of praising Wisdom "always and at all times"; and many of the details of the German are reproduced in the Latin, which is, however, much revised, with a treatment at once more stylized and more academic.

(58) Book II, chapter 6, "A guide for incorporating these matters in sermons and conferences," is a Latin reworking of some of the material from the German *Book* III, the "Hundred Meditations," which Suso had stated in the *Watch*'s prologue that he would not reproduce in full, since they were already available in German.[71]

(59) The Latin Book II, chapter 7, treats "Certain easy daily exercises" by which the devout may espouse themselves to Wisdom and renew their pledges of love.

(60) The concluding chapter 8, "The Manifold Fruits of the Divine Blessing . . ." is original to the Latin; and chapter 8 contains some of the *Watch*'s most effective writing, even though it does not fulfill its rubric's promise to treat of "bridal mysticism."

(61) It will have been seen that, in Book II of the *Watch*, Suso has throughout revised and, in places, suppressed parts

71. Ibid., 57.

of his German text with greater freedom than he used in Book I.

5. *The* Watch *'s Reading Public, and its Contemporary Success.*

(62) It would be mistaken to assume that Suso's only motive in composing the *Watch* in Latin was in order to reach an international readership. Beyond doubt, that was a part of his intention. That he addresses the prologue to his order's master general shows this, but there probably were other considerations. Aside from his own views, which we have mentioned, on the literary superiority of the Latin tongue, he may well have hoped that this statement of his spiritual aspirations would gain greater sympathy, if not comprehension, from his German confreres than would any vernacular composition. Like his own, the whole of their education, from their early days as schoolboys, had been in Latin, and much of it in the beginning had consisted in the memorization of long portions of the Vulgate, so much of which the *Watch* quotes. Latin literature was for them a terrain in which they were at home and at ease, and they enjoyed a facility in Latin composition that they seldom were given for their own languages. For the purposes of philosophical and theological demonstration, a medieval religious could use and could follow Latin more easily than works in the vernacular. We have many instances to prove that this was so. In England in the fourteenth century, Walter Hilton wrote, in English, the first book of his *Scale of Perfection,* a guide to spiritual living, for some anonymous woman anchorite who, he indicated, was far from learned; and although the second book is intended for men in religion, it too is in their native language. But quite soon after the *Scale* was first published, a Carmelite friar, Thomas Fishlake, turned both books into Latin.[72] It is true that this translation was sent overseas, and that we have evidence of its circulation in France, Italy and the Low Countries; but there is nothing to show that Fishlake did not in the first instance intend his Latin for En-

72. Cf. S. S. Hussey, "Latin and English in The Scale of Perfection," MS 35 (1973): 456–76.

glish readers. And in the case of two other spiritual works, *The Cloud of Unknowing* and *The Mirror of Simple Souls*, an English translation from a French original, one English Carthusian of Mount Grace Priory in North Yorkshire at the end of the fifteenth century made Latin versions, as he states, at the request and for the benefit of another monk of Mount Grace, who must have expected the Latin to be easier for him than he had found the English to be. Incidentally, the translator, Richard Methley, shows in a number of instances that he did not perfectly understand the grammatical forms of the English with which he was working.[73] The English of the early thirteenth-century guide for anchoresses, the *Ancrene Riwle*, is notoriously difficult,[74] and this in part must explain the existence of Latin versions of this work, too.

(63) The surviving evidence of the *Watch*'s distribution in its earliest years of publication leads us to several different conclusions. The first is that, as we have shown might be the case, this Latin work scored its greatest success in the German-speaking areas of Europe. Although the manuscripts that have survived, and the records of those that are now lost, show that it was known, read and copied in many parts of the world—in Italy and the Iberian peninsula, in England, the Low Countries, Burgundy and France, as well as Czech-speaking Bohemia—by far the greatest number of copies existed in Germany and the adjacent German linguistic areas, Austria, Bohemia, Switzerland and Alsace. Such was not invariably the case. Walter Baier has shown us recently that Ludolph of Saxony's *Vita Christi* was much more successful in France than in the German territories, and the pseudo-Bonaventure's *Meditations*, though they seem to have originated in Tuscany, circulated throughout the Western Church.

(64) But, whatever Suso's intentions may have been, his own order was anything but his chief patron. Künzle, in the useful ninth chapter of his introduction, "The Readers of the

73. An edition of the Methley translations was prepared by the late James Walsh and Edmund Colledge, but has not appeared.

74. Cf. Mary Baldwin, "Some Difficult Words in *Ancrene Riwle*," MS 38 (1976): 268–90.

Watch, by Communities," shows us that the Benedictines were easily those who most often had copies in their libraries, and that, as we might expect, they were closely followed by the Carthusians and Birgittines, with the Dominicans following only fifth, preceded by Augustinian canons regular. Beyond doubt, these figures tell us much of the different orders' policies and funds available for book-purchase and manufacture, but they also show how many discerning librarians, not concerned merely to promote the prestige of their own orders, considered the *Watch* to be a worthwhile acquisition. Thus it is not surprising that a number of celebrated amateurs of spiritual literature, including the bibliophiles Nicholas of Cusa and John Blackman of Cambridge, were among its owners. Whether they included that other celebrated collector John Gerson we do not know, since his manuscripts, which he so providently presented in his lifetime to the Avignon Celestines, have disappeared.[75] At all events, Suso was spared any attack from Gerson as a purveyor of false doctrine, although, since those whom the chancellor of Paris did so malign included Ubertino of Casale and John Ruysbroek, such attentions can only be regarded as a kind of accolade.

(65) It is not hard to see why Suso's book should have been so successful. We have already remarked on its style, and his ambitions as a stylist, which he realized fully in his German works and also in the *Watch*; and it has been observed that, unlike Eckhart, he was content to compose along traditional lines. He recreates for his readers the spirit and the moral tone of the authorities whom they, and he, most revered, and in this way he obeyed the precepts of every acknowledged master of the art of rhetoric: it is not enough that what one says is true—one must assure the readers of its truth by judicious appeal to those already respected and acclaimed as veracious guides.

(66) Perhaps there is no single work on which Suso relied more to win such sympathy than Boethius's *Consolation of Phi-*

75. Cf. Edmund Colledge and J. C. Marler, "*Tractatus Magistri Johannis Gerson De Mistica Theologia*. St. Pölten, Diözesanarchiv MS 25," *MS* 41 (1979): 354–80.

losophy. Written eight centuries before, it still was, and still is, a "tract for the times," telling us that though civilizations may seem to be disintegrating and bringing men down among their ruins, there is still one love, the love of Wisdom, who is God, which will preserve our souls. That was Boethius's message to his distracted world, and it is Suso's, in the age that witnessed the beginnings of the end of medieval life and learning. Offering his fearful contemporaries comfort and hope, Suso became a Christocentric Boethius.

(67) John V. Fleming, in a recent study, most perceptive and stimulating,[76] has rightly called the *Consolation* "the most important medieval dream-vision and the most pervasive in its literary influence." Among the works that show this influence he lists de Guilleville's *Pilgrimage of the Human Life* and *Piers Plowman,* and as he outlines the plot of any such typical vision as "leading an at first uncomprehending narrator from ignorance to understanding, or from despair to consolation," we can see at once how well he might also have included the *Watch.* Fleming was not the first modern scholar to advance and support the thesis that medieval men regarded the *Consolation* as essentially a treatise on Christian spirituality,[77] and as such, it enriched Suso's work.

(68) One of Boethius's chief contributions to the *Watch* has already been mentioned, the treatment that Suso accords to the personality of Wisdom, so much recalling the characterization in the *Consolation* of Lady Philosophy; but we can also observe that when Suso expostulates against the once-beloved mistress who beguiled him and then became his cruelest enemy,[78] this owes something to Boethius's complaints against the Lady Fortune, "not heeding to wretched men, ignoring their laments," and to Lady Philosophy's spirited defense of her.[79]

76. John V. Fleming, *The "Roman de la Rose": A Study in Allegory and Iconography* (Princeton, 1969).
77. Cf. Pierre Courcelle, "Étude critique sur les commentaires de la *Consolation* de Boèce (ixᵉ–xvᵉ siècles)," *Archives d'histoire doctrinale et littéraire du moyen âge* 14 (1939): 5–140.
78. E.g. *Watch,* 185. (Book I, chapter 13).　　　79. E.g. Book II, Prose 1.

(69) Yet there are few works even so close as was Boethius' to the thought of the pre-Christian world of which Suso shows any knowledge. It may be that in his remark to Wisdom in Book I, chapter 8: "Truly, if I find you more distant towards me than before . . . I lament the long tedium of my banishment as if a thousand years were passing by, yes, a whole Platonic year,"[80] he had learned of this notion of the "great year" from Macrobius's *Commentary on the Dream of Scipio*: ". . . when all the stars have returned to the same places from which they started out and have restored the same configurations over the great distances of the whole sky";[81] but this seems to be as close as he ever came to ancient scientific thought. He shows a nodding acquaintance with Aristotle's writings, but, as with pseudo-Dionysius, there is little or nothing to indicate that his knowledge extended beyond the contexts in which they were quoted by such authorities as Thomas Aquinas. He displays a moderate familiarity with Aquinas, as also with Augustine; but he seems to have known Augustine best through the *Confessions* and the *Rule*, which he must have known by heart from its regular conventual repetition. He betrays no special interest in the scriptural commentaries of Aquinas or Augustine, or, indeed, of Eckhart; and the new, complete Latin translations of Greek, Hebrew and Arabic spiritual classics that were becoming available through the labors of such men as William of Moerbecke seem to have passed him by. Almost the most recent literary source he cites is Alan of Lille, and of William of St. Thierry he appears to have known only the *Golden Epistle* (which, as did most of his contemporaries, he would have considered to be the work of Bernard), William's most copied and most celebrated but by no means most profound treatise. Suso knows which authorities he requires to produce an exact effect—witness his extended and almost verbatim quotations from Hugh of St. Victor, in *De arrha animae* on "the game of love." He has the ready command of every medieval religious

80. *Watch*, 138 and note 12.
81. Cf. William H. Stahl, *Macrobius: Commentary on the Dream of Scipio* (New York, 1952).

of the Scriptures and the liturgy, but one suspects that he was most strongly attracted by the Vulgate and the Church's prayers for the matchless language in which they had clothed every man's wishes and hopes and fears.

(70) Comparing the two versions, we can observe one minor point, not without interest. In the description of the saints in glory, Bihlmeyer accepted the reading of his preferred manuscript, "the confessors shine in verdant beauty," *die bihtere luhtent in gruenender schonheit,*[82] and although he quoted the Latin, *confessores radiant igneo fulgore,* he justified *gruenender* with a statement that in Suso's day green was the liturgical color for confessors. Clark and Jeanne Ancelet-Hustache in their translations followed Bihlmeyer in all this, but it is more probable that *gruenender* is a scribe's error for *glueender,* and that Suso's German said, as does the Latin, "gives a fiery light."[83]

(71) Chapter 12 of the Latin, "A Determination of Certain Objections Previously Omitted," has no equivalent chapter in the *Book,* where, at the end of chapter 12, the servant, enraptured by his sight of heavenly joy, asks to be permitted to remain there, but is told by Wisdom that he must return to the battle and bear without complaint what he must suffer. In the Latin, this has been much elaborated in the style of "books of consolation"; "examples" are supplied, in a preacher's fashion: Paul's constancy, the waywardness of his flocks, the decline of religious living in modern times, the stubborn animosity with which the friars receive criticism of their degenerate ways—all these seem to have been much in Suso's mind as he ventilates the subjects here.

(72) The topic of "consolation" is continued in chapter 13 in both the *Watch* and the *Book,* in the *Watch* at much greater length. The Old Testament theme, so dear to Suso, of the kind-seeming mistress who turns into a cruel enemy, is used once again; and in his account of his afflictions he seems to be describing in veiled fashion opposition and harshness which he had received from his brethren in religion. More

82. Ed. Bihlmeyer, 244.   83. *Watch,* Book I, chapter 11, 167.

openly, when he tells of the grove that he had planted and of
how he was robbed of it, he is alluding to his failure to gain
promotion from the ranks of Dominican teachers. The Disciple perceives that this narrative is "the mystery of espousal
with Eternal Wisdom, who is accustomed to try her lovers with
worldly tribulations";[84] and she offers him consolation in examples of the sorrows that the saints have bravely borne, and
by commending to him what he already reads with such profit
of the desert fathers. Very much in Boethius's style, he asks
for and receives instruction about the divine providence that
sends suffering, and how suffering can, though involuntary,
be meritorious. In both the Latin and the German, Wisdom
makes the shrewd observation: "This is the habit of every
wretched man, to judge that his scourges are sharper than
those of others,"[85] and she encourages him to show fortitude
and patience.

(73) We know no more of what Suso himself represents as
his failure to win academic renown than he chooses to tell us,
but the whole tenor of the *Watch* suggests that he had pursued
his studies and teaching in philosophy and theology with
something less than enthusiasm, that he became persuaded
that his true vocation was in literature, and that he relin-
quished—or, he would have us think, had wrested from him
—his place in his order's teaching program, for the sake of
others, whose names, unlike his own, oblivion has claimed.

(74) It would be unjust to suggest that Suso, frustrated in
his ambitions for one kind of success, consoled himself with
another, which brought him a fame that he had not sought.
We may rather think that he found in his adversities the way
to discover where his best gifts could lead him, and that he
followed this way, using those considerable powers which he
had already labored hard for many years to develop. He is
remembered as a master of affective language, celebrating
"love's good and evil gifts": what love of the fickle and feigning
world can give, that bitterness which, whether he had tasted
it or not, he could so well describe, and that perfect love, which
casts out fear, of the crucified Redeemer.

84. Ibid., 188.   85. Ibid., 193; ed. Bihlmeyer, 249.

(75) Walter Baier has called Suso "the first German Passion-mystic,"[86] and he goes on: "For Suso, no one can attain to the vision of God without going through 'the humanity which suffered.' His God reveals himself in the historicity of the Passion and death of Jesus of Nazareth, and so for him every single human suffering is important for this way of imitation, is exalted, grasped, mourned and praised in the Passion of Christ."[87] We may ignore superficial linguistic resemblances between the *Watch* and the *Imitation*,[88] most of which derive from their authors' use of common sources, chiefly scriptural, and yet appreciate how deep was the response of the Common Life brethren to this view of human existence, lived in the shadow of the cross, in which the human race can find light and hope.

(76) The *Watch* is indeed a chronicle of suffering, but dignified and redeemed and divinized by Christ's suffering; and so there is no place in it for the despair that is a denial of the Christian message. Suso writes much of the miseries of human existence, but he is not forgetful of its joys and its triumphs. This may be why he called it "Wisdom's *Horologium*," her "Watch," naming it after what seemed to the men of his age the astonishing achievement of human ingenuity, mathematical science and mechanical skills, which had produced the first automatic chronometers to replace the ancient water clocks and sundials. Suso was not the only writer to give such a title to a spiritual treatise; his fellow Dominican and contemporary, Berthold "the German," had written a *Horologium devotionis circa vitam Christi*.[89] This was composed to a strict plan and offered a meditation on Christ's saving work for each of the twenty-four hours. It is true that the scribe of a mid-fifteenth century Vienna manuscript of the *Watch* from the "Scottish Cloister" states that Suso had given his book its name "because as the natural day contains twenty-four hours, so this work contains twenty-four chapters by which divine Wisdom makes

86. Baier, 298.   87. Ibid., 299.
88. Cf. Pierre Debongnie, "Henri Suso et *l'Imitation de Jésus-Christ*," RAM 21 (1940): 242–68.
89. Cf. Künzle, 8.

herself known to man."[90] But Suso's temperament was too
ebullient and emotional for him to tie himself to any such
scheme as Berthold's, and the sum of the sixteen chapters of
Book I and the eight of Book II does not appear to be significant. The scribe of MS 1711 in the great abbey of Melk was
more probably right when he wrote: "And it is called the *Horologium sapientiae* as indicating well-tasting wisdom and divine
knowledge."[91]

(77) But, teaching us to look on the pursuit of human wisdom with the eyes of divine knowledge, Suso inevitably sees
and describes the quest with an irony which can become satiri-
cal. We have already noticed that the most probable inspiration for his account of the "school of wisdom" and its "three
orders," in Book II, chapter 1, was Hugh of St. Victor, but
when he begins by satirizing the masters of the "school" as
pseudo-scholars, bluffing their way through disciplines only
half-understood, by bemusing their pupils and rivals with ob-
fuscating jargon, he is drawing on Augustine's account of his
early days as a teacher of rhetoric, in the *Confessions*, Book IV,
chapter 16. Suso ends his account of the "first order" in the
"school" with a merciless attack on irreformable religious superiors, seeking to compel their subjects by new legislation
not to commit the very faults that are evident in their own
daily lives. This has all Hugh's indignation at the shortcomings
of others, but one misses Augustine's jests at his own expense,
as he describes his efforts to conceal from his charges and
from himself his own inadequacies. Suso the romantic perhaps had less in common with Augustine's cool self-knowledge than he thought.

(78) Beyond doubt, Suso is most deeply moved when he
begins to treat of some of the great themes of romantic literature in the language of romance. Not long ago, William Emp-
son protested at another scholar's writing, of a character in *A
Midsummer Night's Dream*, that he was "quite unsusceptible to
the romance of fairyland," asking, "What on earth can the
weasel-word 'romance' be doing here? As a Greek of the age

90. Ibid., 67, note 1.   91. Ibid., 151.

of myth, he simply worships the goddess."[92] One could rejoin that "myth" is just as much a "weasel-word" as "romance," but "romance" is used here of Suso's writings, and their genre, in a precise sense: characteristic of the treatment found in vernacular literature, first in French and Provençal, and, later, also in Latin secular poetry, of stories of heroes of chivalry, especially when they deal with their relations with ladies.

(79) When in Book I, chapter 1, the Disciple says of Wisdom: "She will be the spouse, and I shall be her poor serf,"[93] he is alluding to the philosophy that sees true love as a willing bondage. So did some of the early Provençal poets address the objects of their adoration as "my lord," and Heinrich von Morungen writes: "She whom in my song I celebrate, I crown . . . never did I see a fairer picture than is my lady; I rejoice in her lordship."[94] In Book I, chapter 2, Wisdom says to the Disciple: "And sometimes it happens that what in a lover is judged unseemly by those who are not in love is praised by those who extol love as seemly above all things,"[95] when she is reminding him that there is for lovers a code of conduct, elaborate and ceremonial, and that those who have not mastered it are excluded from Love's court. So does Heinrich von Veldeke (an enigmatic figure, doubly so, since the Dutch and the Germans both claim him as a "father" of their own courtly poetry) tell his hearers that they must always be grateful to him, for his songs tell those who have loved or are now in love of joys "which stupid men can never begin to understand, for Love has never held them captive or pierced their hearts";[96] and he makes a lady say contemptuously: "How could I have understood that he would make a peasant's offers to me?" So it is that Wisdom says with approbation: "Your love is seeking for the heights and is not content to love as do cooks and

92. *The London Review of Books* 1, 25 October, 1979.
93. *Watch*, 71.
94. E. Lachmann, ed., *Die Gedichte Walthers von der Vogelweide*, revised by Carl von Kraus (Darmstadt, 1926) 12.
95. *Watch*, 77.
96. Jef Notermans, ed., *Hendrijk van Veldeke. 25 Minneliederen* (Gorinchem, 1966) 45.

bakers. . . ."[97] It is evident that Suso was writing for readers whom he expected to be familiar with such conventions and with the poetry which they produced.

(80) Naturally, in Suso's Christianized *Minne* there can be no place for the bitterness and cynicism so often found in the secular courtly poets. Heinrich von Morungen, dying for love of his unkind lady, says that if she expects to be free of him she will be cheated: he will bequeath his pain to his child, that he with his beauty may break her heart and so avenge his father,[98] and Heinrich calls another love of his "Thou sweetest, gentlest murderess."[99] The closest Suso comes to this tradition is the allegorical description, in Book I, chapter 4, of the false love who first ensnares and then betrays him; and it has already been suggested that this may owe something to Boethius's *Consolation*. The theme is indeed perennial, and Suso at least knew that the same allegories are to be found in Jeremias, Ezechiel and Osee.

6. *The* Watch *and Contemporary Visual Art.*

(81) The *Watch* is distinguished by one further trait, which it shares with *Meditations on the Life of Christ* and the *Vita Christi*, and for which it was much esteemed by the connoisseurs of the late Middle Ages; this is the markedly pictorial treatment that pseudo-Bonaventure, Suso and Ludolph all give to their material.[100] Their method, tried and approved by many of their precursors who had composed books to provide pious readers with the matter for discursive meditation, was to conjure up for them, as vividly as possible, the scenes, the personages and the events to which imagination and reflection were to be directed.

(82) Sometimes Suso can create a picture with the delicacy of a miniature, suggesting rather than enumerating the details he wishes us to imagine, as in his account, in Book I, chapter

97. *Watch*, 118.   98. Ed. Notermans, 24.
99. Ibid., 80.
100. The writer is grateful to Isa Ragusa, then of the Index of Christian Art at Princeton, and Roger Wieck, of the Department of Medieval Art in the New York Metropolitan Museum, for discussion of this matter.

1, of Wisdom's first appearance: "An ivory throne in a pillar of cloud, of great and wondrous beauty, appeared, and from the pillar the marvelous loveliness of the spouse, in golden garments bordered with embroidery, shone out. Her crown was eternity, her girdle joyful happiness, her words gentle sweetness, her embrace the perfect fullness of all good."[101]

(83) Yet he knew well, as did the painters of his age, how to produce visions of frightening realism. Here is Christ's narrative of the beginnings of his Passion, from Book I, chapter 3: "Afterwards the sons of darkness came to attack me; they took most violent hold on me, bound me cruelly and led me back into the city. Through that night those sacrilegious men wreaked on me various kinds of torment, they had their fill of my sufferings, they afflicted me with mockery and blows, insults and abuse without number. They spat their filthy spittle in my fair face, they blindfolded my eyes, they rained blows on my neck as they derided me."[102] This cannot but remind us of the many savage and brutal representations of such scenes that were being produced then, for altarpieces and to adorn such devotions as the "Hours of the Passion" as they were copied into prayer books.[103]

(84) At times Suso, to produce an effect of satire, uses devices that are derived directly from contemporary visual art. In his description of the ruined city, in Book I, chapter 5, which is to symbolize the decay of Christian society, Wisdom, acting as guide and interpreter, says to the Disciple: "As for what you also saw there, that great crowd of beasts like human-seeming sea monsters, those are worldly hearts hiding under the religious habit, a habit that looks decent enough outside, but inside there is neither grace nor devotion, and so, within and without, they live crippled lives, and they are truly very like monstrous beasts."[104] This is an example of what contem-

---

101. *Watch*, 71.   102. Ibid., 80.

103. What Suso writes is reminiscent of the representation of the Flagellation, a miniature painted in Bruges in the year 1408, found in MS Downside Abbey 26539, f.34ᵛ; cf. Edmund Colledge, "South Netherlands Book of Hours Made for England," S 32 (1978): plate 11ᵇ.

104. *Watch*, 105.

poraries, such as those making inventories of embroideries or other art objects, called "babooneries," animal figures, often clothed in religious or secular attire, shown engaged in activities meant to ridicule human acts. "The Fox Preaching to Geese" was a favorite subject, and Chaucer's *Nun's Priest's Tale* is an extended "baboonery." The tradition, of course, is as ancient as Aesop.[105]

(85) The *Watch* can also create for us comic scenes by employing detail that is ludicrous or grotesque. Suso's character of the star-crossed man has already been commended:

If one of them crosses the seas, the wind is against him. If he plans to go by land, the sky may have granted peaceful weather to the earth for many days, but as soon as this man of yours, this wretched lover, if I may so call him, comes out of doors and makes ready to travel, the clouds roll up, the land is flooded with torrents, and this man, your servant, is afflicted either with downpours or excessive heat or even with untimely cold. This is something wonderful and astonishing. The very mice in their holes do not allow him to rest. If he goes out by day, sometimes the kites in the sky, or even the crows, croaking at him as if in scorn, pursue him; and whether he be silent or laugh, that makes them angry.[106]

In this there is nothing kind or compassionate. We are reminded of the cruel caricatures of grimacing, slobbering idiots with which illuminators liked to adorn the initial letters of Psalm 52, "The fool has said in his heart. . . ." This may not today be to our taste, but we must not blame Suso for sharing those of his contemporaries.

(86) This pictorial quality in Suso, pseudo-Bonaventure and Ludolph is well attested by the number of artists whose illustrations of their books have been preserved. For our information we have the fine edition of one such copy of the *Meditations on the Life of Christ*, with a stationer's careful instructions to a Tuscan illustrator about which scenes he was to depict, in

105. Cf. Beryl Rowland's entertaining and informative account of the genre: *Animals with Human Faces: A Guide to Animal Symbolism* (Knoxville, 1973).
106. *Watch*, 151.

spaces left blank for him by the scribe, and which details he was to supply.[107] Roger Wieck is now engaged on an investigation of illuminated Ludolph manuscripts, and we may hope for a published study from him. Already, we have one such account, furnished with excellent plates, of a manuscript of the *Watch*.[108] Beyond any doubt, so costly a work as this Brussels manuscript must have been commissioned by some stationer or patron with a knowledge so exact that he could instruct the artist, down to small details, about what was expected of him. Others of the surviving illustrated *Watch* manuscripts, especially in the French translation, are very sumptuous, and their pictures have a degree of fidelity to the text that is reminiscent of the best Italian illuminated Dante codices.[109]

(87) But perhaps better indicative of the marketability of such illustrated works among a clientele less engaged in the minutiae of its narrative, but likely to be attracted by a picture book reflecting more generally the authors' brands of popular piety, is Munich Staatsbibliothek cod. gall. 28.[110] Although this is classified among the State Library's "Tresorhandschriften" —and its three miniatures are certainly of high quality—this represents, better than does Bibliothèque Royale IV.111, the methods that a stationer, with a first-class painter at his disposition, could use to produce books that would command a good price, but could nonetheless be manufactured in quantities and at a speed sufficient to guarantee a high level of profit. Cod. gall 28's pictures are most attractive, but they have little more than a general relation to Suso's text.

(88) Each miniature occupies a third of the entire page,

107. Cf. Ragusa and Green, note 28.
108. Eleanor P. Spencer, "L'Horloge de Sapience: Bruxelles Bib. Royale MS IV.111," S 17 (1963): 277–99.
109. One should consult, for example, Gian Alberto dell'Acqua, *Arte Lombarde dai Visconti agli Sforza* (Milan, 1959) 61–62 and plates 81–82, XXVI, describing and illustrating MS Paris BN 2017, a copy of the *Inferno* with pictures by "the Master of the *Vitae Imperatorum*," a Milanese Olivetan brother in charge of an atelier which in the second quarter of the fourteenth century produced many such works for the Visconti and other Lombard magnates.
110. Cf. *Catalogus codicum manu scriptorum Bibliothecae Regiae Monacensis* VI, *Codices gallicos . . . complectens.*

and margins are filled with continuous, intertwining botanical designs. The first, f.1ʳ, contains a lady in a steeple hat and veil mounted on a horse, the others uninhabited. The execution is in grisaille, slightly heightened in color and picked out with gold. F.1ʳ, below, center, are the arms of some branch of the French royal house, supported by couching lions; but it was a common trade practice to leave such a lozenge blank, so that a purchaser's arms could be inserted, and this is no indication that the book was commissioned by some prince or princess.

(89) The first miniature shows Wisdom, dressed as a religious, with the Holy Spirit as a dove over her head, standing before a chair of state in conversation with the Disciple, who is in modish lay attire. The second, f.5ᵛ, which illustrates Book II, chapter 2, "When the Disciple heard these words . . . ," depicts a sick man in bed, attended by a layman, by an angel bestowing his blessing, and by a devil, a horned hermaphrodite, menacing the sick man with a scourge. The third, f.51ʳ, which illustrates the beginning of Book II, chapter 7, "How many of the faithful may be wedded to divine Wisdom," represents an oratory. On the left, a friar (perhaps an Augustinian, certainly not a Dominican in indoor habit) preaches to a group of lay men and women. Right, a priest in doctor's robes hears the confession of what seems to be another cleric, while two women sit on folding stools waiting in very close proximity.

(90) This is the work of a popular illustrator, in no way concerned with what is novel or distinctive in the *Watch*'s piety. Had he been, he could have chosen many episodes worthier of graphic comment, perhaps best of all those in which Wisdom appears to the Disciple, not as any kind of nun, but as a queen in the courts of love. The tradition, established by Boethius, Alan of Lille and Jean de Meun, has already been noticed; and one might have expected illustrators of the *Watch* to have followed it as it is reflected and well established in illuminated manuscripts of the *Consolation*, which show Philosophy in the guise of a great lady of the world.[111] Even less is he concerned

111. Cf. Pierre Courcelle, *La Consolation de Philosophie dans le tradition littéraire* (Paris, 1967) and his appendix: "Iconographie de la 'Consolation,'" especially plates 31, 33, 36, 37, 38, 39, all of them from still unedited manuscripts.

with the author's personality; to show him in the first miniature as a young gallant, instead of the earnest, striving "Amandus" of the Preachers, indicates the artist's indifference to the
confessional, autobiographical strain in the *Watch*. The execution and finish of the miniatures are exquisite, but as a comment on the merits of the work which they illustrate, they must
be judged shoddy and inept.

(91) This is regrettable, because Suso deserves better. He
reveals his own interest in pictorial art and his awareness of
the possible analogies between that and the writer's craft, in
Book I, chapter 6, in the passage beginning "A wise painter,
when something is lacking . . . ,"[112] where Wisdom, telling the
Disciple that in her matchless beauty she has no need of
adornment, begins by this somewhat circuitous analogy with
how an artist, skilled with his brushes, will be able to conceal
under the elaboration of his designs the defects of the materials with which he is working. Such comparison of the objects
and techniques of writers and painters is in the West at least
as ancient as Horace and pseudo-Cicero, and is very much in
the style of more recent commentators on the rhetorical skills,
such as Geoffrey of Vinsauf, although no exact parallel to
Suso's thought on the matter has been found.

(92) Another illustration also showing indifference
(though quite otherwise motivated) to the content of Suso's
book is in MS Brussels Bibliothèque Royale IV.iii, a copy of
the French translation, the *Horloge*. Suso is shown, as he should
be, in Dominican choirhabit. Standing before him is Wisdom,
as splendidly arrayed as might be wished; and, in Lynn White's
expert opinion, she is also endowed with the attributes of
"Temperantia," and with a cruciform numbus, a painter's way
of saying ". . . who is Christ." So far, this is wholly in keeping
with the *Watch*'s letter and spirit, but the two figures are surrounded by what Professor White calls "the finest exhibition of
time-measuring devices surviving from the fifteenth century."
He writes: "The intricate development of this picture, beyond
any conceivable requirement of Suso's text, indicates subcon-

112. *Watch*, 120.

scious pressures to inflate the clock-symbol"; and he argues, persuasively, in the present writer's opinion, that the picture is inspired by a wish to celebrate, as one of man's highest achievements, the technological advances represented by these new chronometers, a point of view, as the author rightly remarks, quite alien from Suso's own.[113]

(93) Whether Suso may properly be considered to have himself been a sufficiently skilled draughtsman to plan the ornamentation of the master-copy, "Exemplar," of his major German works with "proverbs" (by which "captions" seems to be meant) and drawings, incorporated in the text, depends on the credibility of Bihlmeyer's opinion that the "Exemplar" is an authentic Suso autograph. Rieder and Lichtenberger seriously questioned this. Others were not convinced by their criticisms, notably A. Niklas, Planzer himself, and W. Thimme.[114] The present writer inclines to Planzer's opinion, but a more expert and detailed palaeographical examination of the "Exemplar," at that time in Berlin and now restored to Strasburg, than that made by Bihlmeyer is required before the manuscript can be accepted so unreservedly as he did. It is very apparent that its illustrations, a number of which he reproduced, are not all the work of the same man; and the hints that we find in the *Vita* (though not in the Exemplar's prologue) that Suso was himself preparing such an illustrated copy are sparse and vague. We shall be wise to treat this as a still open question until more attention can be paid to it.

7. *The* Watch*'s Place in the Literature of Spirituality.*

(94) Time has necessarily been spent in considering which classical theological masters Suso drew on. It has recently been the fashion to belittle such "source-hunting" as an activity of inferior minds, but such an attitude betrays incomprehension of the medieval regard for authority and originality. Suso and his contemporaries knew how to esteem those who had made

113. The writer is indebted to Professor Lynn White for a valuable private communication concerning medieval horologe-pictures.
114. Cf. Künzle's chapter 14, "Later Evaluation and Use of the *Horologium.*"

new contributions to learning, marked by their fresh approach and innovative thinking; but they expected, and had been trained by their instructors in rhetoric to expect, that serious statements, in Suso's case in his chosen field of spirituality, would be shown to have the support of the sages of times past. Suso's special gift lay in his perceptions of affinity between revered theologians and those who derived their philosophies from quite different modes of thought, sometimes pagan in origin—though to use this term begs the question of whether the poets of romantic love had found their ideas and their imagery in oriental, possibly Arabic models, or were adapting to their purposes ancient Eastern hymns of the love between God and the soul.

(95) We can observe these gifts, and what were Suso's talents in employing them, in his presentation of the paradoxes to be seen in the notion of "the play of love," the *Minne spêl.* We find this topic treated in the *Watch*'s Book I, chapter 8, and in chapter 9 of *The Book of Wisdom*; but its development in the German is very different from that which he later gives it in the Latin. Yet even when Suso composed the *Book*, he was already familiar with the most important exposition of the idea that God seems to treat the loving soul as a plaything, in the conclusion to Hugh of St. Victor's *De arrha animae*, "Of the Soul's Espousal Gift," to which many other writers of the late Middle Ages were indebted. When the German reads: "But, Lord, when the bright morning star rises within my soul, all sorrow is gone, all darkness disappears, and as the joyful light grows, my heart laughs, my spirits revive, my soul is glad, the day becomes a very festival for me, and all that is within me, all that I possess is turned into praise of you. All that was difficult and toilsome and impossible becomes easy and sweet— fasting, vigils, prayer, suffering, self-denial and every kind of harshness becomes nothing at all in your presence,"[115] Suso is translating Hugh, as he was to do again in chapter 8 of the *Watch*, but now at greater length. Clearly, the strong affinities between Hugh's presentation of the divine lover as a sportive,

115. Bihlmeyer, 233; cf. *Watch*, 144.

unpredictable power, sometimes wooing, sometimes seeming to repel the suppliant soul, and the romantic poets' praises of the service exacted by their mistresses as a heavy but joyful bondage, appealed as much to Suso as they had to Mechtild of Magdeburg; and his Latin reveals more plainly than does the *Book* the sympathies that he had for courtly literature.

(96) Again, chapter 10 of the *Book* and chapter 9 of the *Watch* treat of the same theme, why God permits his lovers to suffer in this world; but it is dealt with at greater length in the *Watch*, and with a wit hardly found in the German. Yet even there Suso does write: "'As my Father loves me, so do I love my friends. I treat my friends now as I have done from the beginnings of the world until this very day.' 'Lord, that is what people complain about, and so they say that this is why you have so few friends,'"[116] which is faithfully translated in the eleventh and twelfth paragraphs of the corresponding Latin chapter.

(97) This quip is best known to us in the celebrated rejoinder, once attributed to Teresa of Avila, to the Lord in a moment of catastrophe. She could well have been familiar with the contents of the *Watch* in some Latin printed edition, with the help of a learned intermediary; but Künzle, who dealt with the matter, informed us that the difficulty lies in establishing a Spanish text of precisely what Teresa is supposed on this occasion to have said; and experts in her works are questioning more and more the anecdote's authenticity. It is nowhere recorded in her writings, although, one agrees, it could well be one of the dry jests for which she was famous. A possibility is that one of her numerous Dominican intimates read this passage in Suso's Latin (the first printed edition, giving no information about its printer, place or date, was followed by some eight others in the fifteenth and early sixteenth centuries)[117] and recounted it to her; another is that Suso and the originator of the Teresa "fioretto" may have drawn on a common source, quite probably a proverb.[118] One ventures to think

116. Bihlmeyer, 236; cf. *Watch*, 152, 154.   117. Künzle, 220–25.
118. The English and Spanish Carmelites have been helpful in elucidating this problem; and particularly so has been Fr. Otilio Rodriguez' essay,

that if the joke were originally Suso's, it may already have been found so good that it had gained international currency.

(98) In the Latin, the whole chapter is attacked with brio. The description, already cited, of unlucky men, for whom everything goes wrong, until the very mice and birds of prey join in attacking them, is richly, if malignly, comic. Much of the *Vita* manifests the same vein of humor, often at Suso's own expense; and the illustrator of the "Exemplar" had perceived this in his portrait, not far removed from caricature, of "Eternal Wisdom's Suffering Servant," woebegone, passive, assailed by demons, monsters and his own brethren.[119] Wisdom herself joins in this debate with spirit, calling the Disciple a "coward" and "craven soldier," which provokes him to ask: "Am I the only one to make these complaints against you?"[120] Then he reverts to the notion of "the play of love": ". . . they will add that this is why you have so few friends, because you are accustomed to play this kind of game with them."[121]

(99) The presence in this array, in the "Exemplar's" illustration, of Dominican friars among the Servant's persecutors (Bihlmeyer, through strange inattention, stated that they were nuns of Suso's order, whereas his own accounts show that the women who enjoyed his spiritual ministrations were only too well disposed towards him) points to an unaccustomed trend in his thought. Too often one may find in earlier ascetic treatises emanating from religious houses a self-complacency, a certitude that in an author's chosen way of life is a divinely approved path towards God, from which all other ways can be disregarded as aberrant and misdirected. Far from this, Suso, in his *Vita* as in the *Watch*, has harsh things to say about his fellow Dominicans and the treatment, so different from the prescriptions of Augustine's *Rule*, that he had received at their hands; and he is scornful over how he has seen them neglect their manifest pastoral duties to the people.

"Así trato yo a mis amigos," in his *Leyenda Aurea Teresiana*, (Madrid, 1970) 39–44.

119. Edmund Colledge and J.C.Marler, "'Mystical' Pictures in the Suso 'Exemplar'—MS Strasbourg 2929," AFP 54 (1984): Plate 1, "Eternal Wisdom's Suffering Servant."

120. *Watch*, 153.   121. Ibid., 154.

(100) In this he is looking forward to the "Devotio Moderna" and its condemnation of the selfish worldliness that has infected religious life, and we can be sure that his reprobation of his times would find approval among the Brethren of the Common Life. Like Suso, they saw in a return to the discipline and austerity of former days a remedy against the laxity and inferior standards which they saw all about them. In every age, the *Watch*, no less than the *Imitation*, will find a response from those who must deplore the world in which they are placed, a world that changes, but seldom for the better.

(101) So the *Watch* tells us of Suso's longings for a way of life that was fast disappearing. His own father had left his ancestral lands and had followed the crowds, flocking to the cities in search of wealth. Suso writes of how he yearned for the piety of the countryfolk he had known as a boy, for their simplicity, expressed alike in the songs and the tales which were the diversions of those who had inherited a deeply poetic language that they preserved and practiced as an art, which he could transform into the most felicitous Latin. These men and women were the heirs too of the Eternal Wisdom that he worshipped, a Christian wisdom, founded on Christ, found in Christ, which was being lost and forgotten in the new urban cultures where men no longer knew one another, no longer knew their God. The *Watch* bears witness to Suso's deep love of the prophets, and as they appealed to a faithless Jerusalem, so does he to a world which was forsaking its Creator: "Turn back again, turn back again."

WISDOM'S WATCH UPON THE HOURS

Here begins the prologue to
the book that is called

WISDOM'S WATCH UPON THE HOURS

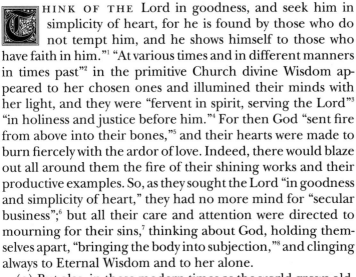HINK OF THE Lord in goodness, and seek him in simplicity of heart, for he is found by those who do not tempt him, and he shows himself to those who have faith in him."[1] "At various times and in different manners in times past"[2] in the primitive Church divine Wisdom appeared to her chosen ones and illumined their minds with her light, and they were "fervent in spirit, serving the Lord"[3] "in holiness and justice before him."[4] For then God "sent fire from above into their bones,"[5] and their hearts were made to burn fiercely with the ardor of love. Indeed, there would blaze out all around them the fire of their shining works and their productive examples. So, as they sought the Lord "in goodness and simplicity of heart," they had no more mind for "secular business";[6] but all their care and attention were directed to mourning for their sins,[7] thinking about God, holding themselves apart, "bringing the body into subjection,"[8] and clinging always to Eternal Wisdom and to her alone.

(2) But alas, in these modern times as the world grows old, this divine love has become so cold in many men's hearts that it is almost dead, and few can be found who are giving themselves to devotion, who are seeking new grace to make them fervent, who rejoice to feel the rain-bearing wind from the

1. Wis 1.1–2. 2. Heb 1.1.
3. Rom 12.11. 4. Lk 1.75.
5. Lam 1.13. 6. 2 Tm 2.4.
7. This is an allusion to Gratian's *Decretals* II.xvi.1, ch. iv, quoting Jerome: "A monk has the office not of a teacher but of a mourner."
8. 1 Cor 9.27.

south[9] again bedewing them with tears, who look for the grace of God's visitation and of his voice from on high. Their minds are all set on the pursuit of folly and "endless genealogies"[10] and bodily delights, and they are held fast in a deadly stupor, as it were. But still, divine Wisdom, caring for the well-being of all men, and always wanting to cure her chosen ones of these ills, intends in this present work not, indeed, to teach those who do not know, because already the earth is filled with the knowledge of the Lord,"[11] but to rekindle dead coals, to inflame the frigid, to rouse the tepid, to awaken devotion in the undevout, and to call those drowsing in the sleep of heedlessness to watch and wake for virtue's sake. So the mercy of the Savior deigned to reveal this present little book in a vision, when it was shown as a most beautiful clock, decorated with the loveliest roses and a variety of "well-sounding cymbals,"[12] which produce a sweet and heavenly sound, and summon the hearts of all men up above.

(3) Now, I entreat my devout readers not to be displeased by my unskilled and crude language, even though it perhaps may seem to sound barbarous to them. For I do not greatly care if I blunder into the errors that polished preachers abhor, provided that I have been able with my earnest words to correct and cure more easily the errors in men's minds. For as "I have received from the Lord"[13] the truths of the fathers, or those things that are known through that most trustworthy witness, the sense of Sacred Scripture, I have put them down in my simple fashion, and it has not been my intention to write more than that. Indeed, because in the past these same matters have been expounded by many authors with such subtlety and style and such frequency that they have now become almost wearisome, I have not attempted to quote the authorities for everything; for if I had named everyone who says as I do, the object of this book would have been defeated.

(4) It should also be noted that I have used the device of

9. Cf. Lk 12.55.
10. 1 Tm 1.4.
11. Is 11.9.
12. Ps 150.5.
13. 1 Cor 11.23.

questions and answers between the Disciple and Wisdom only to convey matters more vividly. It is not to be understood that there ever will be just such a disciple as this, or that Wisdom will be concerned with him to everyone else's exclusion, or that only he, more than all others, will love her so much, or that she will do so many great things only for him, but take him to represent everyone who is like him. So, as teachers do, sometimes he speaks as if he were a perfect man, and then as one who is imperfect, sometimes as if he were one who loves Christ with all his heart and has given himself in marriage to him in faith and love, then later as a sinner, pitifully begging God to pardon him his excesses. And so the style changes from time to time, to suit what is then the subject. Sometimes the Son of God is presented as the spouse of the devout soul; then later the same Son is introduced as Eternal Wisdom, wedded to the just man.

(5) Then, too, all the visions described in what follows are not to be interpreted literally, even though many of them may have a literal application; but they use figures of speech. So we read in the Book of Kings[14] how Nathan the prophet, who was sent by the Lord to King David, used a parable with its characters of two men, one rich and one a stranger, to make the king condemn himself because of the sin that he had committed against his servant, and how the wise woman from Thecua pretended to be someone else, and going to the king with a fictitious story of her two sons, moved his heart to mercy.[15] And when the angel who was sent to Tobias was asked by him who he was, he replied, "I am Azarias, the son of the great Ananias."[16] All these things were true, not, indeed, literally, but according to the sense that they conveyed. So the great preacher, the Apostle Paul, adopted the character of his disciples when, in taking them to task, he said: "I indeed am a Paul's man, but I am for Apollo. Are you not men?"[17] And a little later he says: "I have transferred these things in a figure to myself and to Apollo for your sakes, that by us you may

---

14. 2 Kgs 12.1–7.
16. Tb 5.18.

15. 2 Kgs 14.1–21.
17. 1 Cor 3.4.

learn."[18] Again, a diligent reader will easily be able to discern the mysteries hidden in this figure of speech, if only he will use skill and effort.

(6) Yet I pray and entreat the boundless goodness of him who out of his love impelled me to take on this labor, trusting in his kindness that, since he knows that this undertaking is greater than my ability, he will make good what I lack in the hearts of the devout who wish to read of these matters. May everyone who will read through or listen to this little book with a sincere intention be found worthy to take from it some gift of devotion or some God-given grace. But for any reader to be granted this, he must take the trouble to read it carefully, and not indiscriminately to sample one part and then another as if in haste.

(7) And I, knowing well "my imperfections,"[19] as they may be seen in what I know and how I live, have been careful to send this book to you, Hugh,[20] beloved father of your sons and venerable master of the Order of Preachers. You surpass the rest of us through your authority, and you are esteemed for your mastery of theological knowledge, and more than this, you have been given the light of eternal Wisdom and the gifts of the Spirit. This is shown by your letters, in which as a father you exhort your dear sons to seek peace and fraternal love, to be strict in self-discipline and fervent in devotion, in imitation of Christ Jesus. By this care for us you stir us to strive for the perfection of every virtue. Nor is this enough for you, but you are also mindful of the salvation of the many, of the poor creatures chasing after the things of this world. By word and example[21] you invite them to forsake this transient and deceitful world, and to attain to true and eternal wisdom. So may you, most reverend father, test this book with your expert skill and your spiritual discernment. Decide, as should be done in such matters, if there be here too little or too much, and then do what divine Wisdom may inspire, for her glory and the

---

18. 1 Cor 4.6.   19. Ps 138.16.
20. Hugh of Vaucemain, Dominican master general, A.D. 1333–41.
21. From the Dominican Breviary's prayer for a pope; cf. Humbert of Romans, *Of the Three Vows*, ch. 52.

profit of our fellow man.[22] And for any defects that you may find in this, pardon me, who am the meanest of all your sons in the love of God. Do not think me presumptuous to have written this work, but ascribe it to my "jealousy for God,"[23] and, more, to inspiration from on high. "For God is my witness"[24] that he has not let me rest by day or by night, until I submitted to his working in me. Whether that has been for good, you, who "have unction from the holy one,"[25] must test.

(8) It should be known that this little dialogue between Wisdom and the Disciple had its beginning and occasion in the following way. One day, after matins, this same Disciple did as he was accustomed; he had finished his re-enactment of that most bitter journey on which Christ, condemned to death, was led to the place of his Passion. He stood at the lectern before the crucifix, and complained with sorrowing mind to the Crucified One that he had not, and in all his life had never had, a worthily fervid love for that Passion. At once he was placed into a kind of ecstasy, some sort of heavenly light shone on him, and to his mind's eye there were shown a hundred meditations or considerations of Christ's Passion. He was told that every day he should go through these hundred reflections, making one hundred prostrations as he meditated devoutly, and adding so many petitions that he could, so far as that is possible, conform himself in spirit to the suffering Christ by doing this. For the sake of brevity, I have not here written these meditations in full, but I did faithfully record them in our own German vernacular[26] for the benefit of devout men, both learned and simple. So the Disciple, who before was hard to move with compassion, began, by constantly using this form of meditation, to be softened for the recollection of such sufferings, and in this way to receive various insights, as will be described in what follows. Then, when he started to

22. This alludes to the prologue to the Dominican Constitutions.
23. 2 Cor 11.2.   24. Rom 1.9.
25. 1 Jn 2.20.
26. The "Hundred Meditations" form the third and last section of the *Little Book of Eternal Wisdom*; James M. Clark, *The Little Book of Eternal Wisdom and Little Book of Truth* (London, 1953) 159–69.

write these things down, as he was instructed to do, adversity, that tester of good men, tempted him to turn back. But Christ then appeared to him in a vision, as though he were just leaving the pillar at which he was scourged, and permitted the Disciple to touch his wounds, all fresh and bleeding. And in this way adversity's wounds were healed, and the Disciple was given courage to finish what he had begun.

(9) It should also be observed that the first form of this work was written from time to time, and not without the powerful help of grace. The Disciple of whom we have spoken, whose name and station are not given in this book,[27] did not seem there to act as someone working or composing, but rather as one influenced by God. For when he did not know at all what he should write, that was specially revealed to him, and when he ought to write it, and virtually every chapter that he wrote. Yet at other times, when he wanted to compose according to his choice, or to collect material from other books, or even to make notes, and to add to them what he had collected, what he then did was insipid and inept, as if someone were trying to mix flavors or colors that do not blend. Sometimes he had jotted down on his writing tablet the ideas that came to him, but later, when he thought it over carefully, he would discover that it was no different from what he had drawn from the sayings of the holy fathers. But what divine Wisdom poured into him with the gift of spiritual lights was supported by the authority of "Holy Scripture inspired by God"[28] or the saints, with which he would find that it agreed in meaning, or in language and meaning, or at least in general resemblance.

(10) When the work of writing this was finished, the Disciple was gripped by a certain human fear of jealous men. Prompted by envy, they are as busy now as ever to misrepresent or destroy completely what others do, however good it may be. They call divine charisms superstitious imaginings, and they say that holy revelations are brainsick illusions. Like men who have

27. When Suso does refer to himself by name, he uses his pseudonym "Amandus"; cf. Bk. I, ch. 1; Bk. II, ch. 7.
28. 2 Tm 3.16.

never tasted the fruits of the Holy Spirit, they dismiss the deeds of the holy fathers as idle fictions. They have faith in nothing but their own commonplace inventions and their dubious propositions, which they treat as demonstrations of certainties. It is true that we must exercise great caution in accepting private insights, but they are not to be rejected out of hand. So the Disciple, fearing lest the envious would gnaw his work of devotion to shreds, thought that he should perhaps conceal it or suppress it altogether. But divine Wisdom sent him the clearest signs and beautiful revelations to forbid him absolutely to do this, and the blessed Virgin appeared with her Son to a certain person, to command that these matters should be made known to all who love God.

Here the prologue ends.

BOOK I

The Chapters of the First Book

The subject matter of this first book is Christ's most precious Passion, which itself moves men to much fervent love, and how a true disciple of Wisdom should conform himself to it in his actions. To these matters are added certain more general topics and arguments pertaining to the purpose.

Here begins

WISDOM'S WATCH UPON THE HOURS

CHAPTER 1

How Some Chosen Souls, Divine Grace Going before Them, Are Wonderfully Drawn to God, and Particularly How a Certain Youth Was So Drawn

"ER HAVE I LOVED and have sought out from my youth, and have desired to take her for my spouse."[1] There was a certain youth, known to God, who began in the first flower of his young life to be entangled in worldly vanities. The treacherous delights of the world were dragging him down, and he longed to stray from the preservation of his soul's health into the land of unlikeness.[2] But divine Mercy had pity on him, and sent him light in ways that cannot be described, and he was drawn on by sweetness, and by bitterness too, until at last Wisdom's love wonderfully led him back again into the paths of truth.

(2) When, then, this youth, still only a boy and a novice, and not yet versed in the ways of love, was one day applying himself to reading his Bible, there occurred, among other matters, certain words that invite us to the love of Wisdom, and this gave him such delight that "the witty child"[3] set everything else aside, to write these words down on a scrap of paper as well as he could. After this, very often, when he was present

1. Wis 8.2.
2. This concept, popularized in the West by Augustine, sees man's earthly progress as an exile from "likeness" (to his Creator) into the region where that likeness is lost.
3. Wis 8.19.

at the readings at table, he heard how divine Wisdom shows herself to all men, as an exquisite bride and a dearly loved mistress, so that she may be loved. When in the course of time he grew somewhat older, his heart began to be full of love, but still he did not know whither or to what end he might direct this love, or what indeed love might be.

(3) When therefore he would often hear the praises of such a bride as divine Wisdom read aloud, and she said: "Wisdom is better than the most precious works, and whatever may be desired cannot be compared with it.[4] Length of days is in her right hand, and in her left hand riches and glory. She is a tree of life to those who lay hold on her, and he who will retain her is blessed.[5] Forsake her not, and she will keep you; love her, and she will preserve you. Take hold on her, and she will exalt you; you will be glorified by her when you will embrace her."[6] "Say to Wisdom: You are my sister, and call prudence your friend,"[7] his youthful mind was moved by these words, and he began to feel much favor for this divine spouse and to love her ardently.

(4) But his love was still a childish love, because he did not know as he should how to understand these words spiritually; it was not, indeed, that he intended anything earthly or impure in this love, but that he derived from all this something as it were abstracted, sweetly loving and yet not purely divine or wholly human. And by this loving, in a way that was wonderful and beyond words, he was drawn deeper down by God with a savor most sweet and an inward tasting, and this youth began to think and to say to himself: "Ah, how many good things do I hear of this fairest spouse! So why do you dissemble? What is your reason for not testing whether you are worthy to have her as your beloved? Ah, how blessed you would be if you might have her as your bride! For you are young and made for love, and no heart so fervent as yours will ever by any means be alone and starved of love."

(5) So on another day, when the lector at table was reading

4. Prv 8.11.
6. Prv 4.6, 8.

5. Prv 3.16, 18.
7. Prv 7.4.

from the sapiential books, he heard Wisdom praised as follows: "Wisdom is more beautiful than the sun, and above all the order of the stars; being compared with the light, she is found before it.[8] Her have I loved, and I have sought her out from my youth, and I have desired to take her for my spouse; and I became a lover of her beauty. For her sake I shall have glory among the multitude and honor with the ancients. By means of her I shall have immortality, and I shall leave behind me an everlasting memory to them who will come after me. When I go into my house, I shall repose myself with her, for her conversation has no bitterness, nor her company any tediousness, but joy and gladness. In her friendship there is great delight.[9] If you sleep, you will not fear. You will rest, and your sleep will be sweet. For the Lord will be at your side, and he will keep you."[10] So when he had heard these words, the youth began to burn for love of her, and said silently to himself: "Truly, if you search every land, you cannot find her like for grace."

(6) And then it happened that the inciter of evils, the enemy of the human race, envious of the youth's progress, put in him thoughts hostile to these, and said: "You stupid fellow, do you want to love what you do not know, do you want to espouse what you have not seen? 'A handful that you have is better than two hands full that you only hope for.'[11] For those who build their homes on high cliff tops and try to make their love nests too far up the tree more often enjoy hope than realization, for what they store in their barns for food is the wind. Would it not be better to drink your fill out of a wooden bucket than to take less than will quench your thirst from a golden goblet? This bride would be lovable indeed, if she did not forbid every fleshly delight, if she would allow you to rejoice and feast as you wished. But the fact is that everything that is delightful to the body seems to be contrary to her teaching, for she says: "He who loves wine and fine food will not be wise";[12] and again: "You will sleep a little, and you will slumber

8. Wis 7.29.   9. Wis 8.2, 10, 13, 16, 18.
10. Prv 3.24, 26.   11. Cf. Eccl 4.6.
12. Cf. Prv 21.17, 20.1.

a little, and you will fold your hands in sleep a little."[13] So just consider whether there is on earth a spouse so cruel who would be ready to lay these harshest of laws on her lovers!

(7) To this and to similar temptations of his thoughts a certain inward taste of Wisdom replied thus: "O Amandus,[14] dear youth, consider in your loving heart that it is the mark of all lovers that they sustain hardships for the sake of love; 'for there are as many sorrows in love as there are shells on the seashore.'[15] If therefore it is so, is it not most just that he too, the lover who by a special privilege lays claim to her for his spouse who is of such sublime beauty and incomparably adorned with every grace, should suffer some hardships? And he should be the better able, beyond all comparison, to sustain this who has as the object for his labors one who is so much more desirable. Turn over now in your mind the unnumbered and astonishing travails that, as you have read and heard, the lovers of this world, shameful though it be, have endured for a love completely worthless! Did you not groan when you were told about that lad whom you knew who was so sick with love for a girl that he went around with an iron band cutting into his flesh? Oh, the amazing power of love! Oh, how many have there been, how many are there who have risked possessions and life and honor and their immortal souls, and have exposed themselves to innumerable dangers, when love has bound them, or, better, blinded them! And they indeed did so to receive a corruptible and brief reward, but yours will be incorruptible.[16] 'Give ear, my son, and take wise counsel, and do not cast away my advice. Put your feet into her fetters and your neck into her chains. Bow down your shoulder and bear her, and do not be aggrieved by her bonds.'[17] 'For in the last end you will find rest in her, and she will be turned into your joy. Then her fetters will be a strong defense for you, and a

13. Prv 6.10.
14. "Amandus," (lovable one) is not, as has sometimes been thought and stated, any given or religious name that Suso bore, but the lover's name by which Wisdom addressed him in their colloquies. See II.7.
15. Ovid, *The Art of Love.*   16. Cf. 1 Cor 9.25.
17. Ecclus 6.24–26.

firm foundation, and her chain will be a robe of glory. For in her is the beauty of life, and her bonds are a healthful binding. You will put her on as a robe of glory, and you will set her on yourself as a crown of joy.'[18] 'You will labor for a little, and you will find much rest for yourself.'[19] 'Wine and music rejoice the heart, but the love of Wisdom is above them both.'[20] So do not give up, whoever may urge you, but go on, and 'join yourself from your heart'[21] to the love of that spouse." Therefore, through such consoling words and others like them, he was refreshed and strengthened in his holy purpose.

(8) On one occasion, when he was being urged by most subtle arguments to love the world and give up God, impatient for love, he poured out his heart to God and uttered these laments: "Oh, happy the lover who has found, close by, the place where his love may rest! For if one loves, what helps in loving kindles a happy fire.[22] But alas for me, poor wretch who lacks the fruit and the longed-for reward of love, when nowhere in this world do I find one who will answer to this great love in my heart!" I counseled my troubled mind, telling it to forsake its love, to join the Epicureans' sect and to yearn for the peace of the flesh. "See," my soul said, "how happily in this season the fat rams and the Easter lambs are grazing in the lush meadows and the rich pastures, telling us, not indeed with words but in what they do, that the world knows no joy greater than the belly's joys.[23] But you with your love grow leaner every day,[24] not finding what you seek, not content with what you find. Therefore listen to a wise man's advice: 'Let the milk of the goats be enough'[25] for your serving maids to use, and, again, 'It is better to see what you may want than to desire what you cannot know.'[26] But if it pleases you better to go on loving and to try through your love to reach the mansions of the stars,[27] nevertheless provide yourself here on earth at least with those to whom you can join yourself in love, and

18. Ecclus 6.29–32.
19. Cf. Ecclus 51.35.
20. Ecclus 40.20.
21. Ecclus 6.35.
22. Ovid, *The Cure for Love*, 13.
23. This was a popular proverb.
24. Cf. 2 Kgs 13.4.
25. Prv 27.27.
26. Eccl 6.9.
27. Ovid, *The Art of Love*, 2.39.

who will drive away your depressions and bring joys to your heart. See how many lovers there can be found today who ask for God's gifts, and who yet do not for love of him give up more fleeting joys, who want to be loved by you and still do not want to be severed from their carnal loves. So 'go and do in like manner.'"[28]

(9) When the Disciple, as I say, was turning these things over in his mind, secretly and as it were furtively, he received this inward answer from supreme Wisdom: "The man is very wrong indeed who judges that these notorious carousers, the new hangers-on of an ancient sect long ago condemned,[29] are enjoying happiness as they 'provide for the desires of the flesh'[30] whilst they 'feast sumptuously every day,'[31] unless, perhaps, it is the happiness of beasts in which they are delighting, for beasts they are not unlike. But the noble mind of a rational man, lifted on high by knowledge and love, there finds a happiness by far more elevated and perfect, where he is perfectly joined to the one whom he loves by contemplation and love. Nor does it matter if what is longed for is granted only in part and at times, for a little precious balsam is worth more than a lot of vinegar. 'One bunch of grapes of Ephraim is better than the vintages of Abiezer.'[32] What is more, a man is completely mad who wants to join some girl of his to a love that is divine. You see that two earthly loves cannot be made to agree together; how therefore is a heavenly love to be allied to an earthly one? The man who thinks that he can make a union between such majesty and such vileness is simply attempting the impossible." The mind of this youth for long endured the various conflicts of such thoughts, and his pliant spirit was moved, now here, now there.

(10) "In the meantime it happened"[33] that these words, or others like them, were read aloud a second time: "I have found a woman more bitter than death, who is the hunters' snare, and her heart is a net, and her hands are bonds. He who

28. Lk 10.37. 29. The Epicureans.
30. Cf. Rom 13.14. 31. Lk 16.19.
32. Jgs 8.2. 33. 2 Kgs 11.2.

pleases God will escape from her, but he who is a sinner will be caught by her."[34] Yet on the contrary it is said of the divine spouse: "I have stretched out my branches as the terebinth, and my branches are of honor and of grace. I perfumed my dwelling as the frankincense not cut, and my scent is as the purest balm.[35] He who will find me will find peace and will store up salvation from the Lord."[36] When he had heard these things, the youth replied to a certain clamor calling out, as it were, inside him in an excess of emotion: "It is true, it is true, nor is there anything else that could be said more truly. From now on, 'it is determined.'[37] I have reached my decision! I shall indeed risk death for myself, so that I may win her as my beloved and my spouse. She will be the spouse, and I shall be her poor serf. She will be the teacher, and I shall be her pupil. Oh, if only it were permitted to me to speak to this spouse whom I love above all, if only once it were granted to me to see her! Ah, eternal God, who or what is she of whom I hear such things?"

(11) And as he so vehemently longed to know these things and burned in his desire, he was visited by a certain perception of which words cannot tell, in which this spouse was manifested to him in this way. An ivory "throne in a pillar of a cloud,"[38] of great and wondrous beauty, appeared, and from the pillar the marvellous loveliness of the spouse, "in golden garments bordered wlth embroidery,"[39] shone out. Her crown was eternity, her girdle joyful happiness, her words gentle sweetness, her embrace the perfect fullness of all good. When the Disciple wished to speak familiarly to her, since she seemed near enough for this, she was soon seen to move very far off. First her height would extend beyond the arch of the highest heaven, then she seemed to be very small,[40] and though she remained motionless, she looked to be "more ac-

---

34. Eccl 7.27.   35. Ecclus 24.22, 21.
36. Prv 8.35.   37. 2 Kgs 19.29.
38. Ecclus 24.7.   39. Ps 44.10.
40. This specific detail is borrowed from Boethius's description, *The Consolation of Philosophy* I, prose 1, of Lady Philosophy's first appearance to him, and the whole passage is reminiscent of the *Consolation*.

tive than all active things."[41] She was present, yet she was not descried; she permitted herself to grasp, and yet she was not grasped herself.[42] She "reached from end to end mightily and ordered all things sweetly."[43] First one thought that here one had a delicate young girl, and then suddenly a most handsome youth was found. Sometimes too she put on a most solemn countenance, as if she were the mistress of all arts, and then she appeared with lovely looks and rosy face. Meanwhile, as the Disciple fixed all his gaze upon her, caught up in his longing for her love, she in most friendly fashion seemed to turn to him and bow, and with gracious look and gentle and smiling eyes, yet with a most holy light, to amaze every man's mind, streaming from her most solemn countenance, she saluted him and said: "'My son, give me your heart.'"[44] When he heard this, his heart melted for the exceeding sweetness of love, and as though caught in an ecstasy he prostrated himself at her feet, giving thanks and greatly delighted by her presence.

(12) But as time went on and these things passed from his memory, and once again evil thoughts grew up in his mind and undid these benefits, so that "he was almost sinking"[45] in the ocean's tides, most of all because in all these things which are written he could not grasp the one whom he loved, it happened that they read the Apostle Paul, who gave a clear definition of what has been discussed. For he said that "Christ is the power of God and the wisdom of God,"[46] and that in him "are hidden all the treasures of wisdom and knowledge"[47] of God; yet these words he did not well understand in his immature mind and "with his palate not yet cleansed,"[48] for he did not yet know how to love Christ wisely, that is, according to his divinity, and in his love he was seeking for things more of the present than of the future.

41. Wis 7.24.
42. "grasp . . . not grasped": this is *contentio*: see Edmund Colledge and James Walsh, *A Book of Showings to the Anchoress Julian of Norwich* (Toronto, 1978) 738.
43. Wis 8.1.   44. Prv 23. 26.
45. Lk 5.7.   46. 1 Cor 1.24.
47. Col 2.3.   48. Augustine, *Conf.* 7.16.

(13) When at last the years of his boyhood had gone by and he had come to mature age, on one occasion his mind was illumined as cannot be described, so that, in some way wholly absorbed in the spirit, he was filled with exceeding delight; and then he was most fully informed about these matters which have been discussed, so that the direction of his gaze and the love of his heart "could not any longer be changed or distracted."[49] No physical presence or anything bodily appeared in this vision, and yet that which was seen, not corporeally but superessentially, contained within it every possible delight. In this springing source there was no form or matter or depicted image, but a pure and most simple essence, with a perfect distinction of the Persons. Certainly he did not see God in his essence, as he is in himself, in this abstraction which is being described, but only a certain supernatural emanation of divine rays, brighter than light,[50] and he had not the power to express in words what he saw within himself. Yet that object, flowing with sweetness, containing in itself everything that is good, shown to him on that occasion, was not only the Person of the Father or solely the Person of the Son or of the Holy Spirit, nor was it the deity itself accepted in its most abstract simplicity, but it was that same divine essence accepted according to our fashion of understanding, as it is the supreme and untellable good, the supremely lovable, supremely beautiful and delectable, and the supremely good first beginning of all good things found in created beings. And he understood that this was that spouse of whom we have told, Eternal Wisdom. It is indeed true that each of the Persons may be accepted as being himself Wisdom, and that all the Persons together are one, eternal Wisdom; yet since wisdom is attributed to the Son, and since, by reason of his being begotten, this is fitting to him, therefore it is customary for the Father's beloved Son to be understood by that appellation, at times indeed as God, again as man, as in either nature alike devotion can attain its object and love can find its solace.

49. 1 Kgs 1.18.
50. The thought and language here are those of pseudo-Dionysius, *The Divine Names*, ch. 1.

(14) After this, therefore, the life and the spiritual exercises of this Disciple were spent in a devoted preoccupation with this most divine spouse. For whatever might appear that was lovable or beautiful or delightful and joyous, all of this he referred back to him "from whom all good things proceed."[51] If from time to time there might appear some human beauty, lovable and well formed, and the thought should then present itself that at least this beauty was not to be found in his lovable Wisdom, he would reply: "Be it so. But the light-giving rays of the sun are not such a light as can be produced out of wax or any other fluid, and yet it is a light purer and finer than every light made from whatever material. It is so in what we are considering, for this beauty you see is nothing, compared with the beauty which there is in its exemplary principle, that is, in the divine heart. For if you take away from this lovable creature whatever it possesses of imperfection, materiality and bodily dross, preserving only what has perfection and goodness, all that is present in Eternal Wisdom, in a more noble and eminent way than may be in this or in any other created being."[52]

(15) Through these and similar experiences, this youth at last reached the point where, whenever he heard love songs or suchlike, he would turn all these about and apply them to his Wisdom, whom he loved with the most pure love of his heart, so that they encouraged his love for her to grow. Oh, how often did he press this most sweet, this only love of his heart, in a most burning longing, his eyes shedding tears of weeping for his gentle love, his loving arms stretched out in yearning, enfolding her within his heart in embraces not to be described! Who would be able to tell of the loving looks with which he was very often regaled, of the "secret silences"[53] in which he delighted in the sweetest savor of her presence?

(16) And at times when some of the brethren, after midday office had been said, asked permission to go into the town for

51. This is from the collect for the fourth Sunday after Easter in the Dominican Breviary.

52. Cf. *ST* I, q.4, a.2; I, q.13, a.3–4.

53. The phrase is used by Rufinus of Aquileia (ob. 410) in his translation, *History of the Monks*, dealing with Ammon, the hermit of Nitria.

the sake of visiting their friends, this youth would seek out a secret place and begin to talk to his love, saying: "Ah, mistress of love, impressed before all others deep in my heart, consider what a uniting power love is,[54] joining the lover with that which he loves or, better, changing him into it. Ah, I beg, come, you too, my love, come into the anchorhold of my heart, kept for you alone, adorned with your love as with the loveliest roses; 'come,' I say, and there 'let us be filled from the breasts of your consolation,'[55] and rejoice in the embraces that we long for."

(17) So it often happened, from these and similar experiences, that his heart would feel as if it began to be on fire from the vehemence of his love, and through a violent motion and pulse he evinced the power of love, and by his deep sighs he made known the ardor of his burning affections. And just as a little infant, which cannot yet speak, safely esconced in its mother's lap, longs to laugh up at its joyful mother, and with the movement of its head and the motions of its whole body strives to clap its hands, so this man's heart "in the midst of his bowels"[56] exulted and seemed to be transported in the presence of such majesty, and when his desire was kindled, he made it as plain as he could that his beloved was there. And with inward words he said to his spouse, divine Wisdom, in a voice full of rejoicing: "You are the most noble empress of my heart, fairest queen, and generous dispenser of all graces. In you I possess riches and glory, delights and the plenty of all good things, and whatever there is to desire, through you it is mine." And sweetly ruminating upon this, at once his face began to brighten, his heart to jubilate, his spirit to exult, and in his exultation he broke out with these words: "I loved Wisdom above health and all beauty, and chose to have her instead of light; now all good things came to me together with her."[57]

54. Cf. pseudo-Dionysius, *The Divine Names*, ch. 4.
55. Is 66.11.   56. Ps 21.15.
57. The Dominican Breviary's adaptation of Wis 7.10–11.

CHAPTER 2

How the Passion of Christ May Be a Prelude to Knowledge of the Godhead, and of What Form Christ Assumed through the Bitterness of His Passion

EANWHILE, as these things were happening, the Disciple gathered trust in God, and spoke to the beloved whom he had espoused with these words: "O most loving Wisdom, you who alone know perfectly the nature of a lover's heart, plainly you know that no one can love what he does not know;[1] therefore, since you demand that I love you alone, and that I make you lovable[2] to all men, then grant me to know you better, so that I may be better able to fulfill what you command and teach."

(2) Wisdom: The process by which created things come forth from him who is in the natural order the summit and head of all things, God, is achieved by a descent from things more perfect to things more imperfect, for all perfections of things descend by some order from the supreme pole about which all things turn, God. Yet man, naturally beginning from things that are inferior, and ascending step by step, attains to the knowledge of things that are divine,[3] so that if you want to arrive at a knowledge of the Divinity, it remains for you to learn, through that humanity which the Son accepted, and through the Passion of that humanity to ascend, as it were, step by step along the king's highway to what is higher.

(3) Disciple: O Eternal Wisdom, who bowed yourself low

---

1. Augustine, *On the Trinity* 10.1.
2. *solum . . . dilectum*; here Suso is calculatingly using masculine adjective forms for "Wisdom, who is Christ."
3. *CG* 4.1.

from the high throne, "from the royal seat"[4] in the heart of the eternal Father, into this vale of misery, and bore for thirty-three years long the exile of this world, and who wished to show "the exceeding charity"[5] with which you had loved the human race, by the mystery of your most bitter Passion and your death, by this untellable love of your death, I implore you with all my heart that you will deign to show yourself to me in that form and disposition, most loving, which you took upon yourself in the most bitter sorrow of your Passion.

(4) Wisdom: The more I take on the pallor of death out of the greatness of my love and sorrow, the more hideous I appear in a deathly discoloring, the more lovable shall I become to a loving heart and a mind well disposed. For just as a lover naturally longs to be loved in return, so too does he ask from the beloved some manifestation of love; for a love that is kept hidden is unknown except to the lover. So it is that lovers are accustomed by all the means which they possess to seek for signs and marks of love from their beloved ones, and very often it happens that when the tongue is silent, the inclination that has been concealed shows the power of a hidden love, and what is the heart's secret is shown by outward signs. And sometimes too it happens that what in a lover is judged unseemly by those who are not in love is praised by those who love as seemly above all things.

(5) Disciple: Indeed, in the love of this world I know what you say to be very true; but how such things may be in a crucified man I cannot yet clearly see, for though it be that in one of this world's loved ones nothing could ever be found that would even displease his lover, there are yet many more suitable tokens of love to please anyone who sees them. But this lover is misshapen by the sorrow of death, and how he could appear lovable I do not understand, he whose disposition seems all opposed to loving, since his outward appearance is all hideous with bruises, and inwardly he shrivels up for sor-

4. Wis 18.15, quoted in the Dominican Missal's introit for the Sunday after the Nativity.
5. Eph 2.4.

row, so that he could show "no beauty whatever in him or comeliness"[6] to lovers' eyes, but he is all full of sorrow and miseries. So how can you call him lovable whom plain fact shows to be wretched?

(6) Wisdom: True lovers pay little heed to "the thorn that brings to birth the rose,"[7] so long as they acquire the rose which they yearn to possess. Nor do those who are truly wise prefer lovely gilded coffers that yet contain vile things to the meanest boxes that hide most precious jewels. So the brides of this world make specious offer of what is sweet and mild, yet afterwards "they will spread abroad poison like a basilisk."[8] Outside they shine "with a rosy color,"[9] "bright as the snow,"[10] but inside they are full of poisonous rottenness, and pus and filth; with their words they love, yet with their deeds more often they show their treachery. Against this the bride of your soul, Eternal Wisdom, might be judged by externals to be mean of appearance, abject and despicable, yet within she is made lovely for a feast of living light. Outside the flesh appears dead, yet "the brightness of the divinity"[11] which is not seen, shines within. The flesh appears wretched, yet how it is glorified remains hidden. If you think all this abject, think it splendid too. "Such is my beloved,"[12] he whom you see from without disfigured, because if it were granted to see him only for an instant "in his beauty,"[13] that would make you to faint away for the brightness of his light, for the beauty of his face, for the greatness of his joys, because "no man can see him and live."[14] For this is he "on whom the angels desire to look."[15] Yet the outward disposition and form of his body robbed of life is not to be judged as disfigurement, as you think, but the greatest beauty, for you should pay no heed to how he who is now seen

6. Is 53.2.
7. From the Dominican Breviary for feasts of the Blessed Virgin Mary.
8. Prv 23.32.   9. Est 15.8.
10. From the Dominican Breviary's office for the feast of the Crown of Thorns.
11. *Fulgor divinitatis*, also used in homilies by Bede and Bernard of Clairvaux.
12. Cant 5.16.   13. Is 33.17.
14. Cf. Ex 33.20.   15. 1 Pt 1.12.

looks, but rather to what things he suffered, and why, and for what. If you ask why, it is certain that it was "out of great charity"[16] and love. If you ask for what, it is certain that it was for you, that with his disfigurement he might make you fair, with his "bruises"[17] he might heal you, with his death he might give you the immortality of everlasting life. So therefore you will see your beloved, if you look on him with the eye of love, full of charity and love, who has not loved with words alone as do these lights of love, but who gave proof that he loved by his deeds, for he loved until death and in dying. So therefore it is seen that that form and disposition of the outer man which he drew upon himself from the bitterness of his Passion is more expressive of love than it is indicative of disfigurement. Nor is it any hindrance that this may not be seen by one who does not love, for "to sick eyes the light is hateful that to sound eyes is lovable."[18]

(7) Disciple: Truly and undoubtedly it is so; and "blessed are the eyes"[19] that see so, for this is not for all but for a few, that is, for those who love fervidly. Just as "favor is deceitful and beauty is vain,"[20] he is not undeservedly considered stupid who loves for appearances and not for truth. For because he takes the false for the true, he will go without the fruits he desired.

(8) Wisdom: So that I may revive in your mind the saving memory of my Passion, which should be printed there, and to show how even greater is the manner and the matter of my love, I shall briefly recount for your most devout ears some things about that Passion.

16. Eph 2.4.   17. Cf. Is 53.5.
18. *Conf.* 7.16, quoted in the Dominican Breviary for Augustine's feast, and several times by Eckhart.
19. Lk 10.23.   20. Prv 31.30.

CHAPTER 3

Of Certain of Christ's Sufferings, and How His True Lover Should Conform Himself to Them, and Why God Wished to Redeem the Human Race through Such a Death

"EFORE THE festival day of the Pasch, when the Last Supper was completed"[1] with the disciples, and the time was approaching "when I pass out of this world to the Father,"[2] I went out with the eleven and made my way to the Mount of Olives, where "being in agony and having prayed for long,"[3] and understanding what cruel kinds of torment now threatened me, "my sweat became as drops of blood trickling down upon the ground."[4] It would scarcely be believable to any man living beneath the heavens, with what anguishes, what powerful and terrible terrors of death my delicate nature, horrified at the approach of my death, was then possessed. Afterwards the sons of darkness came to attack me; they took violent hold on me, bound me cruelly and led me back into the city. Through that night those sacrilegious men wreaked on me various kinds of torment, they had their fill of my sufferings, they afflicted me with mockery and blows, insults and abuse without number. They spat their filthy spittle in my fair face, they blindfolded my eyes, they rained blows on my neck as they derided me. "And when morning had come"[5] and I had witnessed to the truth in Caiphas's court, they all cried out that I was guilty and should be put to death. She who gave me birth lamented over me in her mother's heart, and "wept and was utterly disconsolate"[6] when she saw

1. Jn 13.1–2.   2. Jn 13.1.
3. Lk 22.43.   4. Lk 22.44.
5. Mt 27.1.   6. Tb 10.4.

me exposed to such insults and anguish. Then I was led before Pilate the governor, and I was accused and condemned. My enemies looked on me "with terrible eyes,"[7] "and they stood against me as giants."[8] Yet I stood meekly there "as a gentle lamb that is carried to be a victim,"[9] with my head humbled and my heart full of patience. After this, when Herod had dressed me in a white garment, as if I were a clown, to mock me,[10] they flogged my seemly body with most cruel scourges, and pierced my tender head with vicious thorns.[11] My lovely face was all filthy with spittle and my trickling blood, and so at last they led me out, woefully condemned and with a cross loaded on my own shoulders, to the place of my suffering, as they yelled and shouted: "Away with him! Away with him! Crucify" the criminal.[12]

(2) Disciple: O purest pity, if the beginning of your Passion was so bitter, alas, what will be the end and consummation of such sorrow? Truly, for any irrational beast to endure such cruelties would seem to me as misery; so how much more for you, Creator of all things and the fairest of men, to suffer "such monstrous torments"[13] and sufferings. Justly indeed, with the deepest love of my heart and with all my powers of compassion, my soul will suffer with you.

(3) But there is one thing that I long to know from you, for about this I never cease to marvel. To me, seeking your divinity, you show your humanity; I seek sweetness, and you offer bitterness; I ask for milk from your breasts, and your gift for me is to fight in manful battles. O Eternal Wisdom, why do you do this, and what do you want to show by it?

(4) Wisdom: "Be it known to you"[14] that it is not granted to attain the heights of divinity or an unaccustomed sweetness, unless by the paths that lead to a devout faith, and by the progress of love through the bitterness of my humanity and

7. Jb 16.10.
8. From the Dominican Breviary for Holy Saturday.
9. Jer 11.19.   10. Lk 23.11.
11. Mt 27.26, 29.   12. Jn 19.15.
13. From the Dominican Breviary for the Common of Martyrs.
14. Dn 3.18.

Passion. And if this has been evaded, the higher anyone climbs, the farther will he fall. For this is the way by which one must go, this is the gate through which access to that longed-for goal is given. So, therefore, set aside now all your anxious fear, and put on a manly spirit. Act with constancy, and stand steadfastly with me in the front line of the battle, for it is not fitting for a servant to take his ease when he sees his master struggling so strenuously. Look with your mind's eye on David's band of strong men,[15] and if you want to be enlisted as a spiritual soldier of the eternal King, you must cast off your onetime sloth. Follow the example of David's three strong men, and bear yourself unchangingly in good times and in bad, so that you may pass through the thick of your enemies, may draw water at the well of Bethlehem, and may give the great King the drink he desires, submitting yourself to every labor so that you may be obedient to his wishes.

(5) Put on "as a giant"[16] the dress of war. "Take to yourself my armor."[17] An arms-bearer should follow his lord, he does not go before him; and you will be given to drink from the cup of which I have drunk,[18] and the hardships I have borne to the end you too will suffer in spirit, so far as you can. For your heart will know anguish through the daily mortification of your senses as they oppose your reason, and the onslaught of the many tribulations that dispose you to my love, and it will be suffused as it were in a bloody sweat. For I want to enrich the garden you have planted with the rosy blossoms that are anguishes and tribulations.[19] As you conquer the habits that have grown old in you, you will be taken captive and, in a manner, bound; for you will endure from my enemies secret calumnies and open insults and shames, but you will always bear my Passion too in your breast, as a most faithful mother carries her child in her bosom. You will suffer re-

---

15. 2 Kgs 23.16.   16. 1 Mc 3.3.
17. Eph 6.13.   18. Cf. Mt 20.22.
19. On the employment of red roses in the Suso hagiography and iconography to symbolize "the manifold sufferings he must endure," see Edmund Colledge and J. C. Marler, "'Mystical' Pictures in the Suso 'Exemplar,'" AFP 54 (1984): 310–12.

proaches and unjust judgments from many, you will have detraction from the envious, and your head will be crowned as if with thorns when your spiritual endeavors are frustrated by the goadings of envy. Then after these things you will be led with me "outside the camp, bearing my reproach,"[20] when you will abandon, so far as you may, yourself and your own will and all created things that hinder your salvation, as a man about to die abandons everything at the last passing of his spirit. Therefore be strong in spirit, "and prepare your soul for temptation,"[21] for "I have told you the things that are to come."[22]

(6) Disciple: O, abyss beyond all scrutiny, the judgments of God! O, sentence so much to be feared, eternally preordained! Why, if I may say it, did you not decree that the human race was to be saved by some other means less savage? O, if it were permitted to wretched men to say this to you: Why did you do so? Could you not in your eternal wisdom have found another way both to save us miserable ones and to show your love to us and still to have spared such sorrows for yourself, such compassion for us? Justly indeed did a holy prophet of old dare to seem in his secret thoughts to be opposing your design, when he said: "Why will you be as a wandering man, as a mighty man who cannot save?"[23]

(7) Wisdom: The divine substance in its strength surpasses every form to which the human intellect can attain.[24] So, since the intellect cannot grasp that substance, neither will it be able to scrutinize the depths of divine judgment, those depths through which all created things attain their end. And so too let them who depend solely on the gracious favor of the divine will beware of too much restless enquiry,[25] so that "a searcher for majesty will not be overwhelmed by glory."[26] For God in this his immensity could through his omnipotent power call

20. Heb 13.13.   21. Ecclus 2.1.
22. Gn 49.1.   23. Jer 14.9.
24. This is almost literally from *CG* 1.14.
25. This follows the Dominican Breviary in a lesson for the Annunciation, which borrows from a sermon of Basil the Great, *Of Christ's Human Begetting*.
26. Prv 25.27.

human nature back to himself in many other ways, but, conditions being what they now are, there was no way that could be more fitting.[27]

(8) For the author of that nature is not in his working concerned that his might shall prevail, but rather that what is fitting for every creature according to its nature be provided. So since man, because of the imperfection of the human intellect, can know only a very few things that are true, even about natural and mundane matters, by means of scientific deduction, and even those he will not master except by the greatest effort and toil every day, before he perhaps advances by natural means from what is visible to the invisible, from what is bodily to the spiritual, how, I ask you, could the divine mysteries more fittingly be known, and especially those glorious beginnings of the faith, which exceed every power of the intellect, than by being revealed through divine Wisdom, who is infallible Truth, taking flesh, so that "God's attributes, invisible since the creation of the world, are clearly seen and understood through those things that are made,"[28] and that his everlasting might and his divinity should be made known by the humanity that he assumed?

(9) And how should man, who lost his joys through his ill-regulated affections, more regularly have regained what he had lost than through worldly tribulation?

(10) And what is more, since "the way that leads to life is narrow, and the paths are close,"[29] and before the Incarnation they may have been less worn, how could this way be made easier except in this manner, that he who told us of it should go along it before us, making that toilsome path lighter by his own most bitter suffering, and so easing for the creature the road that its Creator had first trodden with such constancy?

(11) Just consider this in yourself. If you were found guilty and condemned to suffer death, and someone were to accept for you the executioner's stroke in his own body, allowing you to go off scot free, how could he show you more charity and

27. Augustine, *On the Trinity* 13.10, quoted in *ST* III q. 1, a. 2, c.
28. Rom 1.20.   29. Mt 7.14.

love, or make you more indebted to him, and urge you more to love him in return?

(12) Ask every created being, "and it will teach you," ask the ordering of the whole universe "and it will answer you"[30] that there was no fairer and more fitting manner to serve justice and also to show mercy, to exalt human nature, to pour out divine goodness and then to bring peace to heaven and earth than by the sorrow of the Passion of such a mediator and by the bitterness of his death.

(13) Nor must you let the labors of the elect terrify you, or the dangers that threaten you break you down, for the untellable sweetness of my presence and the amazing softness of love will provide either that you do not feel any adversity or that you will bear it most easily "by the anointing that instructs."[31] For who will more enjoy the privilege of spiritual consolation or the grace of visitation from on high than he who endures for my sake the bitterest tribulations?[32] Anyone who has often tasted the kernel's sweetness will pay less heed to the shell's sour taste. And a champion known to be a strong and useful man to have by you in a fight, usually people hope that he has already won. So "do not let your heart be dismayed,"[33] but have my Passion always in your mind, and "write it in your heart as in a book,"[34] and take care to conform yourself to it so far as you are able. And now, because I want to instill in you a greater love for the bitterness of my salvific Passion, let us follow further the order in which it is recounted.

(14) When they had led me "outside the camp,"[35] they hung me on the gibbet of the cross between two thieves, merely so that my death might appear the more vile. And as I remained

30. Jb 12.7–8.
31. Cf. 1 Jn 2.27 and Bernard of Clairvaux, *Sermons on the Canticles*, 17.1 n.2.
32. This is paraphrasing Eckhart's German treatise, *On Detachment*: "No one will enjoy more eternal sweetness than those who endure with Christ in the greatest bitterness."
33. Cf. 1 Kgs 17.32.
34. From a responsory in the Dominican Breviary for the fourth Sunday in Lent.
35. Heb 13.13.

nailed in that place, and the cruelest "sorrows of death surrounded me,"[36] my eyes, which once beamed bright, grew dark, my divine ears were filled with mockery, my sense of smell was afflicted with an evil stench, my sweetest mouth was made bitter with a draft of gall. "They struck me, they wounded me,"[37] and they had so lacerated my flesh with cruelest scourgings that torrents of blood spouted out in answer to their savage blows, and ran down my tender body in every direction, so that everyone could see it all spattered with gore. O, if you had seen me in that hour, hanging so wretchedly from my gallows, your soul would have failed for grief! Ah, in that hour and in that piteous time I was robbed of all the wide spaces of the earth, so that I had "nowhere to lay my head,"[38] worn out with wretchedness, but it hung as I bowed it down.[39] They had rained buffets and blows upon my neck, and they had befouled my seemly face with their spittle. My lively coloring had changed to ashen pallor, and all my beauty was so quenched and waning that no longer did I seem as I should, but "as it were some leper, whose appearance seemed to grow loathsome."[40]

(15) Disciple: O, "who will give me"[41] now in this hour to look as I desire upon your lovable face, so woefully changed, that with a heart broken open I may wash it with the tempest of my tears? O mirror of purity, O fairest object of all virtues and graces, "on whom the angels desire to look,"[42] delighting to fasten their gaze on the most joyous of prospects with a happiness that never flags, who will give to my heart a feeling of compassion so great, so extraordinary that in its intensity it may surpass all the pity that hearts burning with this incomparable love can feel? O, that I might shed all the tears that every eye has ever wept, that I might utter the mourning words that every tongue has spoken, that I might be granted to offer some better exchange for your Passion!

(16)Wisdom: No one offers me a better exchange for my

36. Cf. Ps 17.5, 114.3.
37. Cant 5.7.
38. Cf. Mt 8.20.
39. Cf. Jn 19.30.
40. Cf. Is 53.2–4.
41. Cant 8.1.
42. 1 Pt 1.12.

Passion than he who follows after it, not only with his words but also with his deeds, who always "bears in his body the marks,"[43] that is, the works of the cross, humbly following along in my footsteps, so that he treads worldly joys underfoot and has no fear of ill fortune, who ever presses on, with a burning desire, up towards the peak of spiritual perfection. I tell you that floods of tears as plentiful as the rivers in torrent would not be so acceptable to me as are the tears of a loving heart, moved by a feeling of compassion, for they are dear and welcome to God.

(17) Disciple: Most loving Wisdom, for this I long to be taught how I ought to conform myself to you in those sufferings of which you have spoken.

(18) Wisdom: "Turn away your eyes"[44] lest they should see harmful things, your ears lest they hear follies, and for the sweets you long for, accept the bitter. Discard the superfluous and ill-ordered delights of your body; seek for your heart's peace and quiet in me alone; accept with rejoicing every tribulation; endure with patience wrongs put upon you, and long to be despised by everyone. Learn to defeat your own will in everything, and constantly to mortify the desires of your flesh for love of the Savior who dies for you. These, my son, these, I tell you, are the first beginnings which Eternal Wisdom hands on to you and all her other lovers, which are incised, as you can see, in this open book which is my crucified body.

(19) Disciple: So "plentiful"[45] and so boundless is the faithfulness of your Redemption, surpassing all that every mortal could devise, that even if we put aside the multitude of all its other benefits, the great vastness and the loving faithfulness alone of your Passion which you undertook for love would by right compel the love of every heart to itself. But now, O Eternal Wisdom, my soul burns with thirst to hear once again from you that which to wretched men tastes so sweetly. What, I pray you, does such a love ask for itself, or what was in your thought when you undertook to suffer so bitterly? Why did you not

43. Cf. Gal 6.17.   44. Cant 6.4.
45. Ps 129.7.

provide for yourself, why were you not merciful to yourself? For beyond any doubt, if it had pleased you, this could have been more easily accomplished.

(20) Wisdom: The greatness of my love did not permit me to do so. The flames of my love were raging so that they would spare nothing, that they would not suffer tempering. That fire burned so in me that no one ever knew so fiery a thirst for springs of most limpid waters, no dying man ever craved for the life that all mortals cling to, as I for love have thirsted to save sinners and to show myself to them to win their love. It would be easier to bring back the day that is gone, to make every flower that has withered since the beginning of the world to bloom again, to store up once more every countless raindrop that ever fell, than to measure or to estimate the incomprehensible boundlessness of my love; and so it was that my fair body was given over to unnumbered sufferings, for it to bear as certain tokens of my love, so that upon all my crucified body there was not found room even to dot an "i," there was nowhere that the marks of sorrow and love did not shine out. And even here and now it is granted to you through my dispensation in some fashion to look upon this.

(21) See now my slender, lovely hands both cruelly riven by the nails, my arms frightfully racked, my feet pierced through, my legs feeble and twisted and cruelly contorted. Look at my body's tender limbs, penned in as fast as any stockyard beast, and sprinkled and spattered all over with my blood. My body, which had the charm of youthful grace, no longer blooms, but has withered and faded. My tender back was laid to rest on the roughest of woods, the cross. My sagging body dragged upon the nails that held it fast, so that the anguish of my wounds increased. What more? They overwhelmed me with savage wounds and bitter pains "from the soles of my feet to the top of my head."[46] "They have drawn my life down into the lake of death."[47] They did not spare me, but "they have filled me with bitterness,"[48] and with cunning torments they have

46. Is 1.6.
47. A responsory from the Dominican Breviary for Palm Sunday.
48. Idem, and cf. Lam 3.15.

afflicted "the King of glory."[49] And all these wounds of love I have sustained with a great longing of my heart, so that with my bruises I might heal the wounds of sinners, that I might pay the debts of wretched sinners, and that I might reconcile to our heavenly Father all who wish to go back to him.[50]

49. Ps 23.7, etc.; cf. the Dominican Breviary for the feast of the Crown of Thorns.

50. Cf. Lk 15.18.

CHAPTER 4

How the Soul, Which Has Lost Her Spouse through Sin, Finds Him beneath the Cross through Fervent Penitence When She Is Helped by Christ's Passion

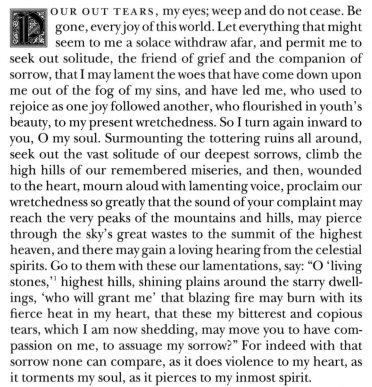OUR OUT TEARS, my eyes; weep and do not cease. Be gone, every joy of this world. Let everything that might seem to me a solace withdraw afar, and permit me to seek out solitude, the friend of grief and the companion of sorrow, that I may lament the woes that have come down upon me out of the fog of my sins, and have led me, who used to rejoice as one joy followed another, who flourished in youth's beauty, to my present wretchedness. So I turn again inward to you, O my soul. Surmounting the tottering ruins all around, seek out the vast solitude of our deepest sorrows, climb the high hills of our remembered miseries, and then, wounded to the heart, mourn aloud with lamenting voice, proclaim our wretchedness so greatly that the sound of your complaint may reach the very peaks of the mountains and hills, may pierce through the sky's great wastes to the summit of the highest heaven, and there may gain a loving hearing from the celestial spirits. Go to them with these our lamentations, say: "O 'living stones,'[1] highest hills, shining plains around the starry dwellings, 'who will grant me' that blazing fire may burn with its fierce heat in my heart, that these my bitterest and copious tears, which I am now shedding, may move you to have compassion on me, to assuage my sorrow?" For indeed with that sorrow none can compare, as it does violence to my heart, as it torments my soul, as it pierces to my inmost spirit.

(2) Woe is me, unhappy wretch.[2] Indeed there was a time

1. 1 Pt 2.5.
2. Here it is not the Disciple but his soul who speaks, calling herself *misera, ingrata*. . . .

when that celestial spouse would go before me in his love, would cherish me, would choose me for his bride, "would betroth me with his ring, and would adorn me"[3] with many gifts. Time and again did I "receive from his lips honey and milk"[4] sweetly flowing. From time to time I enjoyed "the kiss of his mouth";[5] and there were times when he, the spiritual spouse, the lover of the lilies, soothed my spirit with his embrace, and endowed and filled me with every kind of good thing. But I, miserable woman, with no gratitude for all this, "when I was in honor, I did not understand,"[6] but I fled from him, I retreated, I deserted. Alas for me, for I have lost him! Alas for me, for I abandoned the one joy of my heart. "I have forsaken the vein of living waters, the Lord."[7] I who was once the beloved of my beloved have made myself a stranger to him. Faithlessly have I separated myself from him.

(3) Woe is me, wretched woman, why should I have wanted to do this? Why did I desert him, of all men? Alas for what with him I have lost, and how much that is! For truly I have lost myself, and I have offended all the spirits in heaven. Sorrows have come upon me, and every solace has forsaken me. Here I sit naked, "a widow and desolate,"[8] filled with confusion and ignominy, for those who have been my false lovers, and truly my deceivers, they have tricked me, alas, and have abandoned me to my wretchedness, and they have stripped me of all the riches that were my beloved's betrothal gift to me. Alas for the loss of my honor, for the ruin of my joys, for the deprivation of my every consolation, "for in one hour has come"[9] the utter destitution in me of everything that was desirable. From now on, I cannot be consoled, but it will be my greatest consolation to accept no consolation, always to groan and to weep until I achieve my miserable death. Alas for me, where shall I turn? To whom shall I go? "Who will comfort me?"[10] See how the whole world has left me, alone, because I have left my beloved.

3. A responsory from the Dominican Breviary's office for the feast of St. Agnes.

4. Idem.   5. Cant 1.1.
6. Ps 48.13.   7. Jer 17.13.
8. 1 Tm 5.5.   9. Apoc 18.10.
10. Is 51.19.

(4) Woe is me, why have I done this? Alas for that wretched hour in which the notion of this evil first came to my mind. O reddening roses, and you, paling lilies[11] and inviolate violets, you souls who are holy and immaculate, look on this flower of autumn I have plucked. "Attend and see"[12] how like a briar thicket I have become, and take it to your heart, how fast that "flower falls"[13] and fades which the world here has picked; for henceforth nothing now remains for me except, living, to die, flowering, to wither, young, to grow old before my time, and, healthy, to fall sick. But all these things I might easily conceal, and yet not this, that I have struck at your lovely and fatherly countenance, my beloved, that I have brought sadness to you whom I love. For me this is a hell, and sorrow's crown of sorrows. O my sweet one, I am going insane as I remember all the love with which you guarded me, all the sweetness with which you admonished me, how gently you once used to draw me to yourself. Sorrow oppresses me as I think how ungrateful I was for all these things, how little I cared for all your goodness, how lightly I tossed aside such a treasure.

(5) O wretched death, come, for I want you! "Why are you slow?"[14] Why do you not take me away? The human heart is all too strong, that I can suffer so and yet not perish! This heart of mine is hard as iron, for sorrow crushes it and still cannot break it! "Hear me, you divine" flowers,[15] and all you true lovers, mourn with me. "I who was formerly" so much loved,[16] I was adorned with a most excellent name, and I was called the bride of the high King. "The Lord called my name, a plentiful olive tree, fair, fruitful, beautiful."[17]

(6) Woe is me, unhappy wretch, for now I am not worthy to be called his kitchen maid, not fit for the work of his washtub. Henceforth I dare not raise my eyes from the earth, for they are red with weeping and filled with shame; I do not dare to open my mouth again to him. My heart is oppressed, for "I am oppressed on every side,"[18] "and what I shall choose I do

---

11. This resembles a phrase by Jerome in his *Life of St. Paul.*
12. Lam 1.12. 13. Jas 1.11; 1 Pt 1.24.
14. Ecclus 51.32. 15. Ecclus 39.17.
16. Jb 16.13. 17. Jer 11.16.
18. Dn 13.22.

not know."[19] For me to have lost my beloved beyond all hope of regaining him is worse for me than any death, for truly it is considered to be impossible for my most sorrowful soul to find him again as once I had him. See how wherever I go in all the vast space of this whole world I am hemmed in! If only I might be in some great desert place, where no human eye would ever see me, nor ear hear me, so that I might more freely vent all my cries and laments; for that will be the sum of my consolation.

(7) O sin, what have you brought to me? O unhappy fault,[20] O pleasure bought with toil, to what wretched state have you led me? O unclean world,[21] full of deception and dizzying deceits! Woe to him who serves you and submits himself to your will. How many will be the tribulations and miseries with which he will be oppressed! Outward appearances may seem to flatter him, but inside there is concealed the fang that will bite him. Outwardly, he may seem to be happy, but there will be no end to the afflictions of his wretched soul. Alas, alas, deceiving woman, how much you promised me in the beginning when you wanted to mislead me. You laid your snares for me with sweet love letters and all your little gifts. With honeyed words, calculated to entice me, you robbed me of my wits as though with sirens' songs and the sweet playing of flutes. With your whore's face and your sleek throat and your smiling eyes you transfixed this idiot's heart. When I asked for water, you opened a vessel of milk,[22] and you made me drunk on soothing poison and sweet wormwood.[23] With your own hand you held out the fruit to me, lovely and sweet, ripening for my delight alone; you gave me roses from your garden as a gift, and you made great vows that you loved me above all, and that you wished for nothing for me but unending joy and good fortune. You clever little vixen! You venomous viper! This is how you dragged me after you, ensnared with these and numberless

19. Phil 1.22.
20. *O infelix culpa*, alluding to the Easter Eve *Exultet*, 'felix culpa.'
21. *O mundus immundus*, a common pun in medieval Latin. Künzle quotes Henry of Settinello, ob. c. 1194.
22. Jgs 4.19.   23. Lam 3.15.

other false cozenings, to my death, just as they show a green branch to a sheep, and lead it off, happy and rejoicing, to be butchered. You "evil beast!"[24] You are smeared with your victim's gore! Now cruelly you bite what you so smoothly anointed. Viciously you dash to the ground what you so gently lifted up.[25] You feign the siren's voice, but you show that you have a sting. And now everything has turned out in contrary fashion. While I thought that I could sleep in safety on your breast, my hair was cut off, my eyes were torn out, my valor fled, my strength was stolen, and I fell defenseless to my enemies' swords.[26] Remembering this and turning it over in my mind, "I fade within myself, and I have become burdensome to myself."[27]

(8) Therefore happy is the soul, and deserving to be called queen of great possessions, whom dangers from without have made wary, and who has cherished its innocence of mind and body. O, what happiness does such a soul enjoy, even though it may not know this. Let it rejoice in a life that is pure and find happiness in a soul far removed from earthly desires, because "a troubled conscience always forecasts grievous things."[28] It proves that such a state is heavier than lead, fiercer than a lion, more terrifying than the thunderclap, more bitter than wormwood. This is the worm that gnaws at the entrails, which will not suffer men to eat or to rest, but many a time strikes them even while they sleep. So many and so great are the ills that afflict "the conscience that has been defiled,"[29] and they are almost worse than those still undefiled can believe. "For your creature who serves you, the Creator" blazes out "against the unjust for their punishment, and makes its strength gentle for the benefit of those who trust in you."[30] I have said this because experience has taught me to say it, and this present "bitterness most bitter"[31] of my heart has urged me to utter these things. Now, sunk in wretchedness, I am forced to cry aloud and say "that it is an evil and a bitter thing

24. Gn 37.20.
25. Ps 101.11.
26. Jgs 16.19–21.
27. Jb 30.16, 7.20.
28. Wis 17.10.
29. Ti 1.15.
30. Wis 16.24.
31. Is 36.17.

for me to have left"[32] my spouse and not to have obeyed his commands. "Who will give me" sheepskin wide as the heavens,[33] more ink than there is water in the sea, and as many pens as trees have leaves and the plains have blades of grass, that I may write down a little of the sorrow and the irreparable loss that I have suffered, because I deserted my dear one? Ah, to what end was I born into this world? Why did I not die in my mother's womb? I am completely helpless, and what I shall do I do not know. Why do I go on? "Why do I make this tumult, why do I weep?"[34] What more remains for me, but to despise myself and to throw myself down, far from the face of the glory of my God, abandoned into "the pit of my unhappy despair"?[35]

(9) Wisdom: But do you not know that despair is a dangerous matter? Upon no account must you despair of your salvation, for it was for this "that I came into this world to seek and save that which was lost."[36]

(10) Disciple: O, what is this that I hear, that sounds so sweetly in my ears, for me, a man of misery and an outcast cur?

(11) Wisdom: What has happened, that you do not recognize me? How is it that you have collapsed like this, "fallen down on the ground?"[37] Has too much sorrow driven you out of your mind? My son, so dear to me, see, it is I, that same Eternal Wisdom, Son of the heavenly Father, the messenger of mercy, the prince of clemency, the lawgiver of loving kindness, who have opened up the unmeasured depths of mercy, uncomprehended in the infinity of its pity, to every created spirit, and I wait to receive you and all who wish to come back to me into my most loving breast. Look in my face, and know me; for I am he who bore poverty to make you rich, I endured most bitter death to bring you back to life. Behold, I stand here, "Mediator of God and man,"[38] preserving still the marks

32. Jer 2.19.
33. On the source of this conceit, cf. Edmund Colledge: "If All the World Were Paper: Henry Suso's Use of a Much-travelled Commonplace," AFP 50 (1980): 113–16. See also Bk. I, ch. 10, n. 1.
34. Mk 5.39.
35. This phrase is used by Bernard of Clairvaux, *Sermon 6 on the Canticles.*
36. Jn 11.27; Lk 19.10.   37. Jb 1.20.
38. 1 Tm 2.5.

of my cross and holding them out between the eternal Father's
stern judgment and all your sins. So do not now be afraid, for
see, I am your brother, your spouse, ready to pity and conceal
"your sins, and cast them into the bottom of the sea,"[39] and so
to forgive them as if they had never been, if only you are willing
to turn back and will from now on be on your guard. Be
washed in my blood, in the blood, I say, of the immaculate
Lamb filled full of love and of "a rosy color"[40] shining afar.
Raise your head from the earth, open your eyes, and be of
good courage. See how "the best robe is brought out for you,
and a ring is given" to your understanding, and you are offered
"shoes, and the fatted calf is killed,"[41] you are given back a
name that can be loved, so that you may be and may be called
the bride of the eternal King. For "I have redeemed you not
with corruptible things, as gold or silver, but with my precious
blood,"[42] and I have won you with such labor, that justly I may
rejoice over your salvation and be ready to show you kindness.

(12) What I want to say is marvelous and indeed astonishing, and yet it must be believed with a most certain and unwa-
vering faith. See, if the whole world were a globe of fire, with
a handful of tow in the middle of it, the flax would not more
quickly by its natural inclination catch fire than is the abyss of
my mercies moved to wish that a penitent sinner be turned
back to me. For any such natural process needs a little time,
brief and imperceptible though it be; but when a penitent is
forgiven, when someone weeping for his sins is heard, there
is no delay whatsoever.

(13) Disciple: O, the unheard-of pity of this fatherly compassion! O amazing love of brotherly faithfulness! O only joy
of my heart, can it be that you still deign to receive this abject
son of perdition? Why do you want to show your grace to me,
guilty of death, hateful through every kind of iniquity? O, generosity without compare, O, gentleness beyond telling, O,
boundless ocean of divine mercy, not understood by any mortal, exceeding what we might think of, surpassing what we

---

39. Mi 7.19.   40. Est 15.8.
41. Lk 15.22–23.   42. 1 Pt 1.18–19.

ought to ask for, transcending all that every merit might deserve! So "for this cause I bow the knees"[43] of my heart to you, "the Father of mercies,"[44] and falling to the earth I prostrate myself at your most merciful feet, giving you thanks from the depths of my heart, and begging you to look on your only-begotten "Son, whom you handed over"[45] to death, "for the exceeding love with which you loved us,"[46] and that for the multitude of his sorrows you will forget the multitude of all my iniquities.

(14) "Remember," I beg, "your mercies"[47] and your promises of old. For it was you with your holy lips who once gave to the world, lost through the flood, a sign of reconciliation, saying, "I shall set my bow in the clouds, and I shall remember my covenant with you, and it will be the sign between me and the earth."[48] Ah, look now, most loving Father, on the bow which was then prefigured, that is, on your most beloved Son hung upon the cross. Pay good heed to how his every member is stretched out and drawn apart, so that he suffers "all his bones to be numbered."[49] See how his hands and his arms and all his other parts are stretched out wide, worn away with wounds and suffused with blood. Look upon these things, I implore, and by his wounds do you "heal our wounds and forgive us our sins."[50]

(15) Remember, Lord, why you are called "merciful" and "the Father of mercies,"[51] for that is because you who show mercy have mercy upon all, you do not remember the injuries done to you, and you forget men's sins. For it was not for "the just, who do not need penance,"[52] but for us, who "have sinned and committed iniquity"[53] that you will be called merciful. Or was it only the just and innocent, whose singularly chaste lives are constantly read to us as examples, whom you decreed "to

43. Eph 3.14.   44. 2 Cor 1.3.
45. From the Easter Eve *Exultet*.   46. Eph 2.4.
47. Ps 24.6.   48. Gn 9.13, 15.
49. Ps 21.18.
50. From the first prayer for the anointing of the sick in the Dominican Processional.
51. 2 Cor 1.3   52. Lk 15.7.
53. Dn 3.29.

be made of your privy council,"[54] did you plan to give them alone the special adornment of your grace and friendship? Or are you "the God only"[55] of the innocent? Are you not the God of the penitent? Surely you are also the God of the penitent, and of those "who are converted to the heart."[56] "Where sin abounded," did not always "grace abound more?"[57]

(16) Therefore I flee to you, the Father of mercies, and I implore the grace of your protection. And what is more, O Son of the eternal King, with a most burning love and with the embrace of your whole heart I enfold myself in your arms, stretched out, naked, smeared with blood, and never wishing, living or dead, to be separated from you. And for this cause, O sweet and loving Father, forgive me, forgive me for love of your only-begotten Son my sins, through which I have deserved your anger and "have done evil before you";[58] for I have such sorrow because of my sins that I would rather suffer a thousand deaths than ever again offend you, most loving Father. For all "the calamities that I suffer,"[59] or even the hell that I have deserved, or the most cruel purging fires I do not count so much, they do not oppress me so much, compared with the offenses with which I have offended you, my Creator —you, I say, "O my Lord and my God,"[60] my Redeemer and the one joy of my heart—and that I have afflicted you or shown any irreverence towards you. So if now I could fill all the heavens with cries beyond control, if I could beat upon my heart with such violence that it would break into a thousand fragments, that would seem to me a better choice than all the consolations that I have known "in all the days of my life."[61] And the more gently that men deal with me, the more my weeping heart is afflicted, because I have been so unkind to so loving a friend, to so most faithful a Father.

(17) But now, O Eternal Wisdom, "teacher of the knowledge of God,"[62] teach me, I pray, how I may bear in my body

---

54. 2 Kgs 23.23.
55. Cf. Rom 3.29 and William of St. Thierry's *Golden Epistle.*
56. Ps 84.9.   57. Rom 5.20.
58. Ps 50.6.   59. Jb 6.2.
60. Jn 20.28.   61. Ps 26.4
62. Wis 8.4.

your sweetest and gentlest wounds, how I ought to keep them always in mind, so that in this way I may at least show to the dwellers in heaven and on earth the thanks that I shall return for the endless goodness that you have so generously bestowed out of the superabundance of your loving pity on so poor a wretch as I.

(18) Wisdom: You should offer yourself and all that you have to me, nor should you ever take back what you have offered; and you should abstain not only from excess, but even from time to time from what is permitted; and so you will have shown the hands that were pierced on my cross. You must do what is good; and you must suffer steadfastly what ills come to you; and you must control your wavering spirit and your wandering thoughts, and fix them all upon me, who am the highest good; and so you will have fastened your feet to my cross. Do not allow the powers of your spirit and your body to grow tepid through sloth, but learn to exhort yourself with all your might in my service, your arms always stretched out as are mine. Wearied and worn out with every kind of toil, give thanks, and suffer patiently, and curb the motions of sensuality like a man; and so you will imitate me when my legs suffered violence and weariness. So "my flesh will flourish again"[63] through the dedicated and reasonable mortification of your flesh, and, too, you will make for my back, tormented by the harshness of the cross, a gentle resting place through your willing bearing of your various hardships. Always lift up your spirit, encumbered with your flesh, to the Lord; "yield your members to serve justice for sanctification, as before you used to yield them to serve injustice."[64] Let your heart be always ready to sustain all adversities for my name, and so, as a faithful disciple, spiritually crucified with his Lord and in some fashion sprinkled with the blood of compassion, you will make yourself like to me and lovable.

63. Ps 27.7.   64. Rom 6.19.

CHAPTER 5

A Lamentation over the Fervor of Devotion,
Which Has Died in These Present Days in
Various Persons of Either Sex, Whom Christ Recalls
by His Passion to True Love

"OW DOES THE CITY sit solitary that was full of people! The mistress of the pagans has become as a widow," *et cetera.*[1] On one occasion, when Wisdom's Disciple was pondering "in his sorrowful heart"[2] the perilous state of this present world, and how much the love of God had fallen off in his days, and how, too, a love turned away from God but disguised as religion had stealthily grown in many places, it happened that as he poured out his tearful prayers to the Wisdom of God, he was overtaken by a certain sweet drowsiness of the spirit. And then suddenly a certain similitude presented itself to him, which enlightened him more fully about these things. For in a vision there appeared a certain pilgrim, a poor wanderer, standing out of doors, carrying a staff in his hand, full of misery and want. And near him there were seen what looked like the ruins of some most ancient city, the walls and buildings of which had once been most beautiful, strengthened with turrets and moats, gates and bars and other fortifications. But through the neglect of those within, a part of the city had been pierced by invading enemies, and a part had fallen down through the inhabitants' negligence; and even the part that remained was threatened with decay, with high walls here and there that were ready to fall. In this city certain beasts appeared in the likeness of human-seeming sea monsters, and when this pilgrim asked them for help he was driven off with contumely, and those who wanted to help him

1. Lam 1.1.   2. Lv 10.19.

were forbidden by others to do this. And so, confused and pursued and driven out by them, he withdrew, and "he called on heaven and earth to be witnesses against them."[3] I, the Disciple, saw these things that I tell of, and I ask you, O Eternal Wisdom, to show their meaning to me, because you know all mysteries and understand all hidden things.

(2) Wisdom: This is something remarkable, most deserving of compassion. See, I am that pilgrim,[4] and once I was that ruined city's renowned prince and its fair spouse. For the city that you have seen in ruins, it is the mother, the Christian religion, once fervent and devout, in which since the first days of the Church so many faithful, of one mind and of one heart, led a life of outstanding devotion, holy and pleasing to God and full of zeal. They had spurned all worldly things, and they burned only with the love of their Creator, they were always intent upon holy meditations and good works, and they strengthened themselves and their neighbors, "defrauding no one, injuring no one,"[5] but leading a life blessed "in simplicity"[6] and in sincerity, "they crucified their flesh, with its vices and concupiscences,"[7] undertaking great exercises and observing customs full of devotion; and there were men in various monasteries and solitary places and houses of religion, men indeed of might, "most valiant" and strenuous "fighters,"[8] enemies "against the spirits of wickedness."[9] And they would surrender themselves to death itself in the defense of truth and justice. Such, I say, were the illustrious citizens and the most famous sons whom this city, the holy mother, zealous religion, was accustomed to bear and to nourish and to bring up to honorable estate. But alas, in many places in these days, and in the quarters of this city I have told of, ruin threatens far and wide. Some of the citizens and their magistrates have conducted themselves carelessly; the whole spiritual structure

3. 1 Mc 2.37.
4. The representation of Christ as a pilgrim, deriving from Lk 24.18, is common in late medieval literature and iconography.
5. 2 Cor 7.2.   6. Wis 1.1.
7. Gal 5.24.   8. Jos 10.2.
9. Eph 6.12.

of the buildings is weakened and devastated by earthquakes, so that now it is not expected to stand much longer, but it seems likely to perish by its continual deterioration.

(3) For now many of the sons of holy religion and those who profess it have dared to rise up against their superiors with such lawlessness that there is scarcely any place where correction is administered, but if correction should be required by some offense, "a greater rent is made."[10] For, armed with philosophical niceties and with the frivolous appeals to the law that they interpose, they will under no circumstances submit to anyone seeking to put them right, but they overleap "the bounds which their fathers had set,"[11] and involve themselves and others in dangerous dissensions. O, this is a sure sign that this spiritual edifice is falling in ruins, a presage most clear of coming calamity, which is not now far off. How long do you suppose that this spiritual edifice will be able to stand, when the cornerstone has been taken away, and the column that holds up the whole spiritual structure has been thrown down, when, that is, prompt and humble obedience has been put out of doors, and everyone does as he pleases or wants, with no one "who will dare to say: Why are you acting like this?"[12] Alas, alas, where is the obedience of Paul the Simple and those best-tried of his disciples,[13] who, when the fathers of old ordered them to do the impossible, obeyed with the greatest devotion? Let my tongue now be silent about this, but let every pious heart mourn. There will be no profit in talking of it; there will be benefit in silence, for to have kept silence on this subject is to have played the good philosopher.[14]

(4) Now, concerning voluntary poverty, which is the nurse and nourishment of all religious life, which some of the holy fathers chose as their bride, which some called their mistress, and which yet others bequeathed as an inheritance to those

---

10. Mt 9.16.   11. Prv 22.28.
12. 2 Kgs 16.10.
13. This is the Paul who, with others, put himself under the severe discipline of Anthony of Egypt in the Theban desert.
14. This is an allusion to Boethius's *Consolation*.

dearest to them, what shall I say? It is not now loved by many as a wife, but like "Agar, the handmaid of Sara,"[15] "it is cast out,"[16] "and her offspring seems to be opposed to all, and all men's hands seem to be against the wife."[17] For men seek for a thousand ways of becoming rich, and the craft of saving men's souls has been changed for the craft of making money, so that it has to be a very clever young sheep that can save even a little of its wool from the cunning of the thief[18] and the shearers' greed, to keep it warm in winter. And when it is thought unseemly to retain something in the form of cash, they make a show of putting it to a different, pious use. But in truth it is exchanged to serve their cupidity and is changed into a sort of idol. For this they exchange gifts of money into goods of different kinds, books, it may be, or church vestments, so long as they are in need; and so they may "consult the god of Accaron," whom they have stored in their money-bags, as if "there is not a God in Israel."[19]

(5) Then about chastity, which is the ornament[20] of virtues, there is little profit in saying more than a few words. It is pitiful to see the young lambs, fleeing from savage wolves and flocking for protection to their shepherds, falling into traps even worse. They try to escape the teeth of the wolves, and run into the jaws of the crafty rams, to be mortally wounded or to be killed outright. For some "have an appearance of godliness, but they deny its power."[21] They are afraid that their dishonesty may appear in the light of day, but they scheme in secret "to commit robbery"[22] against souls, to violate the violets[23] of the heavenly bridegroom, or to stain them by fondling with their filthy hands. They are like those priests in the Old Law who "thrust a three-pronged fork into the flesh-pot"[24] and stole for themselves what should have been offered to God. And

15. Gn 16.1.   16. Gn 21.10.
17. Gn 16.12.   18. Cf. Jn 10.1.
19. 4 Kgs 1.3.   20. *ST*, II-II, q. 152, a. 5, c.
21. 2 Tm 3.5.   22. Jgs 9.25.
23. "*violasque . . . violare*": this is *adnominatio*, when "a close resemblance to a given verb or noun is produced, so that similar words express dissimilar things." See Colledge and Walsh, *A Book of Showings*, 735.
24. 1 Kgs 2.23–24.

because they do not dare to consume the whole sacrifice, they do at least enjoy the first sampling of the offerings' flavor.

(6) Then what shall I say of love, which binds together the whole spiritual structure? "It is razed, it is razed, down to the very foundation."[25] For they all "seek not the things that are their own, but those that are other men's,"[26] and there is more importance given to dangerous detraction than there is of sincere affection. Brotherly hatred has replaced fraternal charity, and has indeed, to speak more truly, laid it low, so that one might well cry out in weeping and sorrow, and say: "Let every man take heed of his neighbor, and let him not trust in any brother of his, for every brother will utterly supplant, and every friend will walk deceitfully, and a man will mock his brother,[27] and a man's enemies are those of his own household."[28] "Their tongue is a piercing arrow," the prophet says, "it has spoken deceit. With his mouth one man speaks peace with his friend, and secretly he lies in wait for him."[29] And because "they bite one another,[30] provoke one another, envy one another,"[31] deal wounds, it is to be feared lest at last "they be consumed by one another."[32] And yet these things and others like them "are not hidden, so that they will not be known,"[33] or through them "hidden things will be brought into the light,"[34] for, alas, "their sound has gone out into all the earth, and their words to the end of the world."[35]

(7) And if anyone still wished to observe the holy customs and the exercises of piety, following in the paths of the ancient fathers, he would endure scorn, and others would say that he was seeking attention, and because he lived differently from them he would have to suffer many reproaches. Yet in those blessed times when a holy and fervent religious life was flourishing, such things belonged to a state of goodness and perfection. There can be no doubt that then was the golden age,

25. Ps 136.7.
26. Phil 2.4.
27. Jer 9.4–5.
28. Mi 7.6.
29. Jer 9.8.
30. Gal 5.15.
31. Gal 5.26.
32. Gal 5.15.
33. Mt 10.26.
34. Jb 28.11.
35. Ps 18.5.

and indeed "the day of salvation";[36] for in those days men were on their guard against extravagances, they did not deal in flattery so as to receive gifts, nor were they allowed to argue or quarrel, but they occupied their time with works of virtue and holy studies and meditations; and they "had one heart and one soul in the Lord,"[37] living in common, and not each one seeking for something for himself; and therefore they were men perfect "in all power."[38] But of these spiritual exercises of which I have spoken, nothing has remained except "a little here, a little there";[39] for some of the ancient customs, that is, certain parts of their spiritual edifice, are still standing and can be seen, pointing up on high, and in them we find commended not so much new-fangled devotions as the praiseworthy study of the ancients.

(8) As for what you also saw there, that great crowd of beasts like human-seeming sea monsters, those are worldly hearts hiding under the religious habit, a habit which looks decent enough outside, but inside there is neither grace nor devotion, and so, within and without, they live crippled lives, and they are truly very like monstrous beasts. They have, certainly, resounding human voices, just like Balaam's donkey;[40] they roll out their abstractive terms and their spiritual demonstrations, but their lives are all concrete and carnal, for what they preach with their words and their habit they contradict by what they do. "For of this sort are those who creep into houses," taking great pains to "lead silly women captive, always learning, and yet never attaining to the knowledge of the truth,"[41] who with "vanities and lying follies"[42] shut me out from their hearts and from the hearts of other men.

(9) But that you have seen some there who seemed decent in dress and appearance, who have stretched out their hands to me, signifies the number of the elect[43] who live "justly and

---

36. Is 49.8; 2 Cor 6.2.
37. Acts 4.32, as quoted in Augustine's *Rule*, in the form received in the Dominican Order.
38. Col 1.11.
39. Is 28.10.
40. Num 22.28–30.
41. 2 Tm 3.6–7
42. Ps 39.5.
43. Apoc 7.4.

godly"[44] among others, not being corrupted by their example, but "in the midst of a crooked and perverse generation they were as lights shining in this dark world, and with the word of life"[45] they gave light and heat to some of their neighbors. It may be that they are still to be found in great numbers, men and women of every class and religious order and age, yet by comparison with the rest they are few. For truly there are more who go "by the wide and broad way which leads to death"[46] than are those who "strive to enter by the narrow gate and the straight way."[47] And they who conduct themselves among others like "lambs among wolves,"[48] like "the lily among thorns,"[49] give out a sweet fragrance of virtues in their bearing of adversities. These are they whom the Lord has reserved for himself, "who did not bow their knees before Baal,"[50] who "did not make provision for the flesh in its concupiscences,"[51] "who have 'thau' marked upon their foreheads,"[52] which is that they are "always bearing about in their bodies the glorification of Jesus";[53] and the transgressions of other men, which they are unable to emend, they bewail and mourn. Because of the un-numbered hostilities that come up, they can say with the Apostle: "Combats without; fears within,"[54] and after they have suffered every other danger, they may conclude that they have known "perils from false brethren."[55] Not without justice are such men compared with the martyrs, for in addition to many other afflictions, they have been pierced as it were with the swords of a heartfelt sorrow[56] as often as they have seen transgressions committed against God or against justice. "But it will not be reputed as folly in them."[57] For the voice is addressed to them which says: "Tell the just man that it is well, for he will eat the fruit of his undertakings. Woe to the wicked, pursuing

44. Ti 2.12.
45. Phil 2.15–16; 2 Pt 1.19.
46. Mt 7.13.
47. Mt 7.14; Lk 13.24.
48. Lk 10.3.
49. Cant 2.2.
50. 3 Kgs 19.18.
51. Rom 13.14.
52. Ez 9.4.
53. 2 Cor 4.10.
54. 2 Cor 7.5.
55. 2 Cor 11.26.
56. Lk 2.35; cf. the Dominican Breviary for the office of the Compassion of the Blessed Virgin Mary.
57. Ps 21.3.

evil,[58] because the retribution of his works will be given to him. "They will hunger, and you will eat; they will thirst, and you will drink."[59] And as from all around them greater hardships accumulated, as "on the right hand and on the left"[60] fighters joined the battle, not indeed to help them, but, alas, to take the other side, then more than their many predecessors who had found innumerable fellow-workers for their designs, "they will receive" in the time to come a greater "reward according to their labor."[61]

(10) So therefore, that you saw some in that similitude who forbade those who wanted to come to my help means the men who corrupt others who have some good purpose, by their evil advice or example, and, copying the Pharisees, "do not enter into life or suffer those going in to enter,"[62] for they even blasphemed against God's own Wisdom with their most impious mouths, and sought in every way to lead astray those who believed in God, calling him "that seducer."[63] So there are a great many, not urged by conscience but goaded by envy, who find others who excel them in grace and "stone them for a good work"[64] never ceasing to traduce their good works in the hearing of many men. And when they cannot misrepresent a deed done evidently for the sake of goodness, then these envious detractors at the very least try to calumniate the doer's intention, and so those whom they cannot equal in good they outstrip in evil. "For the devil's envy came into the world, and they follow him who are of his side."[65]

(11) The staff which you saw me carrying in my pilgrim's guise signifies the death[66] that I endured on the cross, which I offer to the faithful as a sign of love, so that they may turn away from earthly love, and turn to me with their whole hearts.

(12) The crying aloud that you heard is the severity of my judgment against those who do not turn from their sins, moved neither by fear nor love, but stubbornly persisting in them until their death.

58. Is 3.10–11.
59. Is 65.13.
60. 2 Cor 6.7.
61. 1 Cor 3.8.
62. Mt 23.13.
63. Mt 27.63.
64. Jn 10.33.
65. Wis 2.24–25.
66. Ambrose, *On the Sacraments* 5.2, n.13.

(13) Disciple: When I hear these things with an attentive heart, and I recognize that this is in fact true, "I had rather weep than utter any words."[67] For who would not lament? Who would not mourn and sigh "to see the shrubs growing up"[68] and the thickets sprouting in so holy a place, to see the shining delights and spiritual riches of the one-time city, its wealth of graces, of unction and devotion, and its abundance of every divine charism now reduced to such poverty? Little of grace, and most of malice! Who would not sigh and cry out in sorrow: "Alas, how solitary does the city sit which was full of people?" And, too: "How dim has the gold become, the finest color is changed!"[69] He is very hard of heart or without all religion who could look well upon these losses and not weep from his whole heart. And see how the matter for such sadness and weeping grows, as now "the whole world is settled in wickedness,"[70] and the ancient enemy, as his end draws near, is so clearly seen to be prevailing over many men.

(14) Wisdom: I shall say nothing to you at the present time about "those who are outside,"[71] who "build altars in the streets, and immolate swine's flesh,"[72] who "shamelessly prostitute themselves on every high hill and under every green tree."[73] But I speak of those who openly worship this world, who do not shame to commit "manifest sins, adulteries, thefts and such like."[74] But I desire you to take to heart the overthrow of the holy city, the waning, that is, of the fervor of ancient religious life, and to shed tears of pity for it, and to pour out weeping prayers to God for its restoration and good estate. For this is indeed "the city seated on a mountain, the candle put upon a candlestick, and the salt"[75] of the spirit, with which the men of this world are to be seasoned, "a spectacle to the world and to angels and to men";[76] for by their "word and

67. From the Dominican Breviary for Passion Week, quoting Gregory the Great, *Homily 33 on the Gospels*.

68. 1 Mc 4.38.

70. 1 Jn 5.19.

72. 1 Mc 1.50, 57, 58.

74. 1 Tm 5.24; Mt 15.19.

76. 1 Cor 4.9.

69. Lam 4.1.

71. Mk 4.11; 1 Cor 5.13.

73. Jer 2.20.

75. Mt 5.13–15.

example"[77] others have been accustomed to be strengthened and to be illumined and to be made wise.

(15) Yet when this city sets a bad example, when the light is extinguished and "the salt loses its savor,"[78] alas, alas, what will its standing then be in the world? When they who have renounced this world pursue worldly ambition with all their might? When they "who are called spiritual"[79] will pursue carnal desires and "will entangle themselves with secular business"?[80] O most holy Mother Church, how great will your tribulation then be? Who is there who will arise and restrain the angered Judge? For in this present day, many who should have placated him are greatly offending him. "My soul hates their sabbaths."[81] For their spiritual love has changed into carnal, and that carnal love is imperfectly disguised as spiritual, as "weeds among the wheat";[82] and with this admixture it has grown rotten, like precious ointment that has been adulterated with stinking fluids. They offer to God a corrupted sacrifice. For ambition has conquered everywhere in their hearts and reigns unopposed, as they seek with their whole heart for the worldly glory of authority, and when they cannot obtain what they long for, they are not afraid in their anger "to bring in sects,"[83] and, just as the apostate Jewish people, they seek "to build a place for sport in Jerusalem,"[84] and they fight to have themselves and others transferred to places of pagan learning, "passing beyond the bounds which their fathers had set."

(16) I shall return to what I had intended to pass over in silence, now that the causes of sorrow are increasing, and also the objects of loving compassion and of devout prayer. There was in the city of which I have spoken an important district, one of the chief, in which learning and teaching were most excellently administered to the rest of the citizens. But many of the elders of that people living there were taken from their

77. From the Dominican Breviary's office for the feast of a pontiff.
78. Mt 5.13.
80. 2 Tm 2.4.
82. Mt 13.25.
84. 1 Mc 1.15.

79. Gal 6.1.
81. Is 1.13–14.
83. 2 Pt 2.1.

midst. There was there, moreover, one certain man of God who prayed constantly to him for the safety of the place.

(17) "He beheld in the vision of the night,"[85] and see, from the western part of that place there rose up from the flock a single ram, having two horns and on his head an iron crown, and to him was given the power of reigning in the place of which we have spoken. And he was followed by what seemed like seventy "little foxes,"[86] or they may have been more, who were the ram's supporters, and each one of them received a crown. And they were joined by a multitude of beasts of either sex, some moved by fear, others by greed, and then there were some who followed the crowd in their simplicity. So the ram, who wanted to usurp for himself and his followers the government of the place, went around asserting his strength and raging against everyone who offered him resistance. He cast down the mighty, he humiliated those in authority, and some he condemned to exile. And great fear came upon all the inhabitants and citizens of that place; he and his followers, determined to prevail by fair means or by foul, spared no one at all who opposed them, not for their sex or their age, however deserving their merits or their lives might have been. And so it was that many, cowed by terror, joined them, because they did not want to be wiped off the face of the earth.

(18) Yet some of the people of God were left, fearing "God rather than men,"[87] and they held out in manly constancy through their greatest tribulations, "ready to die bravely for their fathers and the laws of God,"[88] rather than submit to the will of apostates, whose filthy deeds and crimes could quickly bring about the complete ruin of the place. Yet even among these there were some who "did not walk uprightly in the way of truth,"[89] who did not follow the paths of justice and equity as they should, but yet who wished to resist the greater evils that they were beginning to endure from the other side, and therefore opposed them as well as they could. And the leader

85. Dn 7.7.
87. Acts 5.29.
89. Gal 2.14.
86. Cant 2.15.
88. 2 Mc 7.2, 5.

of the sons of God, the supreme governor of that place, a man indeed praiseworthy and magnanimous in all things, zealous for justice, came to their help. And there were various others "who fled from the evils, joined themselves to them, and were a support to them."[90] So the ram was seen to attack with his horns the leader of these people, and to try in every way he could to overthrow him. But still the leader stood fast, in no way to be vanquished. When they saw this, the ram and some of his crew went to the prince of them all, and stirred him up against the man who was leading his people, filling his innocent and unsuspecting ears with their deceitful slanders, and so the ram seized power over the people.

(19) When they heard this, the Church of the faithful lamented with great cries, and some directed their weeping voices to the heavens, caring little for themselves yet much for God's holy laws and the traditions of the fathers, which they saw being openly violated, to the scandal of many, and they made supplications to God that if it were possible, the heart of the prince of the multitude might be given better counsel. And when many who were guiltless "were oppressed by this most bitter service, they cried out to the Lord, and their cry went up to God, and he heard their groaning,"[91] and he came down to set them free. For "good works were still found in Israel."[92]

(20) So on one occasion the iniquitous assembled upon a certain island against the sons of obedience, strongly armed and superior in numbers, "trusting in their own strength."[93] When those who were on the Lord's side saw them advancing, they were greatly afraid, and despaired of escaping; for it was a great and mighty force, "trained up to war"[94] and prepared. And there were very few indeed on the other side, and they were simple men who knew nothing about warfare.

(21) But one of those who were aiding the side of the Lord was constantly exhorting the rest, utterly terrified, to stand

90. 1 Mc 2.43.   91. Ex 1.14, 2.23–24.
92. 2 Par 19.3.   93. Ps 48.7.
94. 1 Mc 4.7.

fast, and he urged them to take refuge in their prayers. And he went to the place where they prayed, and prostrate on the ground in prayer, he said "these and such like things": "'O Lord and ruler, King' of heaven and earth, 'all things are in your power, and there is no one who can resist your will.'[95] You know that these men 'come against us'[96] in their audacity, and 'trusting in their multitude,'[97] wanting 'to reign, but not by you,'[98] and to violate 'the laws of God received from our fathers,'[99] and that they long to wipe us wretched ones off the face of the earth. Alas, Lord and God, 'open your eyes and see'[100] our tribulation and that of your holy flock, and 'turn our mourning into joy.'[101] 'Scatter them by your power and bring them down,'[102] so that they may know that you still have care for your people. Show now 'that the success of war is not in the multitude of the army but in your will,'[103] and have mercy on us, so that this great tribulation, which 'we suffer for our sins'[104] 'we may overcome with you to help us,'[105] and that as our fathers once did, so we too may serve you in peace and tranquillity."

(22) "When these things were done,"[106] God, "who has never forsaken those who hope in him,"[107] listened to the voice of his servants imploring him, and destroyed the power of their enemies. For on the next day, in the same place, in the sight of the force that had assembled, the ram fell to the ground, and one of his horns was broken, while all gave praise to God. And from that time on his power began to fail and wane, day by day. For many understood his trickery, and moved by penitence they began to desert him, and the side of the sons of obedience began to grow and to benefit the Lord's people, with his help as he pursued the enemies of peace. Blessed be the Lord in all things. Amen.

(23) Disciple: It is an astonishing and wonderful thing that

95. Ex 34.6; Est 13.9.
96. 1 Mc 3.20.
97. Jdt 9.9.
98. Os 8.4.
99. 2 Mc 7.2.
100. Dn 9.18.
101. Est 14.17.
102. Ps 58.12.
103. 1 Mc 3.19.
104. 2 Mc 7.32.
105. From the Dominican Breviary.
106. Est 2.1.
107. Jdt 13.17.

the inscrutable abyss of the judgments of God permits his elect to be so afflicted, yet has never deserted them, but frees and protects them as a most loving father. But I should like to know the secrets of this similitude more plainly.

(24) Wisdom: I have said enough for those who can understand. Do not you ask for anything more. From what you have you should gather no small profit. Firstly, you should learn never to despair in any adversity, but to put all your hope in God and to seek refuge in prayer in every tribulation; and never forsake the way of justice because of the savagery of any persecution, however cruel, and, above all, in your dealings show a proper caution and circumspection. Now that you are the ruler or superior of your brethren, however minor your office may be, learn from these things not to put your trust in those who are always denouncing others. Do not always be willing to agree to the suggestions of your associates, when these are made only for self-protection. Nor should you easily accept accusations made against men of good repute, for this is the ruin of all discipline, and it makes those who infect communities impudent in their resistance, and it destroys the strength of religious life. But you should inquire very carefully, either by yourself or through men who are prudent and just and God-fearing, about any dispute that you do not understand; and so in the end, when you have found out the truth and achieved a proper balance, you may give a just decision, and then, without doubt, you will find that some of the disputants have in the dispute been guilty. For sometimes those who allege that they suffer unduly at the hands of their superiors want to avoid all censure of monastic discipline, they make absurd and lying claims that they are the champions of justice and the defenders of truth, when what they want is to escape the corrections of the authorities, and they have this inane desire to put themselves before everyone else. This, this is how you should inquire about any dispute you do not understand; learn to see clearly what is not true, and that what the impious have plotted against the just "return upon their heads,"[108] so

108. 1 Kgs 25.29.

that "their sword may enter into their own hearts, and that their bow may be broken."[109] So "will the unjust be caught in their own snares."[110] This is how the two old men full of evil thoughts were stoned to death, who wanted to stone Susanna as she trusted in the Lord.[111] This is how Amon died, most cruel enemy and adversary of the Jews, who was striving through his wicked suggestions to the king to destroy the people of God.[112] And so that most proud man Saul died upon his own sword, who was not afraid to persecute his neighbor unjustly.[113]

(25) Disciple: O most gentle Judge of all disputes, Eternal Wisdom, who for your elect turn both good and evil to good, I think that in this matter there is only one thing for me, your most humble servant, to do, and that is with a devout heart to return for refuge to prayer. Therefore, O "Father of mercies and God of all comfort,"[114] I humbly entreat you to have mercy on your people and your inheritance, and grant peace to our hearts and tranquillity in our days; and, too, have mercy "on those that hated peace,"[115] because of your blessed name. Pour into them, I beg, a good spirit, so that they may turn back from their errors and return to unity and peace, so that we all may serve you in the bosom of our holy mother the Catholic Church, and that we may be valiant to attain to the glorious city of our heavenly native land. Amen.

109. Ps 36.15.
110. Prv 11.6.
111. Dn 13.34–62.
112. Est 3.8–13.
113. 1 Kgs 18.11.
114. 2 Cor 1.3.
115. Ps 119.7.

CHAPTER 6

Of What Is the Divine Spouse, Eternal Wisdom, and of the Nature of Her Love

"HOW DOES YOUR beloved differ from any other, O you most beautiful among women?"[1] If anyone wants to hear the answer to these words, let him now listen with the ears of divine love. Give me a lover, give me someone burning with incomparable love, and he will understand what I say.[2] But he does not love out of love for anyone at all who may speak to him; he perceives the power of love not by what he feels within himself, but it is my own words that he hears, resounding so greatly that he will think himself drunk rather than sober. And drunk he is indeed, but not "with wine, in which there is luxury,"[3] but in that in which there is the outflowing of spiritual joys. So let us, who are so far off from such an overflowing of love, keep silent, though we long with all our hearts to be brought near to it, and let this loving mind speak its thoughts; let them, set on God's love, be cried aloud, and let this lover tell us how his beloved goes before him, how he is drawn to the love of his beloved, and from all this we shall see "how his beloved differs from any other." Nor should he be too bashful, for a burning love will often show itself, even against its own will. "Come," the loving spirit says, "and hear what great things the Lord has done for my soul."[4]

(2) When in the springtime my blossoming youth and the freshness of my mind summoned me sweetly to the flowering meadows and their blooms of many kinds, so that with fellows of my own age and of either sex I might enjoy the solaces I

1. Cant 5.9.
2. Augustine, *Tractate 26 on John*, n. 4, quoted in the Dominican Breviary for the Wednesday after Pentecost.
3. Eph 5.18.   4. Ps 65.16.

longed for, many there would sing with resounding, wanton voices as we played our various games. Nodding their heads, clapping their hands, and like "young rams skipping,"[5] they would tread a measure, and, as they danced, cry out: "The time that we have to live is short and full of cares, and in man's end there is no solace; and no one has been known to have returned from hell, for we are born of nothing, and after this we shall be as if we had never been. Come, then, and let us enjoy the good things that are here, let us hurry to use what has been made for us while we are young. Let us fill ourselves with costly wine and unguents, and do not let the flower of our days pass us by. Let us crown ourselves with roses before they wither; let no meadow escape our riot. Let us leave tokens everywhere of joy, for this is our portion and this is our lot."[6] Saying, as I have told you, things of this sort, they would yield to concupiscent madness, and each one would gather what flowers he could. But I for some time hesitated, debating in my mind what I should do; and I saw how those flowers of human flesh, which not long ago were lovely, newly blooming with a vernal beauty, suddenly withered and drooped, and all their beauty perished. Startled by this strange sight, and turned back into myself, I began to vow that I would never give my love to any of these perishable blooms, which I had watched as they flowered for so short a while and then withered away so fast.

(3) Therefore one day, as my restless mind was searching all around, like a young roe seeking a shady spot to rest in as the midday heat declines,[7] suddenly there appeared high up among the mountain tops just opposite me, as it were, "a flower of the field,"[8] striking to see, delightful to look at, incomparably lovelier than all the flowers I had ever seen before. And as I hastened to gaze on it, suddenly it changed, and there stood before me no flower but what instead seemed to be a goddess of all beauty, who, blushing as a rose and shining "with snowy brightness,"[9] glowed more brightly than the sun,

---

5. Ps 113.4.   6. Wis 2.1–2, 6–9.
7. Cf. Gregory the Great, *Homily 33 on the Gospels*, n.7.
8. Cant 2.1.
9. From the Dominican Breviary for the feast of the Crown of Thorns.

and spoke as only beauty speaks. She presented herself as the sum of all desirable things, exuding the sweetest perfume, in the manner of a panther[10] diffused all about far and wide, drawing every man to her love; and with the gentlest voice she said: "Come over to me, all you who desire me, and be filled with my generations. I am the mother of fair love, and of fear, and of knowledge and of holy hope."[11]

(4) When I had heard these words, I stood amazed, my eyes fixed on the ground, and I kept silent. For astonishment at the greatness of such beauty had so overwhelmed me that I could find no word of answer at all. But she gently stretched out her hand and touched my heart, and gave me strength to reply. My eyes were opened, and I regarded her with more care, and in my heart I silently pondered these things. Anyone like her "there is not upon earth, in look, in beauty and in the sense of what she says";[12] and to myself I said: This indeed is where the depths of love now meet with the depths of all beauty,[13] for what you have so long been seeking for, now you have found, and what you have met with is more by far than anything you could have imagined. And so at last I turned to her, and in the jubilation of my heart I said in clear tones: O you, fairest of all creatures in this whole universe, you who sprang from the joyful mind of the Creator of all things, tell us your name and your lineage, and whether these are worthy of your great beauty and befitting it. And she with serene countenance and sparkling eyes pronounced with mellifluous lips words that pierced my bodily hearing and winged their way to the seat of my heart like fiery darts, and to my heart, as it melted in the sweetness of love, she said this: "Because 'you are a man of desires,'[14] I have come to show you the hidden treasure of all that is desirable, the center and the circumference of all that can be longed for,[15] 'the length and breadth

10. This alludes to one of the many legends about the nature of the panther, which was regarded as typifying Christ.

11. Ecclus 24.24–28.   12. Jdt 11.19.

13. Cf. Ps 41.8.   14. Dn 9.23.

15. This is an allusion to pseudo-Hermes Trismegistus, *The Book of the Twenty-Four Teachers*: "God is the intelligible sphere, whose center is everywhere and whose circumference is nowhere."

and height and depth'[16] of everything that is to be loved.

(5) "So first of all, if you want to know the reason and the meaning of my name, understand that the dwellers on earth call me 'Eternal Wisdom,' which indeed best of all befits my nobility. For there is nothing in created beings that could be of sweeter savor in the heart of the Creator and of all who love him perfectly. They are not more pleasing, "the sound of the trumpet, the flute and the harp, of the sackbut and the psaltery and the symphony" sweetly sounding, or "of all kind of music."[17] The harmonious notes of the nightingale, sweetest of all bird-song, do not so allure young folks' ears, nor did ever any earthly melody or celestial harmony offer a greater cause for joy. For the savor of my name is like 'a cluster of cypress in the vineyards of Engaddi,[18] cypress with spikenard, of spikenard and saffron, sweet cane and cinnamon with all the trees of Libanus, myrrh and aloes with all most precious perfumes'[19] and most costly scents. 'And I perfumed my dwelling as the frankincense not cut, and my scent is as the purest balm.'[20] And these things I say that you may understand my name.

(6) "Then next, because your love is seeking for the heights, and is not content to love as do cooks and bakers and perfume-makers and others like them, and you, unlike us, ask me if I am well born and of a famous line; and to answer this properly would require a rational sequence of thought, would demand that one had the ability and that the difficulties were not too great. But the secrets of my begetting are such that they surpass the wits of every mortal being. For I am she of whom it was written: 'Who shall declare her generation?'[21] 'I came out of the mouth of the Most High, the firstborn before all creatures.'[22] 'And my emergence is from the beginning, from the days of eternity.'[23] 'I am like a brook out of a river, like an aqueduct that has come out of paradise.'[24] 'I was established from eternity, and from ancient times before the earth was

16. Eph 3.18.   17. Dn 3.7.
18. Cant 1.13.   19. Cant 4.13–14.
20. Ecclus 24.21.   21. Is 53.8.
22. Ecclus 24.5.   23. Mi 5.2.
24. Ecclus 24.41.

made. The depths still did not exist, and I was already conceived, nor had the fountains of waters yet sprung forth. The
mountains with their huge bulk had not yet been established;
before the hills I was produced. He had not yet made the earth
and the rivers and the poles of the world. When he prepared
the heavens, I was present, when with a certain law and compass he enclosed the depths. When he set firm the sky above,
and poised the fountains of waters, when he compassed the
sea with its bounds, and gave law to the waters, that they should
not pass their limits, when he balanced the foundations of the
earth, I was with him, forming all things. And I was filled with
delight every day, playing before him at all times, playing in
the world, and my delight was to be with the children of men.'[25]
'Blessed is the man who hears me, who watches daily at my
gates, and waits at the posts of my doors. He who will find me
will find life, and will have salvation from the Lord.'[26] And so I
remained, always beloved in my beloved, and always, beloved,
flowing out from my beloved, and always from the beginning
playing in my beloved. And so you have what I seem to be, and
what is my ancestry. And yet, so far as full understanding of
what my true essence may be is concerned, reason requires
you not to inquire, because a well-ordered nature should not
strive for impossible things."

(7) Disciple: When I hear with such great emotion these
things, my heart rejoices so that I can scarcely control myself,
and all my spirit greatly exults in the Lord. O, "who will give
you to me" as my beloved bridegroom, born of a beloved Father,[27] "that I may go abroad and find you, and that I may kiss
you so that now no man may despise me?"[28] But I implore you,
my beloved, tell me for what reason it is that you have been
accustomed so often to compare yourself in your loving with
fleshly things, when according to your words and the judgment of all who reason well you cannot be either the body or
the body's strength?[29]

25. Prv 8.23–31.   26. Prv 8.34–35.
27. *dilectum sponsum*, masculine, just as towards the end of her previous
speech Wisdom has called herself "beloved in my beloved," *dilectus in dilecto*.
28. Cant 8.1.
29. Cf. *CG* 1.20: "God is neither the body nor the body's strength."

(8) Wisdom: The human intellect cannot understand simple truths about matters that are most sublime, and therefore it is necessary to convey them through images and accepted comparisons. My beauty is indeed so great that if anyone were to submit himself for many years to great torments so that for the twinkling of an eye he might look on me in all my loveliness, beyond any doubt what he would suffer would be less than his reward.

(9) Disciple: Since, as you assure me, we cannot speak of supercelestial and divine matters except by means of bodily things,[30] let his simple disciple propound to my most wise master a simple word,[31] the explanation of which I long to have. See how the beauty of the heavens is deduced from the glory of the stars, and the fairness of the meadow from its profusion of flowers; and so sometimes the loveliness of young maidens or brides of this earth is judged by the richness of their clothing. So they appear, covered in gold, "dripping with glittering jewels,"[32] clothed in rich embroidery, enriched with intertwining precious stones, all beautiful. So how are you adorned?

(10) Wisdom: A wise painter, when something is lacking in his subject, is accustomed to fill up his picture with what is not essential; and when he knows that his surface is pitted with spots, he will take care to conceal them in flourishings, so that no one will know that underneath his elaborate design there is a snake hiding in the grass. So he deceives the human eye, and produces a pleasing appearance by concealment from the senses, as he covers up what is ill-made and makes it seem pretty by the glowing colors of his design. In truth, this is more to the credit of the artist than to that of the artifact.[33] But, on the other hand, the sun surrounded by the brightness of its rays has no need of any alien, borrowed beauty, for its immense luminosity alone invests it with true beauty. So it is that

30. From pseudo-Dionysius, *The Celestial Hierarchy*, ch. 1, quoted in *ST* I, q.1, a. 9, c.

31. *simplici . . . simplex: traductio;* cf. Colledge and Walsh, *A Book of Showings*, 747.

32. From the Dominican Breviary for the feast of St. Agnes.

33. *artificis . . . artificiato:* this too is *traductio.*

Eternal Wisdom, "the sun of justice,"[34] that very Wisdom "at whose beauty the sun and moon marvel,"[35] "inhabiting inaccessible light,"[36] "in the brightness of the saints, begotten from the womb before the day star."[37] surrounded by its immensity of light, has no need of any alien addition from without, for it is everything that is, that is fair, that is beautiful, that is seemly. To it, to be is the same as to be beautiful, to be delightful. For "all its glory is within in golden borders, clothed round about with skilled embroideries."[38] Indeed, as "it is clothed with light as with a garment,"[39] so is it everywhere suffused with the beauty of light, so that the human eye could not bear the splendor of its brightness. "For man will not see me," Wisdom says, "and live."[40]

(11) And the fairness of every created thing, what else is it than a sort of mirror in which the mastery of the supreme craftsman is reflected? If you tell me that you wonder at the lily's beauty and at the whiteness of its array, why do you not wonder at the lily's Maker? If sometimes a lovely face and an appearance fittingly adorned have been pleasing to your worldly eyes, how rightly will Wisdom, fairer beyond words than all others, beauty in her very essence, be pleasing to the eyes of your heart? For if you will look at things as they are, everything that has been adorned, and all its ornaments, resound to the praise of his ingenuity, he who produced the substance in being, with its quality and its other characteristics. Therefore it is plain that those things that in your days of vanity used to attract you towards what is created should rather have attracted you to the Creator of all these things, "besides what is hidden within."[41]

(12) Disciple: And what is this which is hidden within?

(13) Wisdom: The most joyful vision of my most simple essence, the longed-for enjoyment of my supersubstantial divinity, "the possession, complete and also perfect, of a life that

---

34. Mal 4.2.
35. From the Dominican Breviary for the feast of St. Agnes.
36. 1 Tm 6.16.   37. Ps 109.3.
38. Ps 44.14.   39. Ps 103.2.
40. Ex 33.20.   41. Cant 4.1.

cannot end."[42] For when all these multitudes of blessed spirits
are assembled, such joy is given, such cause of rejoicing is
made that through the greatness of their love and the immensity of their exultation "a thousand years may be in their eyes
as yesterday, which is past."[43] And indeed the whole concourse
of heaven, ceaselessly looking on so many marvels and hearing
new songs,[44] have their eyes always fixed upon me. They stand
with lifted faces, and they look on me with hearts burning in
love; and their feet are placed as if ready to dance for joy, and
their faces are open[45] to contemplate me. So they "lift up their
hearts," and they open wide the heart's mouth to the waters
of the fountain of life, flowing down from on high. O, how
blessed the man who will merit to take part in this most happy
rejoicing, this most joyful happiness,[46] who will be one of the
choir of heavenly virgins who will with me lead the chorus
singing happy songs of praise of heavenly things, where "the
holy choirs of virgins hasten after me sounding sweet
hymns."[47] See how a single word of love from my loving lips
uttered to a loving heart surpasses the melodies of all the
angels, all the harmonies "of harpers harping on their
harps,"[48] and every consort of instruments and every symphony.

(14) Ah, see, I beg, as your mind rejoices, how skilled in
love I am, how disposed I am for the embraces and the kisses
of a soul wholly mine, how delectable above all others. O,
sweet and most precious kiss, bestowed in love from lips so
sweet! O, how blessed the soul to whom in its whole life this
were given, were it only once! And if for its giving the soul
might chance to die, that would be no grave matter.

(15) And so I am always ready to return my beloved's love,
I am there in choir, I am there in bed, at table, on the road,

42. Boethius, *Consolation*, Book 5, prose 6.
43. Ps 89.4.   44. Ps. 143.9, etc.
45. 2 Cor 3.18.
46. *felicissimae iucunditati et iucundissimae felicitati*: this is *commutatio*; Colledge and Walsh, 736.
47. From the Dominican Breviary's office for the Common of Virgins.
48. Apoc 14.2.

in the cloister, in the market place, so that there can be no place where the love which is God is not present and where I am not answering my beloved with love. So does divine Wisdom lay claim to what is solely its own among all spouses, and can be present everywhere to fulfill the lover's desire, and has known all the sighs breathed for it, the wishes made, the services performed. Because of this, a certain lover of Wisdom said: "I set the Lord always in my sight," and again: "Therefore my heart has been glad, and my tongue has rejoiced."[49]

(16) On the other hand, such is the singular prerogative of my goodness that if anyone were to receive a mere drop of it to taste, from then on "he would count but as dung"[50] all the pleasure of this world. My love lightens the burden of sinners, it purifies the conscience, it strengthens the mind, it gives liberty to the perfect and joins them to their eternal Beginning. What more? Whoever takes me for his bride and loves me above all things lives in tranquillity, dies in safety and in some fashion begins in this present life the joys that last for ever and ever. We are saying many things, and we are lacking in words, for no "tongue of men or of angels"[51] is enough to recount my love's preeminence. It can be experienced, but it cannot be told. Yet let what has been blurted out rather than said tell something of the quality of divine love.

(17) Disciple: O, the immense rejoicing of my heart! For is this not indeed "the hour of salvation,"[52] the hour of spiritual rejoicing, the time of visitation and of grace, "the day that the Lord has made,"[53] in which "the heavens were made to flow with honey,"[54] in which fear has passed over into love, and the graces that you have shown to your servants give me greater confidence to speak more fully? Therefore I shall open my mouth, and the secrets that for so long I kept shut up in the chamber of my heart I shall now disclose to you, and the wound of love, so long concealed in my longing heart, I shall lay bare.

49. Ps 15.8–9.   50. Phil 3.8.
51. 1 Cor 13.1.   52. 2 Cor 6.2.
53. Ps 117.24.
54. From the Dominican Breviary for the feast of the Nativity.

(18) You know, for I have quoted a great expert in his *Art of Loving*,[55] that a compelling love does not tolerate any companion, will not endure any plurality. For we have heard long ago that kingship and love do not easily suffer friends. Even a great river can dwindle away into little rivulets.[56] And love too, when it seeks for companions, loses in stature and knows want.

(19) O one and only possessor of my heart, now are its impetuous yearnings so set on you that, loving you only, it demands to be rewarded by a single-minded love. O, how much I ought to desire you to know me by my name, knowing me, to love me above all, and loving me, to elect me among your own most special friends. O my God, would that you might look on me in grace with the eyes of your clemency, that you might direct all my works, and make me your most familiar friend and servant. O, how joyful I should be if these things might come about as I pray. Indeed I should consider myself to have the wealth of Croesus and the delights of all men. Yet now, as I say with a mournful heart, loving you alone and only you, I am obliged to be content with the common laws of love. I beg you, all you gentle lovers, lend me your ears, stoop down to me, and adjudge between me and my beloved.

(20) See how my beloved is for me my only treasure, and I have made him into my mirror of love. The rocks could have melted more easily than my mind could be called back from love of him. Even if he should dismiss me, I shall not dismiss him, for he lives as my lord. If he should spurn me, I shall go on, faithful and constant; I shall sit like the solitary turtledove until I win my beloved back again. I shall accept no consolation, I shall look for no one to solace me, for truly all such "comforters will be troublesome to me."[57] It is he alone for whom I seek; from him alone shall I be able to find comfort. For him "has my soul chosen hanging, and my bones death."[58] If he should go away, he will draw my heart after him, and if he should return, he will fill my mouth with rejoicing. "Whether I eat, whether I drink, whatever else I shall do,"[59] he is present

to me. He is the one for whom I look, he is the one for whom I ask. "I have become foolish,"[60] for I am compelled by love. Ah, I had not expected to take him to my heart as my lover, until I had grown cold in my old age, and had failed in all my powers, until the rose "in the beauty of its shape would perish,"[61] and wrinkles overrun my face, and then, when I was made hideous and unfit for any earthly love, compelled by necessity, to take refuge in his love because I should not have any other whom I should love or for whose love I should long.

(21) Yet since in the flower of my youth my tender years seemed still to promise a long life, I was surrounded by the glad company of my friends and my natural qualities disposed me towards the love of women, and I found many of them, encouraging me, and then holding aloof. But I scorned them all, and rejected the fairest flowers, which were so sweetly proferred, and with face averted I turned away with weeping. Gladly I rejected all this, and made you the one reward of my love. I fled to your love, and chose you to be my beloved. So therefore, O my love, my joy, the sweetness of my soul, would it be unkind for you to love me specially, and to give me some little return for such a love as mine? I do not indeed ask you to love me alone, above all others, but can you not show a kindly love to me among all the others?

(22) Truly this is what causes me pain and care, that there are so many hearts that love you with a most burning love, and who surpass me in love and in every demonstration of love. Alas, alas, what will then become of me? For I am greatly afraid that when you, the lover of the lilies, "feed among the lilies,"[62] it may go ill for me, and that as you breathe in their perfume you may forget the thistles or the nettles, and that so I shall suffer the loss of your love through your love of others. But forget, O my beloved, what I am saying now. You know well how the power of ardent love can conquer, so that a man cannot control his words, nor turn his mind to anything but his love for his beloved. You are indeed, if I dare say so, very

60. 2 Cor 12.11.   61. Jas 1.11.
62. Cant 6.2.

given to loving here and there. So "there are three score queens and four score concubines, and young maidens without number," and yet "one is your dove, your perfect one, your undefiled one,"[63] who claims for herself to be the ruler over all the rest. So in all the coasts of Israel they sought for young virgins, and only Abisag was chosen and brought to the king.[64] So were many women brought to Assuerus, but one was preferred to them all and raised up to be the royal consort.[65] O singular one, you who are single and who have no follower, you who were so happily made, who were so richly endowed, may you possess that only treasure which is your heart's desire! Who will give me at least to fill myself with "the crumbs that fall from the table"[66] of your leavings?

(23) Wisdom: Love has indeed brought you to "an excess of your mind,"[67] which your words pleading love and your tear-stained face both show. But now, if I were to show you that I do love you with a singular love, according to every desire of your heart, what would you want to do?

(24) Disciple: I should want to embrace you a thousand times, and I should long to kiss you ten times a thousand times with a rejoicing love, and whatever hardships love might command me to bear, willingly should I do it all. For see, my lord, how my soul hangs wholly upon your words and waits for one word of consolation. O desire of my soul, speak to your servant's heart. O loving consoler, why do you dally with me? Why do you afflict my longing soul with love deferred? See how impatient my love is, and it cannot wait any longer. For "hopes deferred afflict the heart."[68]

(25) Wisdom: Your love, however intense it may be, still appears to blind you somewhat, for you judge that one can feel about divine and supercelestial matters in earthly ways; "and so you judge, as it were, through a mist."[69] But it is not so. Beyond doubt, God's wisdom is love, and so, just as his essence, existent in all things, is not divided, or, because it

63. Cant 6.7–8, 52.
64. 3 Kgs 1.3.
65. Est 2.16–17.
66. Mt 15.27.
67. Ps 30.23.
68. Prv 13.12.
69. Jb 22.13.

exists in all things, is not made less in any single thing, so too his love, because he loves everything that he has made, is not diminished.[70] And so he has regard for single things, so that he may seem to be free of all things, and so he presides over all things, so that he may be thought to be free of single things.[71] Nor ought you so to imagine that because in your youth you loved me first, you therefore should want to be loved by me as a right, because in fact it is the other way around. It is indeed because I have loved you from all eternity, and "know you by name,"[72] and have chosen you first by a singular love, that you therefore love, even if it follows that the effect of predestination demands the effect of love. So hold firmly to this, without prejudice to all other lovers, that I have a loving care for you at all times, hour by hour, as though I had put aside everything else, and were keeping myself free for you alone, that I might respond only to your love.

(26) Disciple: Happy is "this saying and worthy of all acceptance."[73] Now "my soul is magnified this day above all the days of my life."[74] Therefore as one let "the whole earth and its fullness"[75] rejoice with me, and rejoice as I rejoice, and wish me joy for such a tender love and for so immense and desirable a loving from my beloved. Ah, my loved one, "turn away your eyes from me, for they have made me flee away."[76] Who could have so iron a heart, or so stony a breast, that he could hear your flashing words and not at once catch fire from your love? And who is there so frigid or so tepid that if he were to place you in all your beauty before his heart's eyes and keep the gaze of his love fixed on you, and often were to listen to "your word exceedingly refined,"[77] and again and again were to ponder it, he would not blaze with fire from the torch of this deepest love? Just as the sun, rising into our hemisphere, and going around the meridian's circumference, kindles the earth with its heat, so your fiery discourse sets cold hearts alight with its love.

70. Cf. Bernard of Clairvaux, *Sermon 69 on the Canticles*, n. 2.
71. Cf. *Conf.* 3.11, and Hugh of St. Victor, *The Soul's Betrothal Gift*.
72. Ex 33.12.   73. 1 Tm 1.15.
74. Jdt 12.18.   75. Ps 49.12.
76. Cant 6.4.   77. Ps 118.140.

(27) "All you who thirst, come,"[78] come now to the fount of all love, and to the longed-for fruit of joy giving greatest delight. Why do you use up your possessions and your body and expose your soul to everlasting peril, and still "you are laboring in vain"?[79] Your state is a constant dryness like dropsy. You gnaw at your parched lips with your teeth so as to have the taste of the bits of meat that remain there. O wretched men, truly you are in love with misery, when what you seek you do not find as you ask. Look, I beg you, look at "how good and how pleasant"[80] it is to love the highest good, to give all one's heart to the bride of brides. "Return to the heart,"[81] sweetest lovers, and ponder how blessed is the man who, "leaving all things,"[82] has pledged himself to that bride, and with his heart's devotion has performed for her alone all the labors that are owed to love. Can you imagine how much consolation this man enjoys, how much inward sweetness, known only to him and "hidden from the eyes of all the living"?[83] So did you rejoice, O gentle lady betrothed to Eternal Wisdom, most blessed Agnes, fairest jewel among virgins, as you uttered the praises of such a bridegroom and said: "He has plighted himself to me with his ring, and with priceless jewels he has adorned me. I have received honey and milk from his lips, and his blood has beautified my cheeks."[84]

(28) Truly I confess, O my beloved, that your sweetest saying, shot through with fiery love, has brought my drowsing soul awake. It has made my sad mind "to melt and to revive."[85] It has given light to what was in shadow, it has unlocked what was shut, and it has filled me with one purpose alone, so that with heart and soul I long to be found worthy of that sweetest of betrothals, which would be with you. For so we have heard and so we have found "that there is no respect of persons with you."[86] You invite all men to your love, you fill them all, and you give them to drink from the cup of salvation.

78. Is 55.1.   79. Ps 26.1.
80. Ps 132.1.   81. Is 46.8.
82. Lk 5.11.   83. Jb 28.21.
84. From the Dominican Breviary for the feast of St. Agnes.
85. From the Dominican Breviary for the feast of St. Mary Magdalen.
86. Rom 2.11.

(29) "I adjure you"[87] all, most ardent lovers of Eternal Wisdom, most happy wooers of this most divine spouse, that you will deign to commend me to her with your prayers. Yet now, O body and soul, "for whom are you waiting?"[88] "Why are you careless?"[89] Why are you holding back so long from an undertaking that will so save you? "Let us put off the old man, let us put on the new man,"[90] and let us rouse ourselves out of this neglectful sloth, which keeps us from so much good. For "why were we born?"[91] Indeed, "we live only in our life."[92] Men who are simple, illiterate, ignorant arise,[93] and they are made drunk with love's most fecund plenty; and we, "weaving fine linen"[94] and showing to others the way of truth, inviting them to drink of the cup of the heart's sweetness, persist in the dryness of our minds. Ah, bestir yourselves, my brethren and my companions, "for God is able from these stones"[95] to beget the fire of divine love. "Who knows but he will return"[96] and will scatter saving grace among those who entreat? "Who knows but he will leave a gentle blessing behind him,"[97] so that even we wretched ones are made sharers of his love, that we may have our lot among his beloved and his elect?

(30) It gives great delight, the memory of this fairest spouse, and to recall that she is above all others and has the prerogative of her rank, is "as music at a banquet of wine"[98] and as the sweet perfume of unguents. Yet there are those who "think themselves to be something, whereas they are nothing, but they deceive themselves,"[99] and all who are not on their guard. O, how often do we love what we hardly know, and neglect what we know to the full. We wait with great longing for one to come whom we hardly expect, yet what we can have as we please we reject with hatred, greater than the love with which

87. Cant 5.8.   88. 1 Mc 7.30.
89. Gn 42.1.   90. Eph 4.22, 24.
91. 1 Mc 2.7.   92. Ecclus 48.12.
93. Cf. *Conf.* 8.8, quoted in the Dominican Breviary for the feast of St. Augustine.
94. Is 19.9; see Bk. 2, ch. 1, note 6, below.
95. Mt 3.9.   96. Jl 2.14.
97. Jl 2.14.   98. Ecclus 49.2.
99. Gal 6.3.

we hope for what we do not possess. I confess that "in the days of my vanity"[100] I used to inquire with great care about these things, and I found this, as the proverb says: My eye that man has never seen whose life is lived without some "might have been."

(31) For wherever I turned I found some fault to prevent my love. For if there was physical beauty, there was not pleasingness of mind. Sometimes one who seemed gently bred was found wanting through some defect of morals, or by a certain stupidity that repelled love, rather than winning it. One would have a beak like an eagle or else a snub nose, another would have crooked teeth or a hairy face that she shaved, or else their clothes were dirty. And if every such matter were all one could wish, there would be grinding poverty, which is no friend of love. If some girl were decked out with riches and beauty, her peasant ancestry would make her loathsome. One would be called melancholy, another ill-tempered, and another was said to have a shady reputation. If all these things were just as they should be, then one wanted the impossible, or men's malice or slandering tongues would mix some bitterness in the sweet cup, and would repel me from this kind of love. My spirit longed for love, it wanted the rose, but it complained about the thorns. Giving lilies or violets to peasants, or feeding beasts with food fit for a prince, only wearied me. A peacock may shine in its golden gown, but its ill-shapen feet make it hard for it to walk. What else need I say? I hastened from one to another, but always I found in everyone some stain or defect, and I said in my heart that I never wished to abandon the quest for love until it chanced that I should find a lover free from every fault. "Why need I delay?"[101]

(32) See, now "deep" has met with "deep."[102] The deep of desires has entered the deep of all graces and perfections. What then? "Behold, you are fair, O my love, sweet and comely as Jerusalem,"[103] virtuous and well-born. In your riches you excel all, in your glory you precede all. You are not only wise,

100. Eccl 7.16.   101. Terence, *The Woman of Andros.*
102. Ps 41.8.   103. Cant 1.14, 6.3.

you are Wisdom's own self. There is no one like to you in the faculty of love and in the school of the art of loving. No one will be distressed by fear or shame who will wish to love you or to wed you. Familiarity with you does not breed hatred or contempt, but the more completely your lovers see you, the more ardently do they cling to you in love. For the celestial craftsman, who has executed with his tools every form, designed the features and the beauty of my beloved, cutting away all that was superfluous,[104] and leaving a form of entire beauty; and in him he set up the perfection of love. For who is there, tell me, I pray, who, if he were to see him with his own eyes, would not lose his wits at his beauty, whose hearing would not be ravished by his "sweet speech,"[105] whose heart would not be vanquished by the power of his love? All his being surpasses eloquence, cannot be measured by the meter of words. The beloved's love makes those who love him wish only to fall silent, and so they bring comfort to their lover. And everything that I possess, which has been "sold gratis,"[106] gives itself to his perpetual service, and "swears by him who lives for ever and ever"[107] never to renounce his good pleasure.

(33) O my sweet one, how sweeter than sweet is your friendship, which has not driven me to wander abroad as an exile, but has preferred itself to my love as its longed-for reward. Oh, how joyful is this food of my love, the taste of which makes bitter all that is sweet, yet sweeter far everything that is bitter. "Let my beloved come into his garden,"[108] and there let me be sweetly restored whom he so greatly loves. "Come, my beloved,"[109] let us together gather the roses of your garden. I shall show you the fruits that are kept for you alone, nor shall I forbid you to taste all the desirable things growing there. See how I look on my beloved, as he stands surrounded by three hundred young men of most gentle breeding and of the greatest beauty, and they clad in embroidered garments, and each

---

104. Pseudo-Dionysius, *Mystical Theology*, ch. 2, uses this example, which is also found in Eckhart, *Of the Nobleman* and *Commentary on John*.

105. Cant 4.3.   106. Is 52.3.
107. Apoc 10.6.   108. Cant 5.1.
109. Cant 7.11.

of them "girt about the breasts with a golden girdle."[110] Every one has auburn hair reflecting the rays of the sun like gold, so that he seems to be seated on a couch of living light. And my love in the midst of them "with a rosy color[111] and a snowy whiteness"[112] sends back from his face the light of the sun. "His name and his remembrance are the desire of the soul."[113] O, "who will give me" that his mellifluous name may be inscribed in golden letters upon "the largeness of my heart"?[114] What can remain to be a token of his love, except that nothing of all that is may ever bring forgetfulness of him? O my Wisdom, most sweet, most happy, I pray that neither life nor death nor any turn of fortune separate me from you, but that our love may endure forever, "stronger than death."[115]

110. Apoc 1.13.   111. Est 15.8.
112. From the Dominican Breviary for the feast of the Crown of Thorns.
113. Is 2.68.   114. 3 Kgs 4.29.
115. Cant 8.6.

CHAPTER 7

That Divine Wisdom Is at Once Lovable
and Terrible

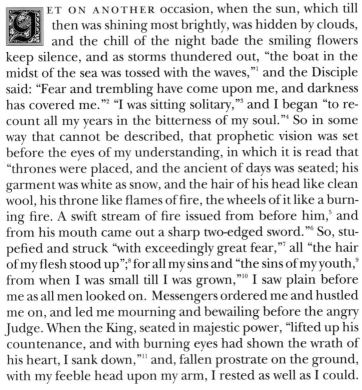ET ON ANOTHER occasion, when the sun, which till then was shining most brightly, was hidden by clouds, and the chill of the night bade the smiling flowers keep silence, and as storms thundered out, "the boat in the midst of the sea was tossed with the waves,"[1] and the Disciple said: "Fear and trembling have come upon me, and darkness has covered me."[2] "I was sitting solitary,"[3] and I began "to recount all my years in the bitterness of my soul."[4] So in some way that cannot be described, that prophetic vision was set before the eyes of my understanding, in which it is read that "thrones were placed, and the ancient of days was seated; his garment was white as snow, and the hair of his head like clean wool, his throne like flames of fire, the wheels of it like a burning fire. A swift stream of fire issued from before him,[5] and from his mouth came out a sharp two-edged sword."[6] So, stupefied and struck "with exceedingly great fear,"[7] all "the hair of my flesh stood up";[8] for all my sins and "the sins of my youth,[9] from when I was small till I was grown,"[10] I saw plain before me as all men looked on. Messengers ordered me and hustled me on, and led me mourning and bewailing before the angry Judge. When the King, seated in majestic power, "lifted up his countenance, and with burning eyes had shown the wrath of his heart, I sank down,"[11] and, fallen prostrate on the ground, with my feeble head upon my arm, I rested as well as I could.

1. Mt 14.24.
2. Ps 54.6.
3. Lam 3.28.
4. Is 38.15.
5. Dn 7.9–10.
6. Apoc 1.16.
7. 1 Kgs 31.4.
8. Jb 4.15.
9. Ps 24.7.
10. Cf. 1 Kgs 30.19.
11. Est 15.10.

(2) When for a time I had kept silent, seized "with exceedingly great fear," at length I came again to myself, and with much lamentation I said to myself these things: Woe, woe "to those walking after the lusts"[12] of their heart. Woe to all "who work iniquity,"[13] for if they knew the future punishment prepared for them and the strict sentence that an angered Judge would pronounce against them, and how he has decreed that this will "begin at his sanctuary,"[14] indeed they would have been more wary of sinning. Truly, they would rather have endured every temporal punishment than have offended the sight of this Judge.

(3) Alas, "O Lord the Lord God,"[15] how very terrible is your face, how threatening and how very sharp your words. I tremble from head to foot at such indignation. O, horrifying sight, so much to be feared, always to be shunned with every care. I ask and with all my power I entreat you, almighty king, by your unmeasured goodness, protect me, I beg, from this fearful sight. Do with me in this life whatever will be pleasing to you. Lay laws upon me, increase my tribulations, multiply my adversities, make my infirmities a hundredfold. Whatever may please you I shall bear most willingly, asking only this, that you will deign to spare me from the face of your wrath. For indeed I have such "fear of the Lord"[16] that even if there were to be only the slightest suspicion that my faults would require you even for a little while "to withhold your face"[17] from me, or that I might have offended you, my judge, there would be no rest at all for me, but I should all waste away in myself for sorrow and grief. And how could I endure that terrifying face, full of wrath and indignation?

(4) Woe to wretched and hardened sinners! Woe to the hellish and damned souls and to the perverse spirits who will see that furious face and its terrible expression without any hope of grace, and will hear that terrifying voice as it thunders: "Go, 'you cursed, into everlasting fire.'"[18] O, everlasting curse!

12. 2 Pt 3.3.   13. Prv 21.15.
14. Ez 9.6.   15. Ex 34.6.
16. Ps 110.10.   17. Ps 26.9.
18. Mt 25.41.

O, "everlasting reproach which will never be effaced."[19] Who will be strong enough to think of "that day to be trembled at"?[20] For your fatherly face is not to be borne, its severity is so amazing when you turn it to your sons to emend them, not to destroy them, that it may seem to be like hell. Who then could look on your terrible face when it held no hope? And so I exhort all men, and, most of all, sinners, that they should never on any account presume upon your silence. For "you hold your peace, and you overlook sins."[21] Yet when "your hand will take hold on judgment, you will render vengeance to your enemies, and you will repay those who hate you."[22] How, I ask, O most loving goodness, can it be true that you are lovable, when you can be so terrible?

(5) Wisdom: I am indeed terrible to sinners, yet lovable to the just and to those who love me. "I am God, who does not change,"[23] and yet I seem different, according to the qualities and diversities of those who look on me. It is profitable for my elect in this world always "to have both fear and love,"[24] so that fear, always urging the soul, "may draw it from poisonous excesses,"[25] and love, gladdening it, may lift it up to the things of heaven.

19. Jer 20.11.
20. From the Dominican Breviary's office of the dead.
21. Hb 1.13; Wis 11.24.   22. Dt 32.41.
23. Mal 3.6.
24. From the Dominican Breviary and Missal for the Sunday in the octave of Corpus Christi.
25. From the Dominican Breviary and Missal for the Monday after the third Sunday in Lent.

CHAPTER 8

How Divine Visitations Come and Go, and How at These Times the Soul Should Bear Itself

HE BEST BELOVED of the Lord will dwell confidently in him, as in a bridal chamber he will abide all the day long, and between his shoulders will be rest."[1] When I hear "these and such like" words which allude to perfect love with the ear of my heart, I sigh greatly, knowing myself to be so far away from the longed-for fruits of this love. For when against the wishes of the lover the beloved is withdrawn, which, I confess, has often happened to me, it seems to me that in love there is chiefly "labor and sorrow."[2] For as often as anyone is gladdened and rejoices in the beloved's presence, so often is he saddened and mourns over his absence. And this is that joyless and most afflicting rule of love, which in earthly loving I sought to avoid, and yet now I find in divine love the same rule.[3]

(2) This is therefore what I have against you, "mother of fair love,"[4] Eternal Wisdom, and I impugn your love, which the day before yesterday[5] you so greatly praised. This coming and going of which I have spoken seems to play a part not only in earthly love but also in yours. For it happens most often that when a lover's mind thinks that he possesses you quite peacefully in his heart's marriage bed, and in "a perpetual covenant"[6] believes that he can strain you to him in the arms of his love so that you cannot be parted, suddenly you who were thought to be present vanish, I do not know where, and you who were believed to be in his embrace disappear far off

---

1. Dt 33.12.   2. Ps 89.10.
3. Cf. Bernard of Clairvaux, *Sermon 51 on the Canticles.*
4. Ecclus 24.24.   5. This alludes to Bk. 1, ch. 6, above.
6. Gn 17.7.

and are not to be seen, but you leave behind you a soul full of sorrow.[7] And while that lover's heart burns for you, his soul thirsts for you, and his sick body languishes, longing with all his powers for you, the one and only joy of his heart, you hide yourself, and give no answer at all that he can understand, as if you spurned him. What is this? Is it not unkind and cruel to refuse to condescend even a little to the soul that "you have wounded"?[8]

(3) Wisdom: The greatness and the beauty of every created thing could answer for me.

(4) Disciple: Will that be sufficient for this loving soul? Even though it may know beyond doubt that your power and wisdom and goodness shine out from created things, and it understands as if from some footprint that you are all that is beautiful and good, still it is very far off from the end that it desires.

(5) Wisdom: If this is not enough, at least let the soul be satisfied by Sacred Scripture, where it can adequately find me if it will take trouble. Let it take every page as a love letter, as a solace of love that I have sent to it, for "all things which were written were written for its comfort,"[9] to raise up its hope and renew its love. Do these proofs of my love not seem to you as if they should suffice a lover?

(6) Disciple: O mistress of the school of all love and fondness, why do you speak so? Are you not a true lover? Are you not also a teacher of love? And, to say better, indeed you are love's own self. So, truly and beyond all doubt, you know the conditions of a loving heart, and it is therefore unbefitting for you to speak so strangely about love. You know, O everlasting love, that anything, whatever it is, counts for little with a lover when it is not his beloved. For nothing suffices a lover except for the one he loves to be with him. See how "there came into my heart as it were a burning fire, shut up in my bones, and I was wearied, not being able to bear it."[10] O most loving object

7. Cf. Bernard of Clairvaux, *Sermon 33 on the Canticles.*
8. Cant 4.9.   9. Rom 15.4.
10. Jer 20.9.

of my love, you have taken strong hold upon the dwelling place that is my heart; I keep you, a fine-wrought jewel, in my heart's casket, and by the power of your love I am all so constrained that even if "the tongues of men and of all angels"[11] were to extol you to me with singular praises, and were to tell me many things about you, or were to show me your love letters, they would be of little profit. No more than they could even sometimes restrain a lover's yearnings, would they be able to fulfill his desire. But all the longings of my heart urge me on to where I may find you, that heart's one and only treasure, and where I may be at rest forever in you, who are the only good. A little while in which I lack your most joyous presence seems to me like the passing of a whole year, so, my loving sweetness, do not, I beg, make yourself strange to your unworthy servant. Truly, if I find you more distant towards me than before, for no more than one day, I lament the long tedium of my banishment as if a thousand years were passing by, yes, a whole Platonic year.[12] For you are "the paradise of pleasure,"[13] you are the supercelestial paradise, indeed more to be wanted than every paradise, for to have you as we desire is to be perfectly blessed.

(7) Now therefore, if it befits all men who are invested with power to be adorned with pity and with clemency, how much more is great mercy and compassion fitting to such a majesty as yours? So why, O benign Wisdom, do you not look in clemency on those poor loving hearts which look on high to you, sending out deepest groans, pouring out fountains of tears, crying after you with loud voice: "Return, return," my beloved, "that we may behold you.[14] Restore to us the joy of your saving presence."[15] Inconsolably they weep, fearing lest they may have offended the desirable face of your goodness. "They sit alone

---

11. 1 Cor 13.1.

12. A "Platonic year" was imagined by the ancient astronomers as the cycle in which the heavenly bodies would go through all their possible movements and return to their first positions, variously reckoned, by some as 25,800 years. The commonest source for the notion in Suso's age was Macrobius's *Commentary on the Dream of Scipio*.

13. Gn 2.8.   14. Cant 6.12.

15. Ps 50.14.

and solitary,[16] for they are full of bitterness,"[17] and in the secrecy of their chamber they converse with one another, and with a longing, sighing spirit they say these words or others like them: "O when will he come? When will he return? Do you think that I shall see him? Do you think that my heart's eyes will see 'him on whom the eyes of angels desire to look'?"[18]

(8) For "to me, the least of all"[19] of those loving you, this sad state of affairs has sometimes happened, and as my beloved departed when I was not aware and was overcome by sweet slumber, I would weep and say: "Alas, 'whither is my beloved gone?'"[20] Alas, where shall I seek him? Do you not think that he will see something to attract him and make slow the return of his affections to me? Alas, alack, why did I not stay awake? Why did I not hold fast to him? My sweet one, show yourself to me, be mine again. For your absence wounds me as greatly as your presence once gave me joy. The uncertainty of your coming and going afflicts me cruelly. So "show me the shadow where you lie,"[21] seeking the cool, shunning the heat, for the sun is mounting, "lest I begin again to wander,"[22] seeking outside myself, I who once used to find myself in you. Ah, how long must I lack that which was once my sole possession and the sum of my desires? Let my surging heart in its longing for you, my beloved, compel your gifts to come down to me. For the violence of this surging robs me of myself, it bears me off to you, and it makes every joy become a burden to me; and so I do not possess myself, yet I have become my own burden. Look on these things with your loving eyes. Now I am failing, I have no strength to go on further. So give yourself, so that in you I may receive myself again, I who have lost myself through you.

(9) O, amazing power of love! Indeed I say that "love is as strong as death."[23] For you, O love, have taken away my heart and have given it to the beloved one, and you have cemented it to him so inseparably that there are certain times when it

16. Lam 3.28.   17. Lam 1.20.
18. 1 Pt 1.12.   19. Eph 3.8.
20. Cant 5.17.   21. Cant 1.6; Is 25.4.
22. Cant 1.6.   23. Cant 8.6.

seems somehow to have left my body and not to know to whom it belongs, whether to the subject whom it enlivens or to the object whom it loves with such devouring heat. O heart, tell me, I ask, whose you are, whether you are his whom you love with all your powers, or his to whom you give life? If you are mine, alas, how seldom you are with me! O, how often you are somewhere else! I do not know where you are, if you are not with him whose you are. Indeed, I would not have sent you to anyone so willingly except to the beloved one, whom I love more than my own life. And since I love him more than myself, therefore the more you are mine, the more you are his to whom I too belong. For you are bestowing on him not only yourself, but all of me too at the same time as you, signing the bond that makes both of us over to him. So then, if you are his, rather, indeed, because you are his, it is not only by your creation and redemption and the other similar reasons that apply to other rational creatures, but it is by a certain singular privilege, which is your willing and free gift, that you are his. For you are truly that jewel which in the first days of my amorous youth, deprived of every worldly and earthly love, I gave to him as my betrothal gift, as the jewel of my delight and as the token of my love, and I signed it with his name in letters of blood, and I made the ivory throne,[24] the bed of gold,[25] and the nuptial couch[26] for him to rest in.

(10) So tell me how you consider that she should be received, she your lover and your spiritual bride, who is Eternal Wisdom, when she returns and "stands at the gate of the heart and knocks and asks for it to be opened to her."[27] I, she says, shall not delay long, nor shall I keep my dear one waiting longer, but I shall run swiftly to our meeting, with the arms of my desires most lovingly stretched out, I shall enfold the beloved of my wishes in my fondest embrace, whilst I utter words of greeting. And just as John, shut in his mother's womb, danced for joy for the coming of the eternal King,[28] so

24. 2 Par 9.17.   25. Est 1.6.
26. 1 Mc 1.28.   27. Apoc 3.20.
28. Lk 1.41.

I, my treasure chamber locked, shall rejoice in my inmost heart at the coming of such a bride, and shall with an exultant voice utter words of greeting taken from the treasury of love, and shall say: O my beloved, the deepest abyss of my desires and the strength of my bones and the whole sum of all my powers salute you from the profoundest and most heartfelt longings of my soul, offering you so many greetings and such devoted service as there are leaves on the trees and stars shining in the heavens and grains of sand along the seashore. So, when he has been so devoutly received, I shall lead him to his own place, that is my heart's couch, the spiritual marriage bed; and yet, alas, this is what compels me to mourn even before it has happened, his waywardness, that is, his comings and goings. For this greatly afflicts my spirit, still not strengthened by attaining to a most perfect love. "These and suchlike things," the deep sighs of my heart and my words of love, O Eternal Wisdom, you hear but you do not heed, and you do not even pretend that you notice or that you care.

(11) Wisdom: I see every single thing, and with my heart's warm longings I look down upon all that is. But wait a little while, and tell me the word that I long to hear from you. For "will not he who speaks much also himself hear,"[29] or will not one who asks many things also give answers? So you too answer, and tell me what I ask. What is it that the spirits of heaven ought to seek and want in their working above all else?

(12) Disciple: O most prudent measurer of all powers, Eternal Wisdom, how shall I, a simple and inexpert man, answer this question? But you, greatest mistress of the heavenly disciplines, reply for me, I entreat.

(13) Wisdom: Then you should know that the angelic spirits and the perfect travelers seek as they work for nothing so much as for the conformity of all their actions to my will. "My food," divine Wisdom says, "is to do the will of my Father who is in heaven."[30] This is the food of angels and of the perfect travelers too, that they might find their delight that their Lord's will is fulfilled in them and universally in all creatures.

29. Jb 11.2.   30. Jn 4.34; Mt 7.21.

So they would find more delight in being put to work which is in itself mean than in performing more dignifying tasks, if that would be more acceptable to my will.

(14) Disciple: O great Wisdom, the answer you have given now is a concealed reprimand, with which you strike at my shortcomings. If I am not mistaken, what you want is to rebuke, in courteous fashion, my querulous talk, and to condemn my want of forbearance, as I seek for what is sweet and shun, when I can, the bitter.

(15) Wisdom: That ought to be the perfection of the tried disciple's love, that he would not only have won freedom from bodily delights, but, too, he would not have such longing for spiritual delights that he would prefer to seek for them more than to receive what is in itself the highest good. So consider yourself what it is you seek for or what it is you love. For those who are not perfect seek those things that are the beloved's, they do not seek him. Or, perhaps, they refuse the burdens he sends, as if they were serfs, or they seek after his rewards, as if they were mercenaries. However, so that I may answer more fully your chief question, about the changeability of my visitations, which, as you say, afflict the loving soul: You must know that sometimes, and more often, other reasons ignored, it is the soul itself which is the cause of the withdrawal, as some opacity in a window shuts out the sun's rays, or such discourtesy is shown indoors to a guest that he, "whose delight is to be with the sons of men"[31] is forced to leave his loved one, whom in this respect he does not love. Sometimes, it is true, when I come I give joy, "making my abode"[32] with her, not, indeed, openly, but secretly and hiddenly, so that there are very few, and they only the most expert, who can perceive the mysteries of my presence.

(16) Disciple: Lord, as I see, you are a most experienced lover, so I pray and I request that you will condescend to show me some of the countersigns of your most secret and most certain presence.

(17) Wisdom: If you want to recognize my presence, you must diligently examine yourself. What are you like in the

31. Prv 8.31.   32. Jn 14.23.

absence of grace? Know this, and at once you will find what you are seeking. For since I am the highest good, by my presence I fill all things with every goodness. And therefore, as a cause is known by its effects, and as the sun, invisible in itself, is made visible by the rays which it throws out, so is my presence apprehended through its most fecund goodness. Now, therefore, if you have ever experienced the goodness of my presence or absence's sterility, try for the mean, so that you as an expert can see the flowers growing among the grass.

(18) Disciple: If every part of my body were turned into tongues, and they were to resound with all the powers of the human voice, they could not express or perfectly tell what you are asking me.[33] But, that I may tell the truth, because of this thing very often I have risen up into the vastness of God's marvels "to a deep heart, that God will be exalted,"[34] saying within myself: O, if such is the immense goodness of God's presence in a sinful man, whose life is little and whose efforts nothing, what is it therefore in others, so immensely full of innocence of life and of graces and virtues?

(19) So I offer this little which I have experienced, as you have granted it, so that I may have a fuller guidance from you in all these things. Therefore, O highest goodness, when you turn away from me your gracious face full of goodness and sweetness, when you withdraw your inward consolation, and "in your hands you hide the light,"[35] then suddenly the wretched soul is changed and is made as it were languid and declining. Then a lassitude of the body follows, and a hardness of the heart and a sadness of the spirit is felt. A certain noxious weariness fills every part of me, so that "my soul is weary of my life."[36] Everything that is seen or heard, even if it were good, at that time evokes only a nausea of the spirit. When you go away, that brings me a horror of my dwelling place, a disgust for my cell, and an equal disdain for the brethren living with me; and "my soul begins to slumber through weariness,"[37] and sometimes, through cowardice, my spirit does not know "from

33. Cf. John of Fécamp, *Meditations*, ch. 15.
34. Ps 63.7–8.   35. Jb 36.32.
36. Jb 10.1.   37. Ps 118.28.

where it comes or to where it is going."[38] I am convinced by most certain experience that then I am more prone to vices, weak to resist temptations, and with less vigor for every spiritual exercise. Everyone who would seek me at times like that would find an empty house, because the good householder, who should fill his servants with blessings and joy, had gone off and left his dwelling empty.

(20) But[39] yet, when that brightest "dawning splendor of eternal light,"[40] rising and moving through the midst of my heart's darknesses, mounts in its beauty: O, "change of the right hand of the Most High,"[41] then all the mists collected by my melancholy disposition dissolve, and the cloudy "night is as light as the day,"[42] and all my sadness is taken away. Then see, how my heart is filled with laughter, my mouth is full of rejoicing. The soul is glad, the conscience is clear, all my bones rejoice, praising God and telling him that "he is good, for his mercy endures for ever. And they sing in the ways of the Lord, for great is the glory of the Lord."[43] Then out of joy the will begins to make holiday, out of exultation the reason begins to keep the feast, so that, filled with such joys, sometimes I might have sworn that the earth's light-giver had ushered in a day so wondrously bright to proclaim the Lord's Resurrection to the whole world. Beyond doubt "when I had thought myself consumed, I rose as the day star,"[44] and "to those dwelling in the region of the shadow of death light has risen."[45]

(21) Then everything that before had appeared hard and bitter and somehow impossible was made sweet and easy. Fasting seemed pleasant, vigils brief, and every exercise trifling, because my love was so great. For on such an occasion of spiritual grace I have the intention of emending my life, correcting my morals and doing many good things, but, alas, as grace withdraws, how little of this do I put into effect! The soul is

38. Jn 3.8.
39. The next six paragraphs owe much to the classical medieval exposition of "the game of love," Hugh of St. Victor's *The Soul's Betrothal Gift.*
40. From the *O Oriens* antiphon for December 21.
41. Ps 76.11.   42. Ps 138.12.
43. Ps 117.1, 137.5.   44. Jb 11.17.
45. Is 9.2.

filled with brightness and truth, and bathed in such sweetness that it almost forgets itself and everything else. Sweet meditations flow into it at will, "the infant's tongue is made eloquent,"[46] the sluggish body becomes prompt to obey God's commands, and, to speak briefly, such a dew of grace falls on every side that "whatever the soul asks it may receive, when it seeks it may find, and when it knocks the door may be opened."[47] I think myself raised high above all that I can see, that I have spurned all worldly things and am standing "in the courts of the heavenly Jerusalem,"[48] so that in some way I seem to begin to savor the signs and beginnings of a new age. My every affection is drawn together in the joy of love, and they find rest alone in their enjoyment of my Creator.

(22) "These things and others like them," I say, happen in my heart of hearts, but I ask you to tell me if this is of my doing or of yours.

(23) Wisdom: Your destruction is your own doing, "but your help is only in me."[49] All you can do of yourself is to fall short, and you are going nowhere. You will know that those things and others like them are granted to you because I am with you. For this is the game of love, which I have been accustomed to play in a loving soul.

(24) Disciple: And what is the game of love?

(25) Wisdom: The game of love is joy and sorrow, succeeding one another through the presence or absence of the beloved. For this is ever the property of love, that its greatness is hidden when the loved one is there, but it is better seen when he retreats.

(26) Disciple: This game of love does not seem to me to be a game of joy but of mourning. But I beg you, do you not think that there may be some travelers exempted at such times by a special privilege from these uncertainties of your visitation?

(27) Wisdom: Very few indeed, because so great a participation by man in the divine stability is a kind of entering into eternity.[50]

---

46. Wis 10.21.   47. Mt 7.8.
48. Ps 121.2.   49. Os 13.9.
50. This phrase adapts Thomas Aquinas, "a kind of entering into blessedness," *ST* II-II, q. 180, a. 4, c.

(28) Disciple: O, who are they, or what is their condition, who attain to such a conformity?

(29) Wisdom: They are those, in fact, who are withdrawn from everything base by the utter purity of their affections, and who by long use and exercise have in some fashion been reshaped like God, and are continually united to divine things, who pass beyond the mind, and most perfectly over-come with the greatest swiftness every obstacle that separates God and the soul.

(30) Disciple: When I hear these things, I raise my voice in weeping, because all I know of life tells me how far off from them I am. But since this height of perfection surpasses my abilities, I want to know from you how an inexperienced disci-ple ought to conduct himself during a visitation of this kind.

(31) Wisdom: "In the day of good things, be not unmindful of evils; and in the day of evils, be not unmindful of good things,"[51] so that you do not take too much pride in the pres-ence of grace, or in its absence become unnecessarily de-pressed, but be like "Aod, who used the left hand as well as the right."[52] If you are still "a new plant,"[53] and you need constant watering, at least take care to bear this alternation with pa-tience, even though you should always be seeking diligently for me to appear.

(32) Disciple: O, if you wished to consider it, you would know very well that waiting every day for one's beloved is a great grief to the heart.

(33) Wisdom: There is no doubt: anyone who may have wanted to love will have to endure love's turning wheel.[54] This is no surprise. Things do not always go well for the lovers of this world; sometimes their good changes for the worse. Even if you are perhaps inexperienced, ask someone among them, and he will tell you that anyone who has wanted to love will

51. Ecclus 11.27.
52. Jgs 3.15; the same interpretation is found in Cassian, *Conferences* 6.10.
53. Ps 143.12.
54. In "love's turning wheel" there is allusion to "the wheel of Fortune," common in medieval literature and iconography, typifying the instability of human happiness.

have to work hard. There are indeed some lovers, not made of any stern stuff, it is true,[55] who are serving love for only a short time and who want to be lovers but not to work for it, and then, if the good fortune that they pray for does not at once smile on them, without waiting they give up what they started; and they never obtain the fruits of love, and it is to men so unworthy that it is said: "Love is a kind of warfare; let sluggards retreat."[56] So a fervent lover, to obtain the fruit of love he desires, must be zealous, patient, compliant, he must not easily give up, even though he may suffer rebuff a thousand times, remaining always "of a good hope,"[57] thinking that "unremitting toil conquers everything."[58] What is weaker than water, what is harder than stone? Yet by the water's constant dropping the stone is worn away.[59]

(34) And so that I may add some good news for you, which will also delight true lovers when they hear it, you must know that this most divine spouse for whom you labor wants to be asked, takes delight in men's service. For who ever obtains what will satisfy love, even in trivial matters, so soon? So let a lover ask and beg and implore, and do not let him give up; and I promise him truly that I shall come to fulfill his heart's desire. No woman was ever found "in all the coasts of Israel"[60] so easy to entreat, so quick to hear, so generous in giving as is she, your most divine spouse. For she has not the power to restrain herself long, such is the greatness of her love. She cannot wait until she may be asked, but "she goes in advance of those who covet her, so that she shows herself to them first."[61] She stands in the marketplace, at the crossroads, "at the entrance of the gates she utters her words,"[62] inviting everyone and drawing all men to her love. Whoever will wish to love me must learn always to look on me as one who will love him, just as I am accustomed to look all the time on my lover. For indeed he does not know whether she whom he waits for may come from the east or from the west or from the north or

---

55. Ovid, *Art of Loving* II.235–36.
56. Ovid, *Art of Loving* II.233.
57. Wis 12.19.
58. Vergil, *Georgics* I.145f.
59. Ovid, *Art of Loving* I.475f.
60. 3 Kgs 1.3.
61. Wis 6.14.
62. Prv 1.21.

from the south. He does not even know whether "she may knock at the gate[63] in the morning or at noon or when the cock crows"[64] and ask him to open. For more often, when the spirit in seeking for me becomes anxious, seeking he does not find; but when he will least expect it, he will have his beloved present to him. For I want a lover always to be prepared for love, yet I do not want him to have confidence in his own merits more than in my graciousness. Indeed it is not enough to spend just one brief hour with the beloved, but more often it is necessary "to be still and see,"[65] if one wants to interpret the beloved's secret smiles, and if one longs to possess that longed-for presence.

(35) And so that we may mix with these sweet words some reproofs, though they are not less loving, you are greatly to be chided, because you are indeed blameworthy as you perform the exercises of this kind of love. Why are you not ashamed that you, who have taken up the weapons of love, who have enrolled yourself in the school of our philosophy, and have placed your shoulder under its sweet yoke, why, I say, do you presume to stand before such a spouse with wandering heart and fearful eyes that scan the earth all around, while she always looks on you with an untroubled face, serene and gracious, nor ever once turns her eyes away from you? How shameful it is for you to give ear to all and sundry, so that you cannot hear what divine Wisdom is saying within you! O, how vile it is in a disciple of love to be so forgetful even of himself that he will not heed the inner words of her whose presence all surrounds him! Indeed, anyone who seems so unworthy deserves that she should withdraw, since she finds you occupied, not with yourself or with her, but outside yourself and outside her in the babble of the world. And therefore I ask you to remember to put all this right. Consider how unseemly it is if a soul that carries the kingdom of God in itself seeks anything from external things. For "the kingdom of God is within you,"[66] which is "justice and peace and joy in the Holy Spirit."[67]

63. Apoc 3.20.
65. Ps 45.11.
67. Rom 14.17.

64. Mk 13.35.
66. Lk 17.21.

CHAPTER 9

Why Divine Wisdom Permits Those Dear to Her to Be Afflicted in So Many Ways in This World

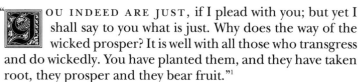OU INDEED ARE JUST, if I plead with you; but yet I shall say to you what is just. Why does the way of the wicked prosper? It is well with all those who transgress and do wickedly. You have planted them, and they have taken root, they prosper and they bear fruit."[1]

(2) There would be no need to go over once again a matter variously aired and frequently discussed and reverted to, but this renewing of my distress, this repetition of my hardships demands that I reply with my complaints against you, O Ruler of the universe. "For do I persuade men"[2] in a vain spirit of ostentation? "God knows it."[3] Or "is my debate against mankind,"[4] or addressed to any one man, and not rather because it has grown cold, the ardor "of a humbled and contrite heart,"[5] vexed from my boyhood until this day with sufferings and miseries? Or who is there who would know better how to feel compassion with all this or worse than you, who "learned compassion by the things which you suffered"?[6] For just as a man born blind reasons illogically about the colors that he has never seen, someone who has not suffered hardships is inexperienced and is no good judge of tribulations. Or how could they believe, those whose "houses are secure and peaceable, and the rod of God is not upon them,"[7] who "spend their days in wealth,"[8] delicately brought up, schooled in comfort, strong, healthy, happy, honored with distinctions, advanced in rank, well connected, whose "bowels are full of fat, and their

1. Jer 12.1–2.   2. Gal 1.10.
3. 2 Cor 11.11.   4. Jb 21.4.
5. Ps 50.19.   6. Heb 5.8.
7. Jb 21.9.   8. Jb 21.13.

bones are moistened with marrow,"[9] what is the lot of those who have "empty months and wearisome nights"?[10] Who are "filled with sorrows"[11] day and night, and live constantly in bitterness of soul? For whom there are "combats without, fears within,"[12] whom you do not suffer to be at rest for the twinkling of an eye, since even the night, destined for human repose, is turned for them into unrest because of "nighttime terrors"?[13]

(3) Temporal honor is taken from them; the glories of the world are made vain. They become contemptible among men; they are laden with reproaches. They are made into "a proverb and an example,"[14] they become "the off-scouring of all, even till now."[15] O, how well he understood, the man who felt all this and said: "There are just men to whom many things happen as though they had done the works of the wicked, and there are wicked men who are as secure as though they had the deeds of the just."[16] Your love seems to be like "a volume flying,[17] yet the taste of it in the mouth is sweet as honey, but to swallow it makes the belly bitter,"[18] because of the labor that goes with it. Tribulations and miseries are the first lessons, the child's exercises of your love.

(4) For the first steps of those who walk to you, the first pages for those reading you, the first gift and jewel for those loving you is this: "Son, when you come to the service of God, stand in fear, and prepare your soul for temptation."[19] Well does he say "for temptation," truly for misery and tribulation, so that in every day of your soldiering you will be in conflict and battle, and the fortune you wish for will seldom or never smile on you. I am not speaking of everyone. "O Lord, you know"[20] whom you will choose for this work so laborious.

(5) If they rejoice in bodily health and strength or comeliness, they are variously afflicted, and begin to fail more and more, and they must languish, weighed down with unheard-of

9. Jb 21.24.
11. Jb 7.4.
13. Ps 90.5.
15. 1 Cor 4.13.
17. Zac 5.1.
19. Ecclus 2.1.

10. Jb 7.3.
12. 2 Cor 7.5.
14. Ez 14.8.
16. Eccl 8.14.
18. Apoc 10.9.
20. Jer 15.15.

pains or severest sicknesses. If they have gold or silver, "thieves break in and steal,"[21] or, what is more difficult, you take away their love for it. If they own fields and "vineyards and olive-yards,"[22] what for others would bring good fortune is destroyed for them by hail or frost. "That which the devouring locust has left the swarming locust has eaten, and that which the swarming locust has left the hopping locust has eaten, and that which the hopping locust has left the destroying locust has destroyed."[23] Give them, O Lord! What will you give them?[24] "Spare bread and short water,"[25] which is this "dish from the king"[26] that is sent to your servants. If one of them crosses the seas, the wind is against him. If he plans to go by land, the sky may have granted peaceful weather to the earth for many days, but as soon as this man of yours, this wretched lover, if I may so call him, comes out of doors and makes ready to travel, the clouds roll up, the land is flooded with torrents, and this man, your servant is afflicted either with downpours or excessive heat or even with unseasonable cold.

(6) This is something wonderful and astonishing. The very mice in their holes do not allow him to rest. If he goes out by day, sometimes the kites in the sky, or even the crows, croaking at him as if in scorn, pursue him; and whether he be silent or laugh, that makes them angry. If someone has become indignant with him when he has said and done nothing to annoy him, everyone joins in cursing him, they sharpen their tongues and they persecute him as he flees from them all, like mad dogs after "the young hare, feeble by nature,"[27] tearing at it and mangling it. Yet even this I shall attribute to your grace, for men do say: "'God loves those who hate him, and he hates those who love him.'[28] To some men he distributes good things, and to others bad."

(7) And what is more than all this, you too, a just judge, show or pretend that you are taking sides against him, when you keep utter silence, as if you were indifferent to the destruc-

21. Mt 6.19.   22. Dt 6.11.
23. Jl 1.4.   24. Os 9.14.
25. Is 30.20.   26. Dn 1.15.
27. Prv 30.26.   28. 2 Kgs 19.6.

tion of your servants. So "the just man perishes, and no one takes it to heart."[29] And "because the wicked man prevails against the just, therefore wrong judgment is given,"[30] now as of old. Was it not that prophet of the Lord, beloved not only for his deeds but also for the meaning of his name,[31] who lamented as if with an impatient spirit, and said: "Why do you not look on those who do unjust things, why do you hold your peace when the wicked man devours someone more just than himself?"[32] See how well he does, and the curses he receives. He serves you to the best of his power, and the envious man despises his life. He is harried with contempt by transgressors of the law, and, what is more, he is afflicted by a thousand punishments of his own making.

(8) And what is yet more than these things, see how "Satan goes out from your presence,"[33] and lies in wait for him everywhere that he may go. "O keeper of men,"[34] O immense loving kindness of God, how can you go on enduring the many kinds of evil that your chosen ones suffer? Or how can you see these kinds of thing without helping? This is why I am now "speaking to you in my spirit's tribulation,[35] in the bitterness of my soul."[36] For you alone see my toil and my sorrow, and you know that these words full of sadness have not come from any levity of spirit, but out of the fullness "of the bitterness of my spirit," words interspersed with so many groanings, and my tears as they flow, hindering my pen as I write.

(9) Wisdom: You are a womanish soldier, to fear hardships so much. "For you have not yet resisted to the shedding of your blood,"[37] nor have you fought to the death in the valley of the champions. "Are you not a man?"[38] But it is shameful how you are like the bravest rhinoceros when things are going well, but frailer than "the spiders' web"[39] when they are against you. A dauntless warrior, to exert and prove himself, desires to experience tribulation and find misery. Was he not fittingly

29. Is 57.1.   30. Hb 1.4.
31. Jerome interpreted "Habacuc" to mean "embracing."
32. Hb 1.13.   33. Jb 1.12, 2.7.
34. Jb 7.20.   35. Jb 7.11.
36. Ps 9.14.   37. Heb 12.4.
38. 1 Kgs 26.15.   39. Jb 8.14.

given glory who said: "Gladly shall I glory in my infirmities"?[40] For if there has not first been combat, there cannot be victory. A pilot is recognized in a storm, a knight is tried in the battle line. A coward can seem brave, when there is no danger, but to contend against hardships is the test of truth.

(10) Disciple: But am I the only one to make these complaints against you? They are not to be numbered, those who have been oppressed with tribulations like this, and who agree with me about it, so that even if I cannot overcome you with reasoning, I shall convince by the vast multitude of my witnesses. Would it not be easier to have one's head cut off once, than every day to be "killed for your sake"?[41] You cannot contradict me or reply that perhaps we are suffering these ills because "we have sinned against you, and have not obeyed your commandments."[42] Are we, then, the only sinners? Do sinners not abound, do your sons not forsake you? And it is the just who are oppressed, and the impious flourish in the world.

(11) Wisdom: "As the Father has loved me, I also love mine.[43] The disciple is not above his master.[44] If the world hates you, know that it has hated me before you."[45] But nothing fresh has happened to you about which you have to complain. It is our custom to test every one of the elect, and especially manly spirits strong in power, with temptations. Why therefore are you pouring out words, heaping up your vehement reproaches, as if something unusual had happened to you, "wrapping up sentences in unskillful words"?[46] See if there is anyone among "the number of the elect,"[47] among those, that is, who will be singularly pleasing to God, who will pass through this world without trials. "You have heard of the patience of Job," it is said, "and you have seen what the Lord intended."[48]

(12) Disciple: Now, if it is permitted to speak, I know what

40. 2 Cor 12.9.   41. Ps 43.22.
42. From the Dominican Missal, the introit for the Friday after Passion Sunday.
43. Jn 15.9.   44. Lk 6.40.
45. Jn 15.18.   46. Jb 38.2.
47. From the Dominican Missal's daily Mass for the dead.
48. Jas 5.11.

I want to say. See, this is what I am lamenting, this is what I bewail, why I am groaning and sighing from the bottom of my heart. Hear, I beg, your servant. Look at those who are saying: "There is no salvation for him in his God.[49] They labor in vain who serve God."[50] And why? They say that their reason is what I have said, that is, the constant tribulation of the just. Nevertheless they will add that this is why you have so few friends,[51] because you are accustomed to play this kind of game with them.

(13) Alas for me, pitiable and unhappy as I am! This is what has driven me, woe is me, to weep many times, now and since long ago, most bitter tears, and it has piled sorrow upon sorrow for me. It is loss to my spirit and the frustration of my labor, as I have sweated for nothing to save my neighbors' souls. For though I had brought many with the greatest effort to mend their ways and to produce "the fruits of a better life,"[52] "giving them birth"[53] with suffering, and gently "carrying them on my shoulders,"[54] and offering to the tender little ones "the milk of consolation,"[55] and "giving my whole self to their service,"[56] I have indeed endured many adversities, when your accustomed times, of temptations, that is, and trials would overtake them, so that "passing through fire and water they might be brought into refreshment."[57] Some of them turned back and followed Satan, saying: "This is a hard word, and who could bear to hear it?"[58] and, as that common proverb says: "It is hard to be good very long." And so these wretched ones leave you, to their loss and my misery, entangling themselves again in their pernicious ways.

(14) Wisdom: This question of theirs often perturbs minds that possess little faith or knowledge; they consider that the

49. Ps 3.3.   50. Mal 3.14.
51. Künzle has pointed out how closely this resembles the celebrated anecdote in which Teresa of Ávila, overtaken by disaster on her travels, and told by the Lord: "This is how I treat my lovers," is said to have rejoined: "It is little wonder that you have so few!" But modern experts on her writings question this story's authenticity; cf. Otilio Rodriguez, *Leyenda Aurea Teresiana* (Madrid, 1970).
52. *The Life of St. Barlaam and St. Josaphat.*
53. Gal 4.19.   54. Lk 15.5.
55. Is 66.11; 1 Cor 3.2.   56. Cf. Phil 2.17.
57. Ps 65.12.   58. Jn 6.61.

merits of the saints, which are not rewarded in the present
but are stored up for the future, should be repaid during the
shortness of this temporal life. They do not know "how incomprehensible are God's judgments, and the depth of the riches
of his wisdom and his knowledge,"[59] and that God does not
see as man sees. For man looks only at present things, but God
at what is to come and is everlasting. But you, who have been
brought up differently in our spiritual philosophy, stand up,
and with your mind pass above everything that can be seen;
"for the things that are seen are temporal, but the things that
are not seen are eternal."[60] So rise out of the ensnaring foul-
ness of temporal delights. Open the eyes of your mind, and
see what you are, where you are, and where you are going;[61]
and then at once you will have the strength to grasp the reason
of all these things. For you are a mirror of the godhead, because God can be reflected in you more clearly than in other
created things;[62] you are an image of the Trinity, because his
image can shine back in you; you are a pattern of eternity,
because you can rejoice in an inviolable incorruption. And
just as I am in my essence infinite, so the desire of your soul
is like a boundless abyss, to fill which not all the joys together
of the world could suffice, no more than a single drop could
fill the vastness of an ocean.

(15) Then you must consider where you are: in a vale of
misery, in exile, on pilgrimage, where good things mixed with
bad are revolved in an endless whirl. Here "laughter will be
mingled with sorrow, and mourning takes hold of the end
of joy."[63] True, the world has duped its lovers from the start,
promising them prosperity and giving them hardships, nor
has it now stopped doing this. But we ought to turn aside for
a while, so that we may more fully dispel all these troubles
of which we have spoken, and go back in more detail to the
principles of the faith.

59. Rom 11.33.   60. 2 Cor 4.18.
61. Cf. pseudo-Bernard, *Most Devout Meditations.* This also alludes to the
famous distich of Augustine of Dacia: "The letter teaches what happened,
allegory what you should believe, the moral sense what you should do, the
mystical where you are going."
62. Cf. Augustine, *On the Trinity* 9.2, etc.; *ST* I, q. 93.
63. Prv 14.13.

CHAPTER 10

Of the Torments of Hell[1]

SO THEN IT WAS DONE; and the Disciple then began "to think upon the days of old, and to have in mind the eternal years";[2] and when he had recollected deeply, and had drawn his understanding, so well as he could, away from sensible things, there appeared to the eyes of his faith in a far-off vision what seemed to be some shadowy place that he did not recognize, and that was very terrifying. When, terror-struck, he asked what this could be, the answer was: "This place, as you see, is that set apart for future punishments, which various souls after they have left the body will receive for the punishment of a variety of their sins;[3] some of them must purge these sins, others must indeed suffer eternal damnation. And just as had been previously shown to them, 'these or their like' were the kinds of torment that awaited them, horrible and monstrous, such that no tongue would suffice to tell them, nor could mortal senses weigh them fully." So when he had returned to himself, and was back from another world, as it seemed to him, he was so shaken by the things that he had seen that he lay for a while like a man half dead, wasting away in himself. Yet some of the things that he had seen he regarded only with the common eyes of faith.

(2) So therefore he looked and saw how from these places we are talking of an intolerable stench was rising. Resounding

---

1. Edmund Colledge has shown that the chief source for this chapter is "The visions which George, a knight of Hungary, saw in St. Patrick's Purgatory": "'If All the World Were Paper': Henry Suso's Use of a Much-travelled Commonplace," AFP 50 (1980): 113–16.

2. Ps 76.6.

3. "for the punishment of a variety of their sins": ". . . diversae animae . . . pro diversitate culparum." This is *conduplicatio*: see Colledge and Walsh, *A Book of Showings*, 738.

hammers were heard, the deepest darknesses were gathering, and the horrible faces of demons were seen here.[4] There was lamenting and groaning, and the wicked were pitilessly torn by one suffering after another. "They passed from icy waters to excessive heat."[5] Meanwhile he considered the equity and the greatness of the judgments of God, and while terrors oppressed his heart, pierced by the horror of what he saw, and he poured with sweat, he remembered that "by the things in which a man sins, by the same is he tormented";[6] and so it was for them. In their lifetime they had lived insensately and unjustly, and they were receiving torments like the sins that they had practiced.

(3) For robbers and plunderers and their accomplices, and those who had despoiled the poor and the friends of God while they had lived, or had afflicted men by unlawful exaction, were violently dragged to some hellish gibbets, excruciating beyond what the human mind can conceive, and hung up and tormented on them; yet they were not dying but being tortured in unspeakable fashion. And some who had gone around in lamblike clothing that concealed their lions' dispositions, who like mad dogs had molested the servants of God with curses or insults or violent words and had wounded their brethren with wicked persecution, were being gnawed at there by the dogs of hell with cruelest bitings. There the proud were being buried contemptuously in hell, "with the burial of an ass"[7] like any other stinking carcass[8] and were given over to the "everlasting reproach which will never be effaced."[9] And for the worldly glory and the pride of mind in which the vainglorious fought for precedence over others, they were oppressed with as great a load and weight of pains, as much as anyone could be burdened with if he had the greatest tower laid on him. And bibbers and drunkards and those "who serve

---

4. Cf. Bernard of Clairvaux, *Sermon 42 on Diverse Topics*, n. 6, quoted by Bonaventure, *Soliloquy*, ch. 3: "Intolerable stench, hammers striking, darkness that could be felt . . . the horrible faces of demons. . . ."

5. Jb 24.19.   6. Wis 11.17.
7. Jer 22.19.   8. Is 14.19.
9. Jer 20.11.

their own belly,"[10] like ravenous wolves they were afflicted with incredible hunger and intolerable thirst, longing for the least drop of cold water to refresh their tongues, burnt with the fire of the flames, "and no man gave to them";[11] but the most frightful demons with burning urns stood at their side and forcibly poured a sulfurous drink like molten lead, glowing with fierce heat, down their throats to burn holes in their bellies.[12] And the lecherous, and those who had fed their flesh with delights and had obstinately persisted in their ways, were being devoured by serpents, and were being tormented in their very bowels by toads with fiery stings. Those who had been given up to the carnal and earthly love of either sex were in their sorrow biting the ground in hell, for demons were most cruelly afflicting them. For they had burning darts and were pursuing their victims with the fiercest fire and covering them with most savage wounds. As companions in torment they had their erstwhile companions in crime. The greedy and the avaricious and the moneygrubbers were being yet more cruelly tormented. For they were being ducked in pits filled with boiling metals, and as they tried to escape they were mercilessly pushed back again.

(4) "A most severe judgment was being made for those who had borne authority. For the more mighty, a greater punishment was ready, and the mighty were there being mightily tormented."[13] O, who would be able to say how much punishment cruel judges, unjust rulers, clerics greedy for filthy lucre, lascivious monks, violent laymen, shameless women, dancing girls and streetwalkers and all the other kinds of false Christians have received there? And what wretched roarings and what lamentable cryings they were uttering, so that merely to see this affliction seemed somehow to exceed every pain of the world? For there were "a multitude of hellish bears and

10. Rom 16.18   11. Lk 15.16.
12. Caesarius of Heisterbach, *Dialogue of Marvels* III.2, relates how such torments were inflicted on the Landgrave Louis of Thuringia, evidently a celebrated glutton.
13. Wis 6.6, 9, 7. In "fortioribus" . . . "fortior", "potentes" . . . "potenter", we also have *conduplicatio*.

ferocious lions, and beasts of a new kind, full of rage, unknown
monsters breathing out a fiery vapor, giving off a stench of
smoke, and shooting horrible sparks from their eyes, and tearing them to pieces with cruelest bites."[14] And then many of
them were being thrown into "the bottomless pit," out of
which fearful "smoke"[15] and an intolerable stench was rising.
They had the look of burning molten iron, glowing like hot
embers, and they were being thrust down again by demons.
"They were gnawing their tongues for pain, and they were
blaspheming the God of Heaven, because of their pains and
wounds; and they had done no penance for their works.[16] They
were fettered with the bonds of darkness and long night, held
in a dim and shadowy veil of forgetfulness. Noise descended
on them to oppress them, and sad visions appearing to them
struck fear into them. Nor could the bright flames of the stars
enlighten that frightful night.[17] For they had all been bound
together with one chain of darkness. The whole world was
illumined with a clear light, but only over them was spread a
heavy night, an image of darkness, but they were to themselves
more grievous than the darkness,[18] and the smoke of their
torments will rise up for ever and ever.[19]

(5) After this a certain voice like thunder was heard above,
which scoffingly and, as it were, accusingly said: "Where are
they now, those who from the beginning, 'from the days of
old'[20] served this world in their every desire, living volup-
tuously and enslaving themselves to their different cravings?
Ah, what use to them are now 'all those things that have passed
swiftly away like a shadow?'[21] A brief delight, what a long rope
of eternal misery does it drag after it! O foolish and senseless
ones, where are now those words that you used to say with
such gladness and rejoicing of heart: 'Come, then, and let us
enjoy the good things which are here, let us hurry to use what
has been made for us while we are young.'[22] What help is now

---

14. Cf. Thomas Aquinas, *Commentary on the Sentences* IV, d. 50, q. 2, a. 2.
15. Apoc 9.2.   16. Apoc 16.10–11.
17. Wis 17.2–5.   18. Wis 17.19–20.
19. Apoc 14.11.   20. Lam 1.7.
21. Wis 5.9.   22. Wis 2.6.

all the sweetness of the world, which you were so quick to enjoy? But now against that it is time for you to mourn, and mourning to cry out and say: 'Woe, woe to us, now and forever, woe that we were born, nor have we now the power to die. Woe for our cruel torments, nor shall we ever be released from them.'

(6) "O, who is there who will consider these sufferings, and take these our torments to heart? For they are such that whatever is horrible to be thought of in the world would not be comparable with them in cruelty. O, how happy is a man not stained with sin, who has not followed the joys of this world, 'who has not regarded vanities and lying follies.'[23] 'We fools esteemed their life madness, and their end without honor. See how they are numbered among the children of God, and their lot is among the saints. Therefore we have strayed from the way of truth, and the light of justice has not shone on us, and the sun of understanding has not risen on us. We wearied ourselves in the way of iniquity and perdition, and we have walked on hard paths; but the way of the Lord we have not known. What has pride profited us, or what advantage has the boasting of riches brought to us? All those things have passed away like a shadow.'[24]

(7) "What was only temporal passed by, but, alas, what remained will remain for eternity. O, eternal, never to be ended, perpetual torment of death! O, end without ending, death heavier than every death, always to be dying and yet not to be able to die![25] O my dear father, who brought me into this world, O sweet mother who with your mother's breasts gave me milk, O all you, my friends and dear companions, farewell now, you so dear to my heart, for the hour has come of most bitter parting, bitterer than every death. Farewell, earth, farewell, companions, whom I have cherished with so kind a love.[26] For we are being led to the fearful gibbet of hell, we are being

---

23. Ps 39.5.   24. Wis 5.4–9.
25. The same conceit is in pseudo-Bernard, *Most Devout Meditations*, ch. 3, and Bonaventure, *Soliloquy*, ch. 3.
26. This is a literal quotation from one of the *Carmina Burana*, "Dulce solum natalis patriae . . ."

dragged to the dreaded torment, never again to see you with joy. O tears, flow unceasingly, O eyes, weep, and let us mourn aloud with our whole hearts for this unhappy separation, from the highest good, from that glorious and happy vision, and from the angelic company, and also from that most joyous number of the elect, to be added to that wretched and accursed and savage rabble of the damned who are to be tormented without end. O, sound of hands beating in grief! O, rending cries from many hearts! O, 'gnashing of teeth'[27] and endless wailing of the shades! O, vast company, entreating and wailing! O, clamor that will remain eternally, that will always last and will never have an end, that will always be renewed and will never win mercy! Our wretched eyes will never see anything but misery, our ears never hear anything but 'Woe, woe' and sadness. O loving hearts, look on this interminable and pitiless eternity. Bewail and weep.

(8) "O 'hills, fall upon us,'[28] mountains, cover us.'[29] Whom are you sustaining, for whom do you wait? 'Hide us from the face of the Lord's terrible wrath, from the face of his anger,'[30] of the glory of God. Alas, alas, why did we not prevent this greatest of future evils when we had the power, and when the opportune time was there? If only one little hour could remain to us, of all that time so uselessly spent that was granted to us as a remedy for such ills. But, alas divine justice has spoken, the way of salvation is shut to us, mercy is denied, all hope is taken away. O, the sorrows and miseries and the terrors that will endure forever in this 'land of oblivion,'[31] where no order but everlasting horror dwells.'[32]

(9) "What more? We wretched and miserable ones are so afflicted, and mourn so over that eternal woe than any end that could be thought of; if it only were the finish, would be a solace to us. So, to suppose the impossible, if there were some millstone so vast that it stretched to the circumference of the heavens, and if some little bird of the smallest size were

27. Mt 8.12.   28. Os 10.8.
29. Lk 23.30.   30. Apoc 6.16.
31. Ps 87.13.   32. Jb 10.22.

to come, after a hundred thousand years, and to take away from that stone only so much as it could peck with its bill, the tenth part of a millet seed in size, and then after another hundred thousand years had gone by were to do as before, to take away a particle of the same size, and go on, particle by particle, so that in ten times a hundred times a thousand years the amount of the stone would not be more reduced than by the size of a millet seed: see, alas, how very thankful we poor wretches would be if after so long as the full consuming of the entire stone would take, there might be an end to the sentence of our eternal damnation.[33] But alas, even this consolation is completely refused to us wretched beings by divine justice. All these are words of the unfortunate damned—so, O my son, will they be chastised who here on earth are spared 'the chastisement of children.'"[34]

(10) Disciple: O fearful judge, see now how my soul is terrified and prostrate at this so terrible vision, and my knees shake so that I can hardly stand. O "my God, my helper,"[35] turn away, O God, I implore, your anger from me. Let this sentence of eternal damnation, so greatly to be feared, not be mine. But if I must endure hardships, "your will be done"[36] here to me; have my full permission for this, and you will not henceforth have in me a querulous disciple. But do only one thing: do not permit me to be separated from you[37] forever.

---

33. Künzle observes: "This similitude of eternity, as Bihlmeyer pointed out, is not found before Suso, but is often encountered in later writings."

34. Ecclus 30.1.   35. Ps 17.3.

36. Mt 6.10.   37. From the prayer *Anima Christi*.

CHAPTER 11

Of the Joys of Highest Heaven.

"ARISE, O my glory, arise, psaltery and harp. I shall arise early."[1] Let us move on to happy themes. See, now we are taking up the "pleasant psaltery,"[2] we are singing hymns to you on the sweet zither, we are sounding dulcet melodies, so that when all the fear that oppressed you has been vanquished and the sorrow driven away, we may raise you up from the depths and bring you with joy to the heights. So now "arise, arise,"[3] lift up your mind's eyes, shake the wings of your desires, and make yourself ready to fly, "to fly upon the wings of the winds."[4] "Lift up your eyes"[5] to the east, and look on the things that are being shown to you. See the promised land, the place of immortality, the heavenly native land, "the paradise of pleasure"[6] and the kingdom of everlasting happiness. For truly in this world you are a stranger and a pilgrim, and therefore it is for you, sent as it were into exile, to hasten to join that number so vast of beloved ones who are waiting for you with such great longing, so that they may sweetly receive you among them in their blessed embraces, and "may make you sit with them"[7] for all eternity. O, if you could know with what love they always long for you that, when you are at last established in the heavenly citadel, you would be shaken by no dread of this world's storms and whirlwinds. But since you are "a stout hunter before the Lord"[8] and a valiant knight, you must in all things act forcefully and prudently, so that no good fortune may elate you, "no hazards

1. Ps 56.9. 2. Ps 80.3.
3. Is 51.9. 4. Ps 17.11.
5. Jer 3.2. 6. Gn 2.8.
7. Eph 2.6. 8. Gn 10.9.

break you,"[9] nor adversities terrify you which these blessed ones themselves so courageously and so happily overcame, now recollecting those days and the years of their affliction in the sweetness of their hearts.

(2) And truly, the more in this world you will have sustained some great labor for the Savior's name, so much greater a reward you will receive in eternity. O, with what glory will he be raised up, with what exceptional honor will this soldier be distinguished, who for the triumph of his patience and the showing of his constancy will be gloriously commended by so great a king before his beloved Father at the heavenly throne, will be surrounded by the cohorts of angels! With how much glory do you think that a crown of victory will shine, which has been won with so much toil? More brightly than the sun, more purely too than the star of heaven will shine the wounds, the bruises and scars received in this world for my name. What is more, in that heavenly native land a multitude not to be counted waits for you of friends most faithful from that noble stock, so that even if each one of them be now infinitely far away from you, he will be joined more closely to you in true love, and will cherish you with heartfelt loving, more than any mother on this earth could love her only child.

(3) Disciple: O Prince of the heavenly court, I beg that you will deign to tell me yet more of this heavenly fatherland, so that my desire for it may grow, and that I may be given still more patience in adversities. Ah, my Lord, tell me, I entreat, how is that King's hall prepared, or who are the citizens or dwellers of such a city, or will they know those things that are happening to us, as your words seem to say?

(4) Wisdom: Now is the moment to "arise, stand up,"[10] and to hasten with me, so that I may lead you to the place for which your soul is longing, and there you will see the deepest mysteries of the divine marvels. Look up to the eighth sphere, more than a hundred thousand times greater than all the earth, yet there is a certain heaven higher still, which is called

9. From the Dominican Breviary for the feast of St. Dominic.
10. Is 51.17.

the empyrean; and it has its name for its extraordinary luminosity, uniform, immobile, perfectly luminous and immensely capacious.[11] And this is that King's hall, the heavenly court of blessed spirits, where "the morning stars praise me together, and all the sons of God make a joyful melody."[12] There the heavenly seats and the luminous thrones are placed,[13] from which that wretched company of malign spirits will flee away, to be replaced by the assembly of the elect.[14]

(5) See now that glorious and sublime city, its gold and its gems wondrously glowing, from the gates of which a fragrance most reviving issues. "Its streets are paved with purest gold, like transparent glass.[15] Its foundations are laid in sapphires. Its bulwarks of jasper"[16] are suffused with pulsing light. It is built "of living stones,"[17] its ways covered in flowers, and it is adorned throughout with gleaming pearls. O, loveliness to be admired by all!

(6) Yet why should I detain you longer? Look at it yourself with your own eyes for what it is, and see that vast and most lovely plain, adorned with its splendor of starry mansions and with delights of every kind. Ah, how various they are! Here is the loveliness of spring and the fruitfulness of autumn, summer's serenity and nuptial rejoicing. Here is the vale of joyfulness and the vision of love. Here heavenly hymnody resounds, divine viols ring out, and jubilating voices sing praises. The joyous crowds exult, and their sweet melodies mingle with the glad choirs. Here the troops of virgins follow after their Lord. Here all who rejoice have but one voice, all hearts have but one ardor. Here is a plenty of delights, an abundance of the heart's desires. Here are no sorrows, but all things rejoice.

---

11. Cf. Thomas Aquinas, *Commentary on the Sentences* d. 2, q. 2, a. 2: "since they [the blessed] participate fully in the eternal light and rest and eternity, therefore it is fitting that the empyrean heaven be luminous and immobile and incorruptible."

12. Jb 38.7.   13. Cf. Apoc 4.2.

14. Honorius of Autun (ob. c. 1156) and Thomas Aquinas both state that man was made to replace among the company of the blessed the fallen angels.

15. Apoc 21.21.   16. Is 54.11–12.

17. 1 Pt 2.4.

Here is the new beginning of happiness and an everlasting safekeeping.

(7) Ah, what joys! Now that with their sweet savor your heart has been wholly freed for a heavenly love, look around you and behold this countless multitude, and consider how with thirsting lips they drink from that first source[18] and "are inebriated,"[19] how by looking into that most divine mirror, from which all things shine out,[20] they are made glad. They are filled with wonder and they do not lack, they enjoy to the full and they do not weary, and what they delight in they thirst for more and more.

(8) And now, as you draw closer, listen, as I tell you how the Queen of virgins, whom you have venerated with your greatest love, by the privilege of a singular honor and glory has mounted up above the highest rank of the orders, "leaning upon her beloved,"[21] in her tenderness among "the beds of spices,"[22] "surrounded by blooming roses and lilies of the valley."[23] See how her matchless beauty has brought joy, arresting everyone in wonder. Now too let that vision of delight which for so long you have desired with all your heart appear. See how the mother of clemency and pity, the mother of "the Lord of mercies"[24] has turned, towards you and towards all sinners, "her eyes of mercy,"[25] how imperiously, how powerfully she gives commands to everyone, defending the wretched and reconciling the guilty.[26]

(9) After this, turning the eyes of your understanding to the nature of the angels, see how those supreme ones of the order of the seraphim and the spirits of their choir, burning with a

18. *de fontali principio*: the adjective 'fontal' is from pseudo-Dionysius, as latinized by Thomas Aquinas and the other Western scholastic philosophers.

19. Ps 35.9.

20. On the Word of God as the "eternal mirror," see Thomas Aquinas, *Commentary on the Sentences* d. 11, q. 2, a. 11, ad 4, adducing Boethius and pseudo-Dionysius, *The Divine Names*, ch. 4.

21. Cant 8.5.   22. Cant 5.13.

23. From the Dominican Breviary for the feast of the Assumption.

24. Is 63.7.   25. From the *Salve Regina*.

26. Bernard of Clairvaux, *Sermon 2 for Pentecost*, n. 4, says that the dwellers both in heaven and in hell look to Mary, "those in heaven that they may be perfected, those in hell that they may be delivered."

divine love, are drawn up towards God, fervently and unflaggingly as a blazing flame. See how the order of the cherubim, receiving the fullness of divine light, pour it out copiously upon others, how the thrones and their confederates find sweet rest in God and God in them. Then see how the second hierarchy is given light from the first, and how they are assigned to their particular acts. Ah, see, my beloved, how, most fairly and most nobly, order is given to their innumerable multitude, and how distinct each order is in the diversity of its merits.[27] O, wondrous joys, O, semblance of amazing beauty and unmatched delight!

(10) And now that you have been brought so far, see how the holy Apostles and "my friends"[28] are seated before all others with the highest honor, and are given power to judge,[29] and how the martyrs shine out "with rosy color,"[30] the confessors give a fiery light, the virgins appear "in snowy brightness,"[31] and then how all the company of heaven abounds in divine sweetness and is filled with rejoicing. These heavenly hosts, all as one, leading the choirs with untellable rejoicing, utter their melodies before the throne. Then "the stream of the river"[32] flows out, and "makes drunk with pleasure,"[33] their minds and fills their mouths with joy. O, how happy the city where there is always such festivity, and how joyous the court that never knows any care! So, no less blessed and happy are those bidden to such a banquet and elected by God to merit that they join in such a company!

(11) The faithful spouse who is to reign forever will be led home in happiness into this heavenly land, this glorious country, and she will at last be robed in a glorified body.[34] She will have on her head a crown of gold, and above that "another little golden crown."[35]

27. This is the teaching of pseudo-Dionysius, *The Celestial Hierarchy*, ch. 6–9, which is summarized in *ST* I, q. 108, a. 5, ad 4, 5, 6.

28. Jn 15.14.   29. Mt 19.28.

30. Cf. Est 15.8.

31. From the Dominican Breviary for the feast of the Crown of Thorns.

32. Ps 45.5.   33. Ps 35.9.

34. For scholastic teaching on the body's glorification, see, e.g., Thomas Aquinas, *Commentary on the Sentences*, IV d. 44, qq. 1–2.

35. Ex 25.25.

(12) Disciple: Tell, I beg you, loving sweetness, what may be the crown of gold, and what the little golden crown?

(13) Wisdom: By the crown of gold understand the essential reward, in the little golden crown perceive the accidental reward. The accidental reward is a certain joy in the works one has performed to gain some excelling victory, such as the famous triumph of the martyrs, and the excelling triumph over the devil or their own flesh of the doctors and the virgins.

(14) But the essential reward consists indeed in the perfect conjunction of the soul with God, so far as the soul perfectly finds its enjoyment in him as in one who is perfectly seen and loved. For the endless desire of the soul will never be fully satisfied, unless it be absolutely immersed in the depths of the godhead. And so in this perfect enjoyment of that supreme Trinity and most simple unity it will at last be made completely blessed. And as much as now it more perfectly forsakes all temporal things, with so much the more freedom will it rise to the contemplation of spiritual things.[36] And by as much as it surrenders itself to spiritual actions, by so much will it there more happily be absorbed into the depths of the most divine clarity, and will be made one spirit with it, so that the soul will by grace be made that which God is by nature. O, how happy the soul that will be made a companion of the angelic troops, that will be saturated with the nectar of Christ, and that will be joined, clinging sweetly and inseparably, to the supreme Trinity in its blessed embrace! O, untellable ending, and wonderful and utter sweetness of this coming into rest!

(15) And you, the disciple of Eternal Wisdom, brought now to "an ecstasy of mind like Benjamin the youth,"[37] refresh for a little while your troubled heart in this most peaceful resting place, with this most joyful company whom you see now before you. Consider the splendor of their faces, which once with their mad insults and mockery impious men assaulted and with their injuries afflicted. Raise up a joyful heart with thank-

36. This is the teaching of Thomas Aquinas, *On the Perfection of the Spiritual Life*, ch. 7, ". . . which comes by forsaking all temporal things."
37. Ps 67.28.

ful words, and speak, as if you were saluting them from afar, to these "fellow-citizens and 'domestics' of God"[38] of this celestial court. "By your voice"[39] say: "Where are now 'the reproaches of those who reproached you,' that once 'fell upon you';[40] where are the bowed heads and the downcast eyes that showed your heaviness of heart? Where, I ask, are the inward anguishes which gnawed in your hearts? Where are your mourning and tears? Where are those faces that had grown pale and lean through a thousand perils? Your poverty, your want and all your deprivation, what has become of that? How has that woeful voice grown silent that used once to lament and say: 'O my God, how much I suffer, how long I am tormented, affrighted and afflicted.'

(16) "Where are they all now, those who despised you, who persecuted you, who 'robbed you of your labors,'[41] and brought all your life to bitterness? No longer does one hear the voice of those who were exhorting men to battle and saying: 'Do manfully'[42] and fight against the enemy and the world and the flesh, and, again, 'Take your shield,'[43] seize your bucklers, polish your lances, stand fast in your fortress. Be armed night and day, 'gird your loins about with truth.'[44] Nor is this voice of secret exhortation any longer heard, which in the time of the visitation of grace you used to be aware of within yourselves as you said: 'Now prepare your soul for temptation,'[45] so that it may withdraw with rejoicing of the spirit, and may not 'be swallowed up with inordinate sorrow.'[46] No longer does one hear you say as once you were accustomed: 'O my God, why have you forsaken me?[47] Why have you forgotten me, and why do I go mourning, whilst my enemy afflicts me?'[48] Rather now I hear, sweetly resounding in your hearts, that voice of mirth and gladness which says: 'Come, you blessed of

38. Eph 2.19.
39. Ecclus 39.17.
40. Ps 68.10.
41. Wis 5.1.
42. 1 Cor 16.13.
43. Eph 6.16.
44. Eph 6.14.
45. Ecclus 2.1.
46. 2 Cor 2.7.
47. Mt 27.46, where Christ is repeating the words of Ps 21.2.
48. Ps 41.10.

my Father, possess the kingdom that has been prepared for you from the foundation of the world.'[49] Where are now all the tribulations and adversities, the anguishes and miseries and every evil that you have suffered in the world? O God, how fast all these things passed by, and now they are as if they never had been. Astonishingly fast did they appear, and fast did they disappear. O my most loving God, 'how incomprehensible are your judgments,'[50] and deeply hidden from the sons of men!

(17) "Ah, you the elect and the beloved 'sons of the Most High,'[51] see how the hour has come when you will no longer flee so that you may be concealed in corners, dressed in rags as the humble and rejected, unworthy of every honor, and as 'the reproach of men and the outcast of the people.' For now you are crowned with such glory and honor, raised up into eternity and beyond, in such dignity and excellence that no understanding is able to estimate your fame, no tongue is able to recount it. O you heavenly princes, O you most noble kings and emperors! O you sons of the most high God,[52] partakers of the divine Nature,[53] with what great mirth are your faces seen to be suffused, with what copiousness and superabundance are your hearts seen to overflow for exultation! You carry golden wreaths that shine beyond all telling. Crowned with your wreaths you go, your faces shining, your apparel splendid, your singing joyful. O, how sweetly do your gentle voices sound, as giving thanks you say: 'Ah, blessings and glory and wisdom and thanksgiving, honor and power and strength for ever and ever'[54] to him by whose benevolence we are protected, by whose mercy we are saved, and by whose goodness we are to reign in eternity. 'To you be praise and glory in eternity.'[55] Look around you now and see this glorious kingdom, circle upon circle, filled with delights, 'in which all the saints rejoice with Christ.'[56] Behold, this is the heavenly native

---

49. Mt 25.34.   50. Rom 11.33.
51. Lk 6.35   52. Ps 81.6.
53. 2 Pt 1.4.   54. Apoc 7.12.
55. From the Dominican Breviary for the feast of the Most Holy Trinity.
56. From the Dominican Breviary for the feast of All Saints.

land, the mansion of repose, the place of recompense and the kingdom of perpetual felicity."

(18) Disciple: O, the amazement and immense wonder of the profundity of so many mysteries, transcending all understanding, and known in full to God alone! O incomprehensible abyss of the divine deepness, how many marvels are hidden in you! O, what do I hear, what do I see, what indeed do I feel in myself of the great works of God, which no tongue would suffice to recount, in this glorious city? For many are "the glorious things that are said of you, O city of God,"[57] but they are nothing to compare with the wonders that are hidden in you. Truly I now know that "the report is true which I have often heard"[58] of your wonders and your glory, "and I did not believe those who told me until I came myself, and saw with my own eyes, and have found that the half had not been told to me. Your wisdom and your glory exceed the fame that I heard. Blessed are your men and blessed are your servants, who stand before you always and hear your wisdom,"[59] and see your glory.

(19) And now, King of glory, let it be permitted to your servant to present his poor petition to his lord, and "do not put me to confusion."[60] May your servant, I entreat, henceforth remain here close to you, and let him not return to his own house. For truly "it is good for us to be here."[61] Hear, I beg, your serf, humbly prostrate before you, and give him now a place where he may stay with you in this glorious city.

(20) Wisdom: On no account. The humility of Sion is not yet complete. Your hour has not yet come. It is now the time for you to fight, and the hour for you to reign has not arrived. This is the time for you to gain merit, and the time for rewarding is not yet. Act like a man, for there are still many "battles you must fight for the faith of Christ."[62]

---

57. Ps 86.3.
58. 3 Kgs 10.6.
59. 3 Kgs 10.7–8.
60. 3 Kgs 2.20.
61. Mt 17.4.
62. From the Dominican Breviary for the feast of St. Lawrence.

CHAPTER 12

A Determination of Certain Objections
Previously Omitted.

O U K N O W indeed that this happy place of everlasting blessedness has been shown to the eye of your purest contemplation for the reason, not that here and now you should remain there, but so that in every "wrestling"[1] and adversity you may know how to return here, and that you may be able more easily to bear all your adversities, and that you be strong in answering to your querulous assailants: "Why does the way of the wicked prosper,"[2] and why is God accustomed in this world to chastise his beloved ones? To begin, let me reply to your complaint which some time ago you made against me with such grief, and say that it is because of the narrowness of the way "which leads to life"[3] that many of those whom you had rejoiced to have won for the Lord with great labor and sorrow "went back."[4]

(2) For if you will look at this more carefully, you will find beyond doubt that this state of affairs is very common, nor has this happened to you alone, but to some of the most holy fathers, as can be very plainly shown. Did all of those persist who had been brought to believe through my words and those of the Apostles; did Paul, "vessel of election[5] and teacher of the pagans"[6] for this reason complain that his journeyings and his labors had been in vain?[7] Rather, he preached the gospel far and wide to the people with great labor and "solicitude,"[8] traveling most strenuously everywhere; he sent letters, and

---

1. Eph 6.12.
2. Jer 12.1.
3. Mt 7.14.
4. Jn 6.67.
5. Acts 9.15.
6. 1 Tm 2.7.
7. Phil 2.16 .
8. 2 Cor 11.28.

"cherished his children as a nurse,"[9] and "carried the name of Jesus before pagans and kings and the children of Israel."[10] But what came of this? Where are now the Ephesians and Galatians and Corinthians for whose sake he had gloried in having so labored, and exposed himself "to stripes and often to death"?[11] Or did Paul and the other Apostles and teachers therefore desist from preaching and the saving of souls, when they saw that their children had turned back and had been perverted by "false apostles,"[12] or did they on that account act more sluggishly? Not at all. But as everywhere they "published the word of God"[13] and did what was in them, they entrusted the fruit that was to come from this to the decree and will of God. So you read in the Acts of the Apostles: "And as many," it is written, "as were ordained to life everlasting believed."[14]

(3) So truly, provident nature too is wont to adorn the trees with leaves and flowers, so that sometimes in the blossoming season, wherever one may look, a tree may be seen not merely leafy but laden all over with flowers, presenting itself to the senses in lovely colors and giving out sweet perfumes. But when the awaited time of ripening has come, out of many trees the one that had looked so beautiful fails and perishes, so that barely one thousandth part of its yield can be seen to survive. But a prudent husbandman with many trees in his orchard does not stop planting fresh ones because one or more of them may have failed, but where one has fallen he makes haste to replace it with another. Do you not know that "a tree has hope. If it be cut, it grows green again, and its boughs sprout"?[15] But "a just man will fall seven times in a day and will rise again."[16] When Paul says: "The Lord knows who are his,"[17] his judgment remains unalterable. But "who has

---

9. 1 Thes 2.7.   10. Acts 9.15.
11. 2 Cor 11.23, 16. By the plural "mortibus" we should understand "fear"or "danger of death."
12. 2 Cor 11.13.   13. Acts 13.49.
14. Acts 13.48.   15. Jb 14.7.
16. Prv 24.16; this is an ancient and common conflation of the true text, "A just man will fall seven times and will rise again," with Ps 118.164, "Seven times a day I have given praise to you."
17. 2 Tm 2.19.

known the mind of the Lord,"[18] or who among mortals will be able to know who they may be who will be damned, or who are to be eternally crowned, especially because they so often change their own free will? You may see one man, from an anchorite's cell, holy as if he were Christ's own brother, turning away from the highest good, and falling into hell to be damned to eternity, and another coming out of the brothel with a contrite heart and joining the company of the angels to be eternally saved.

(4) Yet the word of salvation will be meted out indifferently to all men, for "the last one you would expect to find in the water will turn out to be a fish, so let your hook hang everywhere."[19] And the she-wolf preys upon many sheep, yet attacks but one.[20] When the struggle's "course is finished"[21] in glory, the man "will enter into the joy of his lord"[22] who has brought back to his master[23] a hundred thousand souls or one soul that he has won by his preaching. Nor will it be less glorious, though he has never gained a single soul, if only he has faithfully and to the best of his ability "done what must be done for salvation."[24] For a knight who has shown himself valiant in battle will be commended, if he has "striven manfully"[25] and steadily, even if he has not gained a triumph for his lord. So also "the teacher of the pagans" exulted that "a crown of glory was laid up for him,"[26] not less than if all those whom he had converted had persisted in the true faith and in the unity of Mother Church. Nor need we doubt what experience also teaches us in this case, that sometimes a teacher's spirit is more afflicted with the toil and sorrow that he has spent on laboring, as he thinks, uselessly, than when he has judged that he has worked fruitfully. For indeed, when this is so, he finds joy in his Lord, but in the other case he sorrows, and "his soul is

18. Rom 11.34.
19. Cf. Ovid, *The Art of Loving* III.425–26.
20. Ovid, *The Art of Loving* III.419.
21. 2 Tm 4.7.   22. Mt 25.21.
23. From the Dominican Breviary for the common of one doctor.
24. Augustine's *Rule.*   25. 2 Tm 2.5.
26. 2 Tm 4.8.

troubled within him,"[27] and, what is more, he is wounded by the poisoned darts of envious men.

(5) Moses, who was accepted and elected by the Lord to lead his people out of the land of Egypt into the promised land—how many thousands do you reckon there were whom he led out? Yet see that out of them, only two arrived there,[28] and the rest perished. "Gideon, on whom the spirit of the Lord came," that he should free his people from the Madianites, had chosen many companions for himself, so that he could fight against them; and when they were tried by the Lord's consent at the waters, there were so many thousands rejected and sent back that only three hundred men remained to give battle with him and overcome their enemies.[29] Isai had many sons who were fine gentlemen, but only David was chosen to be king.[30] So there were many kings of the people of Judah, but among them all only three "carried off the high places."[31] So therefore, going over the single events of your life, you will find that you have gone astray, when you have wanted to twist to your own desires, in generation and corruption and the vagaries of your free will, that fairest order of the universe, which was not instituted except by divine Wisdom.

(6) So from now on pay good heed, lest in the future you behave as faintheartedly as you now are doing, when you have been struggling up towards the Creator of all things on crippled feet, swollen by the toilsome path, and with impatient spirit showing that you want to know why he has no regard for "your labor and sorrow,"[32] because he has allowed some lamb, snatched by you from the enemies' jaws, to stray back again, and that he did not rather make it pass from this world whilst its intentions were still holy, nor did he avenge you or himself forthwith upon the one who occasioned the lamb's ruin. But

27. Ps 41.7.
28. Nm 14.30–38. The two were Caleb and Joshua.
29. Jgs 6.34–7.7.
30. Isai, by the Greeks called "Jesse," was the father of David: Ru 4.17; 1 Kgs 16.1–13.
31. That is, Asa, Ezechias and Josias; 2 Par 14.2, 31.1, 34.3.
32. Ps 9.14.

you will do better to think how much I labored when I redeemed the human race, and yet from many I have had little profit. So it is that when with troubled spirit you were complaining against me, by some heavenly illumination your simplicity received this divine reply: "It is enough for a disciple to be like his master. If they have not obeyed my word, neither will they obey yours."[33] Remember that in the heavenly citadels you did not see "living stones," distinguished by their honor and glory, which had not been repeatedly "polished by pounding and grinding."[34]

(7) But perhaps in your secret thoughts you are striving to evade what I have said, asserting that at one time it was different and that things have now changed, because in these last days "love has almost grown cold,"[35] and that the holy prophets are dead, miracles too for the greater part have ceased to be performed, and the evils here on earth have multiplied. Some of the faithful also who live perverted lives are more difficult to convert, because of the many who entice them, and are more apt to relapse. Therefore, you say, it is time to stop trying to make them bear fruit.

(8) To this I say that the nearer the end of the world comes, and men fail and degenerate, with more danger to themselves, the greater is their need to be renewed with fervent teaching and by grace. And the more damnably the holy prophets and the friends of God have been destroyed and in their place false prophets have risen up, the more necessary has it been to teach fervently and to give one's very soul for the truth that is now falling asleep.

(9) For I call all those men false prophets who belie with their deeds what their words say, such as those who teach that avarice is to be shunned, and thirst with all their souls for money. They cry aloud that the world's glory is to be spurned, and they are the ones who with their whole heart seek after empty honors and promotions. They lay down the law about

33. Cf. Mt 10.25; Jn 15.20.
34. From the Dominican Breviary for the dedication of a church.
35. Mt 24.12.

rejecting what is subtle and pursuing what is simple, they who are enslaved to a subtlety beyond measure.

(10) And to say nothing about the rest, you may see many who are pursuing what is no more than secular learning, but which they dress up as that which our holy fathers in the name of simplicity and innocency commanded their successors to do; but in reality they may be seen to be worshipping worldly vanity. You can see one man arriving, clothed in most costly fabrics, a pleated cloak falling from his shoulders and a surplice pressed into a hundred folds around him, as if he were vested in a philosopher's toga; and he is to be seen walking about "adorned all around in the likeness of a temple."[36] Another has gloves on his hands, and narrow shoes with turned-up toes, as if they were made for dancing, on his feet. Yet others wear tunics of a degenerate new fashion, tailored and trimmed like the garments of worldlings. Their sleeves are cut to be so tight that only with great effort can they get their arms into them. They have dangling ivory writing tablets, gleaming silken girdles, and things like this that show their levity and degeneracy; they want in this way to be pleasing to foolish women, and they are displeasing to God, and to the prelates of churches, and to every decent person of either sex.

(11) What do you think that those men will think whom such prophets have been sent to teach, when they have seen them coming, not wearing sackcloth as did the ancient prophets, but with all these ornaments, which give scandal and offense? They will be utterly rejected, and that proverb may be said to them: "Physician, heal yourself."[37] For a man whose life is despised, someone says, it will follow that his teachings too will be despised.[38] O, how many slanders and mocking gestures and sniggerings will they receive from those who are outside! O, how many men will scorn them, and how often! And they will deserve it. For indeed all this ought to be mocked. "Be ashamed, O Sidon, says the sea."[39]

---

36. Ps 143.1.   37. Lk 4.23.
38. Gregory the Great, *Homily 12 upon the Gospels.*
39. Is 23.4.

(12) For the same will be said to them as the devil said to one monk who was tempted to wear a long cloak, and who, since he could not have one, wore his mat of rushes for a cloak. But the devil, sitting behind him on the mat's tail which he was dragging along after him, said to the brother: "O monk, if you could go further, you would indeed go further."[40] Could not the devil's dear ones, striving for a worldly kingdom, well make the same excuse for themselves, when they are so often seen to be committing, without any subterfuge, such deeds against the poor and the abject of this world? It is no wonder if they are unhappy and quarrelsome who are striving for an empire, when there is such strife about the meanest kingdom. If this diseased craving for newfangledness were found only in subjects, a remedy for so contagious a disease would more easily be provided.

(13) For now there are many who ought to excel others "by word and example,"[41] and whose dress and conduct ought to persuade others to the religious life, who are doing these things, and, what is more to be condemned, do not shame to defend what they do. For what comes from arrogance or newfangledness is represented by their specious reasoning as decent or useful, as they try to exculpate it either as gifts or as longstanding custom. But, alas, this is the prudence of the world, "a wisdom beastly or devilish,"[42] when temporal utility is preferred to spiritual good. What then should they do, the "little flock,"[43] the weaker vessels, the female sex, when they see manly spirits led astray into such nonsense? Indeed, when all the shepherds rush down the slope, the flock must of necessity follow them over the precipice.[44]

(14) In ancient times men were not only exhorted about the things necessary for salvation, but the works of superogation were praised as much as possible; and pious exercises were commended to the faithful as those by which what was necessary to salvation might be better obtained, and, once

---

40. This may be in some still unedited version of *The Lives of the Fathers.*
41. From the Dominican Breviary's prayer for a pope.
42. Jas 3.15.   43. Lk 12.32.
44. Gregory the Great, *Pastoral Rule*, ch. 2.

obtained, preserved. But nowadays such matters are too often passed over in silence, by those who fear that if their tongues say one thing and their lives another, they will gain a name for insincerity. And, what is more to be condemned, not only are most useful matters much neglected, but such men do not desist from causing to those who practice and praise them whatever troubles they can. So when the holy man Jeremias foretold an early overthrow of Israel because of the people's sins, and by the Lord's command offered them a chain of wood, so that he might more easily move them to penitence, the false prophets opposed him and broke his chains of wood, making many reproaches against him and saying: "Peace, peace, and there was no peace."[45] Did he not prophesy the best about this who said: "He who neglects small things will fall, little by little"?[46]

(15) And you will find this lamentable defect not only in those who, like the eagle, are known by others to fly higher, but also beyond all doubt in men of the same type as a calf, which, so far as appearances go, usually shows a humble and useful character. But such men most resemble the lion, who is said to fill the ears of its cubs with its roaring and clamor so as to revive them. But the fourth beast with mystical significance, man, that is,[47] has become so weakened by his long-persisting shortcomings that no one doubts that there is, as it seems, no hope for him, as he so plainly considers that every unlawful thing is permissible to him, and he follows the desires of his heart without fear. As to the other creatures, dwelling apart in caves and woods, forsaking courts and cities, they turn again to their secular pleasures and engross themselves in them with a deliberation as great as the recklessness with which they began, so that now, alas, there is hardly a place left to flee to, as, the end of the world drawing near, "the man who is an enemy" hastens to spread out his snare "and to sow many weeds."[48] "Blessed indeed are the dead who are now dead in the Lord."[49]

45. Jer 6.14.   46. Ecclus 19.1.
47. The eagle, ox, lion and man, seen in the Visions of Ezechiel (Ez 1.10) and John (Apoc 4.6–8), and used as the symbols of the Evangelists.
48. Mt 13.25.   49. Apoc 14.13.

(16) Recall a notable event, which happened to one of these men of whom I have spoken, who, while he was prophesying or making some exhortation to others for their salvation, produced a great rhetorical outburst to the effect that the love and zeal for God and his saints of many men was dead, and that Christ would not again find his Mary Magdalen in the world to perform so many services for him as once she did. When he had finished his sermon, some young woman came up to him and said, as if in anger against him: "Oh, friar! If Mary Magdalen could find her Christ as once she did, Christ would indeed find his Mary, now as then," meaning that if some of these prophets of whom we have spoken were what they should be, there would still be those to accept them with all devotion.

(17) Yet while I am introducing this pure truth, which does not know how to flatter vice, with words that are temperate and yet quite resolute, I see you alarmed in your mind, fearing lest perhaps what I am discussing in secret with you, if it should come to the ears of those who do such things, will be disregarded, or, what is certain, will be received less than gratefully. This, then, is what displeases me, and this is what makes you blameworthy, that I see you to be very timid in matters that I know to be of concern for the salvation of many. So what are you? You are not Jeremias, you have not been "sanctified in the womb."[50] You are not a prophet. But what are you? A sinful man and a "herdsman plucking wild figs."[51] Nevertheless you have been sent by him who also sent these men, and this is attested by your name, and by your religious profession, confirmed by the supreme vicar of Jesus Christ.[52] Why are you afraid? Even if you are displeasing to empty and dissolute men, still you can be pleasing to the many who do not "walk in levity"[53] of spirit, but live decently according to the institutions of the holy fathers, and win themselves and many others for God.[54] But are you seeking "still to be pleasing to

50. Jer 1.5.   51. Am 7.14.
52. Plainly, this is addressed, if not to an individual Dominican such as the master general, at least to the whole Order.
53. Tb 3.17.
54. An allusion to the Dominican Missal for the feast of St. Dominic.

men"?[55] I say these things not, indeed, to approve singularities, but to define and witness that it is good to proceed along the common path; but, alas, what once was singular begins now to be common, and what is now singular once was common.

(18) Nor ought a "faithful and prudent"[56] disciple desist from what he has begun, by pleading as you do that no one listens to him. Furthermore, what I am saying will gain no hearing from them, because it will contain no subtleties of questioning, no arguments in favor of worldly advantages, which, as likely to bring honors or earthly rewards, are the only matters that they will receive gladly, prize dearly, put into practice, these many who disregard everything else. This present volume should contain only "lamentations and canticles and woe,"[57] which rouse up minds torpid in vices, and raise up hearts to things that are divine. See how the Lord sends Ezechiel to the people "with stiff necks,"[58] the Lord saying: "They will not listen to you, because they will not listen to me."[59] The holy prophet is sent, and yet, even before he is sent, it is foretold that he will achieve nothing. And in this the love of the Lord is considered, who "will have all men saved"[60] and not lacking the remedies of salvation, and the hardheartedness of the Jews is rebuked, who had no gratitude for God's benefits, but persisted in their obstinacy. Regard too the prophet Jeremias, who when he had written the book of the Lord's law, which was utterly rejected by the king and "cut up with a scribe's penknife and cast into the fire,"[61] did not for all this give up, but at the Lord's command went on writing a second volume.[62] Even if you do not want to consider this, at least follow the counsels of some wise man, and go on proclaiming your message to yourself and those who are yours, even if the ears of all others are deaf. Thus it was from the beginning of the world, that various holy men and God's greatest friends, sustaining many hardships and hearing them all patiently, merited the eternal rewards that you have seen,

---

55. Gal 1.10.

56. Mt 24.45.

57. Ez 2.9.

58. Ex 32.9.

59. Ez 3.7.

60. 1 Tm 2.4.

61. Jer 36.23.

62. Jer 36.28.

"and now they are crowned and receive the palm."[63] So it is plain from what has been said how good it is to serve the Lord rather than the world, and how joyful it is to love heavenly things rather than those of the earth, which are to pass away.

(19) Disciple: What should I reply to all these things, far exceeding my powers? There is nothing whatever for me to do but to lay my finger on my lips,[64] and entrust "my imperfect being"[65] to your most benign will and to your most perfect majesty, adding only this, which I know by your grace, that those who attempt to compare your most precious love with the utterly empty love of the world are fools and like those who talk nonsense. For like base men, "they count it delightful to be among the briars,"[66] because their reasoning too is empty, because the whole multitude, of those, that is, who love the world, approve that love, and, on the contrary, there are few who are joined to you in perfect love, and who take the pains to blame your love for being imperfect. Alas, "they are blind, and leaders of the blind."[67]

(20) This is much more easily proved by opposition than by any proposition,[68] for it is agreed that the multitude is not ruled by reason, but rather drawn along by ungoverned emotion. I know that I have gone far astray, and with a sorrowful heart I accuse myself of having thought that I had done much for my neighbor's salvation, when in truth I had given it the least possible exertion, and of having been so impatient in adversities. O, how mercifully you spare us, in giving us adversities here, and how severe is your wrath when you distribute nothing but prosperity![69] Very loving is your fatherly correction. "For whom you love you correct, and as a father with his son, it pleases you."[70] Let no one complain that you have forgotten those whom you afflict. For rather "with an eternal

63. From the Dominican Breviary for the common of Apostles.
64. Jb 21.5.   65. Ps 138.16.
66. Jb 30.7.   67. Mt 15.14.
68. "ex hoc oppositum quam propositum": *similiter cadens*; see Colledge and Walsh, *A Book of Showings*, 747.
69. ". . . adversa . . . prospera": *oppositio contrariorum*; see Colledge and Walsh, *A Book of Showings*, 744–45.
70. Prv 3.12.

forgetting you have forgotten those"[71] whom now for a little while you spare, rewarding them now with some few good things, but it is your will to condemn them eternally, punishing their evil deeds without end. So I think it very fitting that men should here be oppressed with continual adversity for whom you have decreed that they are to be spared such miseries and to possess so immense a glory.

71. Os 1.6.

CHAPTER 13

How Profitable It Can Be for a Servant of God to Endure Many Tribulations in This World.

"BE COMFORTED, be comforted, my people, says your God."[1] A certain sick spirit, subject to the vicissitudes of this world more than should be, when the night of adversity had overtaken the day of prosperity, forgetful of the remedies that have been discussed, began again to be disquieted, and to pour out its soul to God with a most dejected heart, calling to mind again with a burning heart the adversities it had suffered, "like coals laying waste,"[2] crying out in its sorrow for sympathy and shedding great tears.

(2) So, because Wisdom's Disciple had no means at hand with which to revive his spirit in its labors in adversity for Christ, see, as he longed and sighed, in a vision a most lovely youth stood before him, who put into his hands that musical instrument which is called a psaltery, in the shape of a cross,[3] and made his mind to burgeon again with spiritual maxims, bidding him to sing joyfully and skillfully to the psaltery, and to bring gladness in the Lord his God to hearts that were sorrowing or mourning. And there were souls, laboring "with various diseases"[4] and other troubles, who drew closer to him, humbly entreating him to give them consolation for their labors. Taking the psaltery from the youth's hand, coming to himself, and understanding what he was asked to do, in the

1. Is 40.1.   2. Ps 119.4.
3. This analogy, though rare, is found elsewhere. Robert Manning of Brunne, in his English version of the *Manual of Sins*, tells how Robert Grosseteste, explaining why he listened to harp-playing in times of mental distress, likened its sound to the sufferings of the cross, drawing men's souls up to heaven. I owe identification of this to Dr. Frank Mantello.
4. Mk 1.34.

middle of the youth's sad song he began with the words from the prophet: "Be comforted, be comforted, my people, says your God."

(3) But as he pronounced these and similar words of consolation to alleviate the sorrow of his mourning soul, "he refused to be comforted,"[5] but began to grow sadder and sadder. For sweet words, when grief is at its full, sometimes make sad hearts yet sadder, just as harmony, so it is said, makes the joyful man more joyful and the sad man more sad. So too for a devout soul, fragrant with the divine love, the more sweetly it knows within itself the divine presence, after its bitter trials, the more does it become wholly dissolved in tears for this unlooked-for joy.

(4) It happened in the same way in this case, that what was offered to the sorrowing soul as reasons for joy would be turned into the cause of sadness. For it should rather have laughed, yet it began to weep without restraint; but when it was asked why it wept, or what could be the matter, it replied: "Suffer me to bewail my sorrow,[6] for my soul is in great anguish."[7] It was asked: "What are you suffering? Tell me." And it replied: "Ah, unhappy me, when I was still in the days of my youth I went out to seek a lover for myself, so that I might rejoice in her company and lead a happy life. And when I had looked upon many, and could have had my choice among them, there was one, fairer than the rest, it seemed to me, who was pleasing to my eyes. She showed herself to me with gentle words and every kind of promise, so that I rejected all the rest, and agreed with her, and took her as my bride. And after I had dwelt with her for no long time, and was hoping that by living with her I was to have great well-being, alas, out of a lover she turned into an enemy. The lamb was changed into a lion, and by her means my whole life became filled with sorrow and misery. For while I was dwelling, safe, as I thought, in my house, and, like a leafy but not yet full-grown tree near the willows by the stream I was beginning to spread out my

5. Jer 31.15.   6. Jb 10.20.
7. 4 Kgs 4.27.

branches and to bear fruit, she whom I had thought of as my beloved stretched out her hand against me, and nipped and shriveled up with winter cold my tender blossoms, tore off my branches, "stripped the bark from my fig tree,"[8] and, "while I was yet but beginning, cut me off."[9] She roused up my most cruel enemies against me, who spared me in no way as they afflicted me day and night. As I sought to resist them, I was greatly oppressed by their repeated insults, my youthful body began to grow sick, and my joyous spirit wasted away in much sorrow.

(5) After this, "adding sorrow to sorrow,"[10] and inflicting a wound where I was already wounded, she took away from me my dearest kinsman,[11] only solace in this world of my heart, whom as my own soul I had loved, and left me desolate. O, if at that time you had seen me, how I looked up to heaven, weeping and wailing with tearful cries, entreating that our merciful God would turn his anger into clemency, and "lift his hand"[12] so heavy for a little while from the afflicting of this wretched being, your loving heart would have been moved. But see—and this I am compelled to tell you with tears—my most cruel bride intensified her anger against me, which I have described, in this way. For I had only two sheep left to me, eating with me from my platter and drinking with me, and working to help me in every way; and then, when I least expected it, there came "evening wolves,"[13] carrying off my lambs and tearing them to pieces, rending them miserably with all kinds of bodily death. And when, with weeping and lamentation I had run after them, hardly had I with great labor wrested back some part of their carcasses, "as if a shepherd should snatch out of the lion's mouth two legs"[14] of his beasts, when she, my enemy, saw this, dipped her hand in the gore of those lifeless ones, and touching my face and sprinkling me with their blood, "she made me a reproach to fools."[15] She

8. Jl 1.7.　　　　　　　　　　9. Is 38.12.
10. Jer 45.3.
11. Künzle considers that this may refer to Eckhart.
12. 1 Kgs 6.5.　　　　　　　　13. Hb 1.8.
14. Am 3.12.　　　　　　　　　15. Ps 38.9.

added to their death heavier tribulations, and she "put out the light of my wavering lamp."[16] "She took away the voice of mirth,"[17] and carried off everything that was glad and dear. She wounded my heart over its whole surface with most cruel and unbelievable sorrows. Then many loving hearts wept to see these things, and there were those who mourned with louder voice, "striking their breasts,"[18] suffering greatly with me in my affliction. Yet there were some who stood there, making mocking gestures at my misery, "wagging their heads,"[19] making what I was suffering into my reproach. Why should I go on? For this savage tribulation afflicted me so that "there was but one step, as I may say, between me and death."[20]

(6) Nor did she stop at this, she whom I used to love the best, but she added to these fresh tribulations. For from the days of my youth, with great labor and care, I had planted a grove, fair in the greenness of its leaves, surrounding "a seat of honor,"[21] from which I had hoped that I should receive glory and honor for myself. But when the time was ripe for me to enjoy what I had toiled for, the seat was overturned and the grove was given into the charge of someone else, and all my work was wasted, and the end that I had intended was frustrated. And so, seeming "to have lifted me up, she threw me down"[22] violently. And when these evils, so recent, had increased, a great multitude of what seemed like serpents and poisonous beasts rose up against me, and attacked me with great force, sometimes all together beating upon me, sometimes one by one. Then I was the lions' "brother, and the companion of ostriches."[23] Rabid dogs barked at me, scorpions came from their hiding-places and wounded me. Serpents breathed a kind of fetid breath on me and hissed, "and were not afraid to spit in my face."[24] So, wounding me and mocking me with every kind of pain, "they made my life bitter."[25] What more? There would not be the time, if I should wish to recount

16. Prv 20.20.   17. Bar 2.23.
18. Lk 23.48.   19. Mt 27.39.
20. 1 Kgs 20.3.   21. Ecclus 7.4.
22. Ps 101.11.   23. Jb 30.29.
24. Jb 30.10.   25. Ex 1.14.

all her scourgings, my adversary's, with which she has beaten me "even to this hour";[26] but I may say with the prophet: "My secret is my own, my secret is my own."[27] All these things have broken violently out of the abundance of my heart because of the cheering voice of your consolation, out of the fullness of my heart with flowing tears.

(7) When the Disciple had heard these things, he understood them to be the mystery of espousal with Eternal Wisdom, who is accustomed to try her lovers with worldly tribulations, and then to join those she has tried to herself in her love; and, turning to her, he said: "O divine Wisdom, unsearchable depth! O endless sea of all loving kindness, why do you so afflict those who love you, and permit those who care little for you to go 'with neck raised up'?[28] Do you not know, you who are the shaper of all things, how very weak is that on which human debility rests, and that 'the body which is corruptible is a load upon the soul,'[29] so that it cannot always see the things that are to come, but thinks rather of its inclination towards the things within its view? O most clement God, consider clemently[30] our tribulations, and give us the power to suffer them, and give strength from on high to our weak hearts with your most welcome consolations.

(8) Wisdom: The newborn kid seeks refuge with its mother, it seeks the she-goat's breasts; but when it has grown as it should, it turns away from milk and seeks the heights of the mountains, "it feeds among the lilies,"[31] and is a free member of its flock. Now you are grown in years, and you have outgrown the milk which is the diet for children. It is time for you to be "weaned from milk, drawn away from the breasts,"[32] and to be joined to the company of "valiant men."[33] Learn then from the example of those men what you should do, and how patiently you should sustain all adversities, so that you too, tried by tribulations, may join yourself to their number with joy that will have no end.

26. 1 Cor 4.11.   27. Is 24.16.
28. Jb 15.26.   29. Wis 9.15.
30. "O most clement God, consider clemently . . .": conduplicatio.
31. Cant 2.16.   32. Is 28.9.
33. 2 Kgs 24.9.

(9) So "come up to a deep heart,"[34] rise up and look back, and see the innumerable crowd of all "the saints who are from the beginning of the world";[35] and turn over in your mind how all those who have especially pleased me have also been proved outstanding in their bearing of adversities. And about all the others, whose number is infinite, I shall keep silence; see here, close at hand, that boy, the harpist, "a man according to God's own heart."[36] "What great troubles," he says, "have you shown me, many and grievous, and, turning, you have brought me to life, and have brought me back again from the depths of the earth."[37] Joseph, the future lord of Egypt, sold into slavery by his brothers, and defamed by an evil woman, was given over to imprisonment in a dungeon. For the present I shall pass over Abraham in silence, he who was blessed by the Lord, Moses, the Lord's elect, and the rest of the patriarchs, prophets and friends of the most high God, whose enduring hope ought properly to be your mirror of patience, and give you strength in adversities.

(10) "Ask each generation, and they will declare to you; ask your elders, and they will tell you."[38] For you are a foreigner, "not knowing how to go out and come in";[39] and you will see how laughable what you suffer is, if you wished to weigh it properly and compare it with the sufferings of the fathers. See Isaias, outstanding for his great graces, cut through with a wood-saw.[40] Jeremias, "sanctified in the womb,"[41] who "did not desire the day of man,"[42] was buried under stones and burned.[43] Ezechiel had his brains cruelly dashed out.[44] Daniel,

34. Ps 63.7.   35. Lk 1.70.
36. 1 Kgs 13.14.   37. Ps 70.20.
38. Dt 32.7.   39. 3 Kgs 3.7.
40. This is an ancient tradition, unwarranted by Scripture, but there appears to have been confusion of the allusion, probably in the popular Latin translation, the *Visio Pauli*, to Isaias and Ezechiel: "I am Isaias, the celebrated prophet, and Manasseh, the son of Hezechias, sawed me through with a wood-saw . . . Ezechiel had his brains dashed out on the mountain . . ." (Justin Perkins, "The Revelation of the Blessed Apostle Paul," *Journal of the American Oriental Society* 8 (1866): 217 [A translation from a Syriac manuscript of Nestorian origin]).
41. Jer 1.5.   42. Jer 17.16.
43. This is another such tradition, recorded by Tertullian.
44. This is related by pseudo-Epiphanus, *The Lives of the Prophets.*

"a man of desires,"[45] "was cast into the lions' den."[46] The three children were put "into the furnace of fire."[47] Job, the model of patience, was given into his enemy's hand.[48] Tobias was blinded.[49] The Machabees were slain with most cunningly-devised torments.[50] Yet these fathers "received as a promise"[51] temporal good things. And afterwards, from the beginnings of the infant Church, "the kingdom of heaven has been suffering violence, and the violent are bearing it away."[52]

(11) Do you not see how the Apostles, my dearest friends, have suffered in this world "in hunger and thirst, laboring in cold and nakedness"?[53] They have exposed themselves "to prisons and stripes and deaths,"[54] and have subjected themselves to all the labors and hardships of this present life, nor have they lacked tribulations, yet they did not dwell upon this with complaining words, as you are doing, but rejoiced in contumelies and were joyful in tribulations.[55] And the holy martyrs—who would dare to consider them and still be slothful or complain? They "made trial of mockeries and stripes, they suffered bonds and prisons,"[56] they endured innumerable kinds of torment, and they were most gloriously crowned. Confessors and virgins, enduring their long martyrdom, "crucified their body with its vices and concupiscences."[57] What did Alexius[58] do? What did Eustace[59] suffer?

(12) And if in this present day what "young men and virgins"[60] and married women too and most devout widows through all the wide regions where the faith is kept suffer for the love of God, if the greatness of their tribulations were known to you, would that impose silence on your querulous

45. Dn 9.23.
46. Dn 6.16.
47. Dn 3.20.
48. Jb 1.12.
49. Tb 2.11.
50. 2 Mc 7.
51. Heb 11.39.
52. Mt 11.12.
53. 2 Cor 11.27.
54. 2 Cor 11.23.
55. Acts 5.41.
56. Heb 11.36.
57. Gal 5.24.
58. St. Alexius's legend tells of his solitary years, for long disguised as a beggar, at the doors of his father's palace in Rome. His feast was introduced into the Dominican liturgy in 1305.
59. Probably the saint of that name venerated as a martyr under Hadrian.
60. Ps 148.12.

lips? Do you not call to mind the very memorable example of the married woman, most devoted to God, who came to confession to you and revealed how for twenty years she had lived with her husband, who, acting not like a man but like a raging lion, assaulted her again and again, with his sword drawn, and rained down innumerable blows and insults on this holy and shamefast woman, so much so that from hour to hour, when her husband appeared, she was filled with terror of sudden death? All these things that devout woman bore most patiently; she was not complaining or moaning, but she was entreating you devoutly to pray for the salvation of that beast. Did you not then look up to heaven and beat your breast, and with a shameful heart acknowledge that you had suffered nothing, but had been wandering around at your ease?

(13) Furthermore, you still have a place in which you can better find shelter and may more profitably reflect. I put forward the Achilles of your heart, the *Conversations*,[61] that is, and *The Lives of the Fathers*, which you read and reread every day, and from which you would not willingly be distracted, even for a short time. If you have diligently examined them, it will be surprising enough if you have not made sufficient progress to have learned patience in adversities. Where is your friend Arsenius?[62] What has become of Macarius? Have you forgotten Anthony? Paul and Hilarion, have you rejected them? "Gather together the dispersed"[63] ones of your heart, and be mindful of the most godly fathers who, dwelling in the Thebaid and in the districts of Egypt and in other places in the desert, and searching for mountain fastnesses, clefts in the rocks and thickets in the woods, sought out the harsh wastes of the emptiest desert, and there, remote from every human face, suffering innumerable hardships with great devotion, led a life admirable to all men.

(14) Do you not blush when you look on these men, do you

61. Of John Cassian.

62. Arsenius, Macarius, Anthony, Paul, and Hilarion are all desert monks whose histories are narrated in *The Lives of the Fathers*.

63. Ps 146.2.

not long with all your mind's desire to be numbered in their company, and do you not shame that you have no wish to imitate, even a little, what they endured? Do you want to be idle among so many most valiant fighters, growing torpid and drowsing? Let it not be so. Time is now passing. You have changed into a man, so from now on throw away childish things, and prepare yourself for more rugged battles.

(15) Disciple: Truly, the remembrance of so many fathers is "as music at a banquet of wine,"[64] and it will be made sweeter than honey in every troubled soul. When I, poor worm, see with my heart's eye these glorious men, the famous "knights of the heavenly hall"[65] and their astounding deeds, truly I exclaim with weeping heart that I am nothing and that I suffer nothing; and if ever I thought that anything saddening had happened to me, when I see them, that passes, and I breathe gently again.

(16) But I should have wished to know whether casual misfortunes and involuntary sufferings may be beneficial or even meritorious, and also why it seems to be your custom to occupy your friends with adversities rather than with good fortune.

(17) Wisdom: In one question you have asked, it seems, for three of your doubts to be solved, that is, about the occurrence, the manner and the causes of tribulations. As to the first, keep this statement firmly in your mind, that no tribulation or any other fortuitous happening can be called "casual," when it is related to the first Cause of things, even though by reduction it may seem to fall under this or that law of causality. So, whatever adversity may happen to you, it is brought about at the instance and by the providence of him by whose power all things were created and are preserved in their being.

(18) Furthermore, about involuntary tribulations, you must know that even though something involuntary may not as such be meritorious, yet still if a prudent spirit will wish voluntarily to suffer what has been brought to it involuntarily, and will

---

64. Ecclus 49.2.
65. From the hymn *Aeterna Christi munera*, used in the Dominican Breviary for the common of Apostles.

bow its will, until now rebellious, to the rod of God, making a virtue of necessity,[66] it can hardly be doubted that that which before seemed noxious will be made beneficial and meritorious, and will help towards a spiritual growth in virtues. So truly the wisdom of God since the beginning of the world has been drawing countless unwilling men to itself, and "compels" the rebellious "to come in."[67] But why the elect, as so very often, are oppressed here with adversities, you may have this for your quick answer: It is because "man's thoughts are prone to evil from his youth";[68] you must know that the way of the elect is through the thorns of tribulation, lest noxious delights give them occasion for sinning, but when one of them is borne down into the depths by continual tribulations, he may be compelled to make his way up on high, even though he may be unwilling.

(19) Disciple: I do not doubt that worldly tribulations are useful and even salutary, if they do not go beyond the capacity and possibilities of the man who suffers them. But I see them here so afflicting men, harassing and driving them so forcibly, that they sometimes seem to exceed every human power.

(20) Wisdom: This is the habit of every wretched man, to judge that his scourges are sharper than those of others, and that anyone who sees his misfortune should lament it more than anyone else's; and if anyone thinks himself crushed to the very ground by this kind of affliction, however else he may be oppressed, he will still bear the burden of his own complaining. So once you have put away every notion that you are exceptional, submit yourself to the divine will, and receive in love God's chastising. "For God is faithful, and he will not suffer you to be tempted beyond what you can endure, but for the temptation he will provide a happy issue, so that you may be able to bear it."[69] So why do you still tremble? What are you afraid of? For he is most loving, so that he wants, and he is most wise, so that he knows best what is best for every man,

66. The phrase seems first to be found in Jerome, *Against Rufinus,* and he is adapting one by Quintilian.
67. Lk 14.23.   68. Gn 8.21.
69. 1 Cor 10.13.

and he is most powerful, so that when a man's own powers fall short, the hand of the Almighty will supply. So, "cast your care upon the Lord,"[70] entrust yourself to God, believe that you belong to him, and "cast all your care upon God, for he has care of you."[71] Draw near, and say with confidence to him: "My Father, let not my will but yours be done."[72] And so when tribulation will come, go out to meet such a guest, receiving him kindly, and say with a glad heart: "Welcome, tribulation, my friend."

(21) Disciple: O God, how easy it is to say this, and how hard to make one's deeds fit the words, for the savage wounds of grinding afflictions are cruel indeed!

(22) Wisdom: If tribulations did not afflict, they would not be worth calling "tribulations." When tribulation is at hand, it imposes its power, but after it has passed and been vanquished, it brings great joy. It brings a short bitterness and a long consolation. Often tribulation is in the end overcome by usage, so that it seems as if it were not tribulation, or to be easy. Anyone who has become accustomed to monsters will pay little attention to what is monstrous. Yet any part of the immense fullness of divine sweetness that you may so gain may not be for you so truly meritorious or so praiseworthy as when tribulation is patiently and steadfastly suffered out of a fervent love. We have found more who were overwhelmed by elation when everything has been going well, than who were broken by adversities and forsook their spiritual undertakings. So you may have blossomed out as a student of astrology, you may have penetrated every secret of the liberal arts, you may have seemed wonderful in your mastery of all wisdom, you may have outstripped every rhetorician and dialectician in eloquence and subtlety, but this will not bring you to a good life as will that one thing which is necessary for salvation, that is, to abandon yourself out of "love from a pure heart and a good conscience and an unfeigned faith,"[73] and to commit yourself wholly to God in every tribulation, and patiently to conform

70. Ps 54.23.   71. 1 Pt 5.7.
72. Lk 22.42.   73. 1 Tm 1.5.

yourself to his will. All that is common to the good and the bad, but this can only be in his elect. Such is the preeminence of eternal glory over every temporal and transitory suffering that anyone who takes care to see things as they are should rather choose to want to be tormented for many years "in a furnace of burning fire"[74] than wish to be deprived of the smallest reward reserved for him in the future; for labor has its end, the reward has no end.

(23) Disciple: O, highest and ineffable love, how sweetly and melodiously do these instruments resound in a saddened ear! "O, wonderful condescension of your love towards us,"[75] that "you set your heart"[76] upon a man wretched and afflicted and desolate, and that you deign so to assuage the mourning and to console the sad and mournful. For when you sing your songs so sweetly, the spirit oppressed with sadness is lightened, and your heavenly melody drives sorrow's recollection from the spirit, at least for the time, so that it may bear its sufferings more easily. Then, even if it were given to me to choose, I should prefer to go on suffering adversities and so to be supported by your sweetest consolation, than to be free of adversities and not to have your most precious anointing. Ah, do now what you have begun, for the man to whom Eternal Wisdom sings so sweetly on the harp in adverse times considers that it is as though he suffers nothing.

(24) Wisdom: If you wish to hear the harping of this spiritual music resounding sweetly, rouse yourself up, and pay careful heed to the precious fruit of temporal adversities. For as in a harp the strings tunefully stretched make the sound sweet, so any one of the elect, when he is oppressed by adversity, is stretched as it were by some outside force, and so is made more able to give out a sweet and heavenly melody.[77] So you must know that temporal tribulation is vilified by this world, which is indeed quite insane, but by God, the supreme Judge, it is esteemed as most precious. Tribulation quenches the

74. Dn 3.6.   75. From the Easter Eve *Exultet*.
76. Jb 7.17.
77. Gregory the Great, *Moralia* XX, ch. 41, compares holy men's self-chastisement and abasement with the tuning of harps.

Judge's anger, and turns his severity into friendship and kindness. Whoever suffers adversities willingly for God is made like
to the suffering Christ, and so is drawn into his embrace and
secured by his love as one who is like to him.

(25) The fruit of tribulation gives a strength as anointing
and incorruptible as balsam. As the morning star heralds the
sun's coming as it rises on this world, so likewise does man's
tribulation do. For it shows the joyful nearness of that sun
which is above all the heavens, wishing to seek out the troubled soul, and it declares the inward consolation that will follow. And as the dark night precedes the bright day, and winter's rigors go before the joys of summer, so tribulation is
accustomed to precede the inward and eternal consolation of
good minds. As "the rainbow giving light among the bright
clouds"[78] is the sign of divine peace towards the human race,[79]
so cruel tribulation is the sign of divine appeasement towards
the contrite spirit.

(26) It is the forerunner of grace, the companion of hope,
the mother of love. It protects the active life with its defenses,
and it subtly sharpens the eye of contemplation. This it is that
makes a fleshly man spiritual, and turns an earthly into a heavenly mind, for it forces that to rise aloft which it forbids to
waste itself upon itself. It begets a shunning of this world, but
it bears friendship with God. It makes men's friends to grow
fewer, but it causes grace to grow greater. For it often happens
that what is spurned by this world as abject is chosen by the
highest good, and is worthy to be singularly adorned by its
love. This is the "narrow way," but it is safe and quick, and
"leads to life."[80]

(27) Let anyone endowed with sense consider now how
foolish it would be for a man always to be counting his own
profit, and to think that this will give him support. They cannot be numbered, those who have fallen into sin's deepest
sleep and have died the death of the spirit, whom wretched
sinfulness has swallowed up, but, when the rod of divine cor-

78. Ecclus 50.8.
79. Gn 9.13.
80. Mt 7.14.

rection struck them, roused up, as it were from deep slumber and "the empire of death,"[81] changed their lives for the better, and, "casting off the works of darkness, put on the armor of light."[82] O, how many are there, imprisoned in the world, on whom tribulations have pressed, and are held fast by the hand of the Most High, like untamed beasts and uncaged birds, who if they had the ability, roused up from sloth, would flee from the place which they sought for their own well-being. O, how many are they who may have committed the greatest sins, who may have perpetrated many crimes, if they had not been saved by a loving dispensation of God through their tribulations.

(28) For what is it that makes a man of haughty heart and puffed-up mind and ambition learn to know himself better, and "not to mind high things,"[83] but to remain humbly within himself and to fear, and to teach others to stoop down to their suffering neighbors? Tribulation is the nurse of humility, the teacher of patience, the guardian of virginity, the bringer of everlasting felicity. Tribulation is considered to bring such well-being that it can hardly be that anyone will hide himself when it sprinkles its goodness around, whether he belong to the beginners or to the proficient or even to the perfect. It takes away the rust of sins, it promotes the growth of virtues, and it confers the fullness of graces. What can be of greater use than this most precious treasure? For it takes away sins, it shortens purgatory, it repels temptations, it extinguishes carnality, it renews the spirit, it strengthens hope, it enlivens the countenance, it brings peace of conscience and it offers the unending fullness of inward joys. It is the health-giving draft, the plant more healing than all those of the earthly paradise. It does indeed chastise the corruptible body, but it nourishes the immortal soul. A devout soul grows well fed on tribulation, as the roses and the lilies are made fecund by celestial dew. It gives wisdom, it attracts circumspection, and it makes a clumsy man more adroit. Anyone who has not suffered adversities, what does he know? "He who has not been tried, what kind of things does he know?"[84] It is God's chosen

81. Heb 2.14.   82. Rom 13.12.
83. Rom 12.16.   84. Ecclus 34.11.

gift, the loving rod, the father's stroke. It calls to those who are willing, and it is accustomed to draw rebellious wills to itself.

(29) To a suffering man, adversity and prosperity are equally serviceable; friends and enemies are alike helpful to him. How often, I ask you, have you silenced the raging of furious adversaries and enemies crying out upon you, when you have made them powerless by your gentleness, your patience and your heart's cheerfulness? I who have created all things out of nothing[85] bring unforeseen tribulations from anywhere at all upon my elect, lest they be deprived of this benefit, which is so great to them. For strength is tried by adversity, and your neighbor is strengthened, God is glorified. Patience in adversities is like "a pillar of cloud of aromatic spices, of myrrh and frankincense and of all the powders of the perfumer,"[86] whose sweetest odor, rising from the fire of tribulation, always ascends before my eyes, making me appeasable towards him and rousing all the court of heaven in wonder.

(30) The men of this world are not accustomed to watch some earthly knight fighting valiantly in tournaments so often as the whole company of heaven are used to approve and watch a spiritual man, in his manly battle along the way. For all the saints have provided the suffering man with the confidence of faith, for throughout their lives they had tasted before he did "the Lord's mixed cup,"[87] and now with their thoughts, which then were so fearful, they persuade him that he will have no harm, but that this is a health-giving drink they all proclaim with one voice. The virtue of patience is more than the raising up of dead men and the performance of other miracles.[88] It confers the glory of martyrdom, and it offers the victorious palm. It is clothed in a purple robe, it is given a wreath of glowing roses, it is adorned with a golden scepter, it is invested with a royal diadem. It is a carbuncle, shining in golden necklaces; and this is patience, showing itself when

85. 2 Mc 7.28.   86. Cant 3.6.
87. Ps 74.9.
88. Gregory the Great, *Dialogues* I, ch. 2: "I believe that the virtue of patience is greater than signs and miracles."

hardships occur. Gleaming gem, perfume breathing sweetness, and honeycomb distilling everywhere—so is a religious walking patiently among his brethren and equably suffering their faults.[89] His voice sounds sweetly from a joyous heart in the palace of heaven, he claims as his own a special song that they do not know how to sing who have not merited to sing it by their spirits' toleration in the adversities of this life. What more need I say? "There is no tongue that can tell, no letter can express"[90] how very profitable it can be to suffer adversities in patience. But of all the things that have been said, let at least this not escape from your memory, that those who know tribulation are called wretched by this world, but I count them blessed, for they are to reign with me without end.

(31) Disciple: O, how plainly it appears now who you are! For you are that most celebrated Wisdom, not to be compared with any mortal being; that is most manifest, and you make truth known and bring it to the light with a mellifluous savor and a most sweet taste, nor do you leave us any room for doubt. Therefore it is not wonderful if anyone willingly suffers all adversities, who in them is so gently consoled by you. My sweetest Father, see me now prostrate at your feet, giving you thanks with the devout love of my heart for all my present adversities, and also for all the direst punishments of the past with which you have deigned until now to chastise and teach me. Once they seemed to me so severe, for I thought that they came from an enemy's severity. But in a wonderful way all these fearful things quickly "passed away as a morning cloud,"[91] and so through your doing they are in my sight as if they never had been; and I am compelled to say with the wise man: "I have labored a little, and I have found much rest for myself."[92] For when I place you, my heart's one treasure, as a mirror of love before the eyes of my loving heart, and I embrace you in perfect love with all the desires of my heart, I forget everything that could make me sad, and all that could ever bring me toil or sorrow passes into oblivion.

89. Cassian, *Conversations* XX, ch. 9: "That man is truly perfect and not only in part who endures solitude's desolation in the hermitage and his brethren's weaknesses in the community with equal generosity."

90. From the hymn *Dulcis Jesu memoria*.

91. Os 13.3.   92. Ecclus 51.35.

CHAPTER 14

How Profitable It Can Be to Have Christ's Passion Constantly in Mind

E GO ON from roses to roses, and, leaving the violets, we hasten to seek out the lilies, when we turn our heart's eyes back from the seed that can grow into the flowers—which are the sufferings of some godly men[1]—to your sufferings, roses in full bloom, O you "the flower of the field,"[2] you rose without thorn, Eternal Wisdom, whom we desire above all else. For it is through your fruitful and adorable Passion that the matter of which our every spiritual good is formed is most copiously imparted to us. "Where is then our boasting?"[3] Where is the hope and joy of our heart? Truly, it is in you alone, the highest and true good, and in the most precious treasure of your Passion. And so it is an unfailing delight to store so priceless a treasure in the heart, and unceasingly to speak of it, and at all times, with all one's mind and body, to be occupied with it. Would too that it might never fade in our hearts, but always go on, burgeoning anew and putting out fresh shoots.

(2) And how happy too are you, O glorious light "of all the churches,"[4] winging your way on your pinions above every changeable thing, and reaching up to touch the secrets of the godhead, for you have gone within, to look with purer eyes into the abyss of the divine clarity, and you have heard the words "which it is not granted to man to utter";[5] and yet, descending into the depths, in a certain honeyed mood, so as to proclaim the praises of the Passion you have cried out to all

---

1. "flowers—which are the sufferings of some godly men": see note 19 to Bk. I, ch. 3, above.

2. Cant 2.1.   3. Rom 3.27; 2 Cor 11.28.

4. Rom 16.16   5. 2 Cor 12.4.

from the riches of your heart, saying to men: "I judged myself to know nothing among you but Jesus Christ, and him cruci-fied."[6] O words sweet as honey, "sweeter than honey and the honeycomb,"[7] constantly to be pondered by devout minds, from you the distillation of virtue flows, offering to wretched mortals the joys of salvation in full measure.

(3) And so you too, heavenly viol, sweetly adorned with dul-cet eloquence and illumined with the Eternal Word's most divine majesty, most blessed Bernard, to whom the Word, made flesh and hung up upon the cross, tasted so sweetly[8] that you entreated him with all tenderness, with "these and words like them": "A bundle of myrrh," you say with the spouse, "is my beloved to me; he will abide between my breasts,"[9] mean-ing the bitterness of the Lord's Passion. And, as you say, "this wisdom have I given myself to meditate; in these things have I established my perfect righteousness, in them is the fullness of my knowledge, the riches of salvation, the plenty of merits. From these things sometimes I drink a healing bitterness, and then again I find the sweet unction of consolation. It is this that has lifted me up in adversities, has brought me low in prosperity; and among the joys and sorrows of this present life, as I make my way along 'the King's highway,' it offers me everywhere a safe conduct, thrusting aside the evils which threaten me. I do not ask, as does the spouse, 'where he lies in the midday,'[10] he whom I embrace 'abiding between my breasts.' I do not ask 'where he feeds in the midday,'[11] he whom I see, my Savior, hanging upon the cross. There he is more sublime, here he is more sweet and closer to hand. There he is bread, here he is milk. Meanwhile, this will be my higher philosophy, 'to know Jesus, and him crucified.'"[12] I have accepted these things, O teacher so much to be vener-ated, as they are commended by your lips.

6. 1 Cor 2.2.   7. Ps 18.11.
8. This probably alludes to the legend (which Bernard of Clairvaux and Thomas Aquinas share with others) that makes a crucifix bleed and speak to the adoring saint.
9. Cant 1.12, quoted by Bernard in *Sermon on the Canticles* 43.
10. Cant 1.6.   11. Cant 1.6.
12. 1 Cor 2.2; Bernard, *Sermon on the Canticles* 43.

(4) For the rest, O Eternal Wisdom, I lay up for myself this highest wisdom, that whoever may wish to have everlasting salvation and a wealth of rewards should choose to mount to the apex of all virtues, to gain both knowledge and wisdom, to stand equably between prosperity and adversity, to tread a safe path, and to want a foretaste of the bitterness of your Passion and the sweetest draught of your consolation. He must always carry you, Jesus, Jesus, I say, crucified, in his breast. O lovely jewel, chosen "more than gold and any precious stone,"[13] always to be worn "between the spouse's breasts," never to be consigned to oblivion. Never did any precious jewel so adorn some lovely girl who wore it on her bosom so much as the crucified Jesus, enclosed within the mind, makes the devout heart all beautiful. Jesus Christ in the heart of one who loves him is "apples of gold on beds of silver."[14] "A massive vessel of gold adorned with every precious stone,"[15] so is the fervent breast which can contain this name.[16]

(5) Wisdom: The frequent recollection of this Passion makes any dullard most learned, and it turns amateurs and simpletons into teachers, teachers, I say, not of "knowledge, which puffs up, but of love, which builds up."[17] The Passion is as it were "a book of life,"[18] in which all things necessary for salvation are found.[19] This book, more than the books of all the philosophers, "teaches all things,"[20] and its savor is as if it were all anointed with some honeyed sweetness. Does it not seem to you to be so? Do not now both your mouth and the lips of your heart, which it moistens, taste this sweetest honeycomb richly trickling down? Does not each single letter carefully

13. Ps 18.11.   14. Prv 25.11.
15. Ecclus 50.10.
16. The imagery of "Jesus" as a jewel to adorn the breast of a devout soul would certainly be related by Suso devotees to his story, in the *Vita*, of how he did cut the sacred monogram in his own flesh. In the *Horologium* Suso alludes briefly to this episode in Bk. II, ch. 7, below.
17. 1 Cor 8.1.   18. Apoc 3.5.
19. Cf. Thomas Aquinas, commenting on Heb 10.7: "This book is Christ according to his human nature, in which all things necessary to man for salvation are written" (*Exposition of the Epistle to the Hebrews*, ch. 10, lect. 1).
20. 1 Jn 2.27.

read seem to you to show itself like "storehouses of spices"?[21] Happy the man who will apply himself seriously to its study, for he will prosper in the world's contempt and in God's love, and he will receive an increase of every virtue and grace.

(6) Disciple: O most lovable Wisdom, nothing in this life could be sweeter to my heart, as you yourself know better than I, than that I might always weep for your Passion with a devout heart. But alas, I am enclosed in dryness and a certain hardness, so that I do not feel compunction as I should when I remember it; and therefore, O blessed Wisdom of the Father, teach me how else I should act with regard to this so precious matter.

(7) Wisdom: The recollection of my Passion should be made, not perfunctorily, nor with haste, especially when there is sufficient time and opportunity; but it should be done with mature and careful and heartfelt recollection, and with a certain mournful compassion. For unless this sweetest wood be chewed with the teeth of a loving discretion, its savor, however great, will have no effect at all. And even if you are unable "to weep with him who weeps,"[22] or to mourn with the mourner, at least with loving devotion you should rejoice and give thanks for so many benefits freely shown to you by the Passion. Even if you are not moved by a loving compassion and a desire to give thanks, but feel yourself, as you recollect it, oppressed by some hardness of heart, nonetheless, whatever hardness there may be, rehearse as well as you can the memory of this saving Passion to the glory of God, and what you are unable to receive by your own power, entrust into his most loving hands. And so persevere, asking, knocking, seeking, until you may receive.[23]

(8) "Strike twice upon the rock,"[24] that is, with inward recollection and with not less bodily labor, "exercising yourself into godliness,"[25] by directing your hands or your eyes up towards the crucifix, by striking your breast or devoutly bending your

21. Is 39.2.   22. Rom 12.15 and cf. Mt 11.17.
23. Cf. Mt 7.7.   24. Nm 20.11.
25. 1 Tm 4.7.

knees, or by other similar acts of piety, persisting till there come a plenteous flow of tears, so that reason too may drink of the waters of devotion, and that when devotion comes, your animal body may be kindled to receive grace. If perhaps you plead that only seldom do you experience this delectable state, which is "sweeter than honey and the honeycomb," it is not surprising that perhaps you are from time to time disturbed by temptations. You will act more like a man if you will pursue, with all your intention, that virtue, not for the sake of the delight that it may bring, but for virtue's own self, and only to be pleasing to God, even if you are not seeking this with your affections. For a state of love belongs to blessedness, exertion requires strength.[26]

(9) Know furthermore that frequent meditation on my Passion will promote for you two chief consolations among others which cannot be numbered: that is, it drives off inordinate sorrow, and lessens the punishment in purgatory. I shall show you better by example than by word how my sorrow can expel the spirit's sorrow. For there was a certain disciple of Wisdom, "may his name be in the book of life,"[27] whom at the beginnings of his conversion a certain inordinate sorrow oppressed so mortally that he could not read or pray or do any good deed at such times; but one day, sitting in his cell, when he was cruelly driven by this suffering, and afflicted with incredible sorrow, there came into his understanding as it were a voice from on high, saying: "What are you sitting here idle for,[28] wasting away in yourself? Get up, and think with devotion of all my Passion, and with the bitterness of what I suffered conquer what you are sorrowing over." Hearing this, that friar got up, and applied himself to meditating on the Passion, and from then on, cured by that healing medicine, never, through its continual repetition, did he feel any such suffering of his spirit.

26. This is almost literally from Bernard of Clairvaux, *Sermon 5 in Lent*, 7: ". . . They act much more manfully if they pursue virtues, not for the delight that they may feel, but for the virtues themselves, and only with complete intention of being pleasing to God, even if not with complete affection . . . . For such a state of love belongs to blessedness, exertion requires strength."
27. Phil 4.3.   28. Cf. Mt 20.6.

(10) And I shall show you how this most efficacious meditation has the power to relax the punishment of purgatory. For
the Author of nature leaves nothing disordered in that nature,
for divine Justice lets nothing whatever of evil go unpunished,
but subjects it to due correction either here or in the future.[29]
For when do you think that there ought to be an end to the
punishment of some sinner, guilty of many evil deeds, who
may not have achieved worthy satisfaction for a thousandth
part of whatever mortal sins he committed, to pay for which
he is condemned to go down into purgatory's infernal regions, until he has repaid "the very last farthing"?[30] O, very
long must such a wretched soul wait! O, enduring and very
sharp will its torments be, sorrow endless and measureless,
penitence heavier than every earthly torture.[31] But see how
the easiest and briefest satisfaction might compensate for this
punishment, if anyone knew how to obtain that satisfaction
from the treasury of the Passion of the immaculate Lamb. For
this richest treasury, because of his great love, his most worthy
Person and his most immense sorrow, is sufficient and superabundant; and therefore a man could in this way have recourse to that treasury, and devoutly draw for himself on the
Lamb's merits and satisfactions, so that even if he ought to
purge himself a thousand years long, in a short time he would
be set free from it all.

(11) Disciple: I beg, my Lord, that you may teach me, a
wretched and most needy sinner, this most useful skill, for
your goodness's sake; for, alas, my own merits are not enough,
so that it is very necessary for me to look to those of others.

(12) Wisdom: If you wish to change the punishment of purgatory, which is long and bitter, for that of this life, which is
easy and short, you should apply yourself to doing this: first
of all, with compunction in your heart and "an afflicted

29. Cf. *CG* III, ch. 140, 4: "It belongs to God's perfect goodness that he
should leave nothing disordered in things. . . . Therefore it is necessary that
human sins be divinely punished. . . ."
30. Mt 5.26.
31. This is the teaching of Thomas Aquinas, *Commentary on the Sentences*
IV, d. 21, q. 1, a. 1, qla. 3, c.

spirit,"[32] with weeping of the heart, consider most gravely the enormity of your sins, "acknowledging against yourself your injustice to the Lord,"[33] most bitterly recalling what you have done, whom you have offended, whatever you have deserved, saying: "Lord, 'I have sinned, I have committed more sins than there is sand in the sea.'"[34]

(13) Then you should humbly abase yourself before the eyes of the eternal Judge, and esteem yourself as vile, so that with the tax collector "you do not dare so much as to lift your impure eyes towards heaven,"[35] nor "with your unclean lips"[36] to name that glorious name, but only to count yourself "not even a man, but a worm"[37] impure, and to make nothing of your works of satisfaction, as if they were of no moment, and so, wretched and miserable, to wait outside his doors for the judge's grace, and with deep grief in your heart to say: "My Father, I have sinned against heaven and before you, and I am not worthy to be called your son; make me like one of your hired servants."[38] Then with greatest love you must extol and magnify the merit of my Passion, thinking that "with me there is plentiful redemption,"[39] and that the least drop of the most precious blood which flowed freely through my wounds in every part of my body would have been sufficient for the redemption and satisfaction of the whole world;[40] but I wished it to flow out copiously as a proof of my great love and my most overflowing pity, as the consolation of every wretched being.

(14) Then at last you must, with a love that is indeed humble but yet fervent, seek for the hand of your helper, and ask for the infinite merit of the most merciful redeemer as a support, never hesitating, for that fount of love is more apt in always flowing out in mercy, to you who are judged worthy of that mercy, than you are to entreat it.

(15) Disciple: O gracious Word, to be accepted above all others, by me and by those who are like me, wretched sinners,

---

32. Ps 50.19.   33. Ps 31.5.
34. From the Dominican Breviary for the second Sunday after Trinity.
35. Lk 18.3.   36. Is 6.5.
37. Ps 21.7.   38. Lk 15.18–19.
39. Ps 129.7.
40. This is the teaching of Thomas Aquinas, *ST* III, q. 46, a. 5, ad 3.

with the greatest joy, because when we come to this sight of your Passion, from which we can wash away our sins, we can find grace, and be made deserving of everlasting glory. "O, who will give me" only the least drop, as it were the briefest instant, of this most precious drink, the rosy "blood of the unblemished Lamb,"[41] in which to wash my wounds? All my powers, now be roused up if I may in some way obtain this saving medicine as a remedy for my sins. O bedewing drop, coming out from my Lord's little toe, O rosy droppings from the eaves of the royal hall, flowing out, that is, from the cleft in his breast, or even coming from the least pricking of his tender body, heal and make whole again the wounds of my sins. "Hail, O cross, our only hope,"[42] flooded over with noble blood. "Give to those who love you justice, and to the guilty pardon."[43]

(16) O most merciful Wisdom, as these "comforting words"[44] proceed from your mellifluous lips, a question that is not trivial strikes at my spirit, and my great love devoutly entreats that you may answer it. For you have said that by your Passion sufficient and superabundant satisfaction has been stored up for the human race. If this is so, why then is satisfactory punishment enjoined, why is there demanded punishment of a quality according to the quality of the fault?

(17) Wisdom: Because not only should a man seek after the effects of this Passion, he must be conformed to it. He is conformed to it by baptism, in which those who so renounce their past sins are freed entirely from them. But it is necessary that those who sin after baptism should be conformed to the suffering Christ[45] by some sort of punishment or suffering, which they should endure in themselves,[46] even though far less than what the sin deserves may suffice when the satisfaction we have spoken of cooperates.

(18) Disciple: Then let us return to this subject, so full of profit, from which we have digressed for so long, taking, from its fullness, occasion to consider so many mysteries.

41. 1 Pt 1.19.
42. From the Passiontide hymn *Vexilla regis*.
43. Ibid.   44. Zac 1.13.
45. Cf. Phil 3.10.   46. *ST* III, q. 49, a. 3, ad 2.

CHAPTER 15

How a True Disciple of Christ Ought to Conform Himself to Him in His Passion.

HEREFORE WHEN THE SONS of darkness had nailed me to the gallows of the cross, the hideous torments already laid upon me were not enough for them, but, raging more savagely, they stood around me as I lamented and died, and they "derided me,"[1] and "blaspheming me" they gestured at me, "wagging their heads,"[2] and with their insults afflicted me most hatefully in my misery. But I was not moved by what they did, but, enduring patiently, I said: "Father, forgive them, for they do not know what they do."[3] They hung me up, the Son of God, between two thieves, as if I were deserving of torment, and one of these, it is true, mocked me, but the other implored my protection, and I received him at once into my grace, and giving him pardon for his sins, I promised him a heavenly paradise. "I looked about, and there was no one to help.[4] They had all forsaken me,[5] for my acquaintances like strangers had departed from me."[6] For they stood "far off"[7] from what was happening and watched what men were doing with me. And indeed my brethren, in the anguish of my death, scattered and fled away from me. The tormentors dragged off my clothes and left me naked. The greatest "power of God"[8] and his Might, Christ the Lord, stood there in his wretchedness, as one deprived of all his strength, for they had mercilessly maltreated me with cruelest torments. "Yet I was as a meek lamb that is carried to be a victim,[9] and I was dumb

---

1. Lk 23.35.
2. Mt 27.39.
3. Lk 23.34.
4. Is 63.5.
5. Jer 2.29.
6. Jb 19.13.
7. Mt 26.58.
8. 1 Cor 1.24.
9. Jer 11.19.

and did not open my mouth.[10] I was hemmed in on every side";[11] miseries pressed on me everywhere, and wherever I turned I found sorrow.

(2) Then "there stood by the cross"[12] of her Son who hung there that most sorrowful mother, grieving with all her motherly love over each of my wounds, and bearing in her heart my torments and enduring my wounds. So hearing her weeping voice and her woeful lamentation, perceiving her "very great grief,"[13] moved with compassion, I lovingly consoled her; and commending a beloved mother to a beloved disciple, I gave the disciple to her as a son in place of me. How then the sword of sorrow pierced the inmost heart of my sweetest mother, how too the sword of grief transfixed the whole heart of her Son as he hung, no one can perfectly judge that.

(3) Disciple: O most cruel sorrow, most worthy of a deep compassion! O, the endless cruelty and hardheartedness of those who tormented you so monstrously! O cruel beasts, more savage than lions, more fierce than rapacious wolves, how could you so viciously torment that "meekest Lamb,[14] beautiful above the sons of men,"[15] noble and gently bred, loving and meek? O my God, if only your servant had been present when these things were being done, that the pity and compassion that they lacked might have been mine to supply! Truly, had that been possible, and the redemption of the human race might still have been accomplished, I should have offered my soul in return for your life, or I should have perished together with my beloved. Or indeed, if this had been refused, as I lay prostrate for sorrow and embraced with the arms of a most loving compassion the foot of the cross on which my love was dying, I should have wept and cried aloud until perhaps, when "the earth quaked and the rocks were rent,"[16] my lover's heart too would have been broken. O, how happily should I have left this earth, if, as my beloved died, I too with him might have been dead. Have you not recalled

10. Ps 38.10.   11. Dn 13.22.
12. Jn 19.25.   13. Jb 2.13.
14. Jer 11.19.   15. Ps 44.3.
16. Mt 27.51.

what Saul's armor bearer did, who on mount Gelboe, seeing his lord, entrenched against his enemies, die as was not meet, because he longed to give him his loyalty and his company, foolishly "fell upon his sword and died together with him?"[17] O, if a servant, seeing his master's unhappy death, died along with him, would not a lover, seeing his beloved faithfully die for him, the one he loved, have died with him? For how could he live, and not choose "to die manfully"[18] rather than live wretchedly? Therefore truly "my soul has chosen hanging, and my bones death."[19]

(4) Wisdom: I chose this hour for me to die from all eternity, so that then I might drink the chalice of my Passion alone, and that I should endure a death "for all men."[20] But now the time has come for everyone "who wishes to come after me to deny himself and take up his cross and follow me,"[21] and let him know for certain that this loving imitation will be as acceptable to me as it would have been if at that time he had stood fast by me and had died with me as I was dying.

(5) And see that this will be your cross, which you must carry if you want to be my lover. Whenever with all your power you apply your care to the exercise of virtues and the fulfillment of the divine commandments, and yet receive for this, from envious men, their scorn or detraction, and, what is more, in their eyes you become so vile and appear so despicable that they impute to you, not the virtue of patience or "the grace which is in you,"[22] but impotence and cowardice, and so that, wanting to vindicate yourself, you dare not and do not know how, still you must not only endure this patiently and willingly for God, but you must also, out of your superabundance of grace, apply yourself with greater zeal to praying for them to "the Father who is in heaven,"[23] and with devotion you must commend them to me, and show me that they are forgivable. Whoever may have conquered himself in this injurious conflict, for the glory and the imitation of the Crucified One,

17. 1 Kgs 31.1–5.
18. 2 Mc 7.5.
19. Jb 7.15.
20. 2 Cor 5.15.
21. Mt 16.24.
22. 2 Tm 1.6.
23. Mt 5.16.

should know that every time that he has done this, he has caused the death of the Lord to be enacted again as though it were new, and that he will carry my crucified image in him.

(6) And if, as you perform good works and walk in the Lord's path in innocence and simplicity, these good works of yours are spurned by envious persecutors, and they go on to say of you not good, but evil on every side, imputing much to you that is not true, never ceasing to slander your life to those who consider you worthy of honor, you must not be shaken by this, but rather gladdened, and continue to keep a loving heart for those who persecute you, so that you may be ready at all times with sincere affection and your heart's love to forgive every injury, so that it may be so wholly expunged from your memory as if it had never been done. And you should offer such men advice and timely help, for the love of him who not only forgave their offenses to those who wished him to be crucified, even though they were not laying hands upon him, but strove to help them by interceding with his Father for them. Whenever you do this for the love of God the Father, and master yourself, most surely and truly you have been there, crucified beside your crucified beloved.

(7) By fleeing the solaces of the world, and forsaking earthly profits and consolations for love of me, except in so far as necessity asks you to use them, you recompense me with this willing withdrawal for my abandonment, when I was deserted by all men. As often as you will leave your dear friends or kinsmen for the love of your Savior, you will take the place of my beloved disciple and brother, suffering with me beside the cross. When you strip yourself of your own will, that is the garments which covered my nakedness. Whenever it is your will to do nothing to those who attack or accuse and show hostility to you, and accept the anger and impatience of those who use wild words against you, patiently and with great sweetness of heart, gentle words and a cheerful countenance, so that your mild kindness may justly bring shame to your adversaries and their pride should be brought low by your humility, then truly will the image and likeness of my death shine out again in you. And through the example of my most faithful

mother and my beloved disciple, let the memory of my Passion be always with you, in your heart by recollection, in your prayer by devout consideration, and in your works by loving imitation.

(8) Whoever will do these things will be a true imitator of Jesus Christ, who will bestow on him an abundance of delights in his presence. "So let the sign of your love be what you show in your works."[24] Just now you were urging yourself to want to die in the body for me. Now your time has come. Hasten, hurry and accept in the spirit a death for me. O, how much will the heavenly Father glory in such a son, who has accepted this cross! O, how much will the teacher of teachers rejoice in so most faithful a disciple! With how much glory do you suppose that he will be lifted up in the heavens, a beloved one dying for him whom he loves, and so responding to his suffering, that "he may feel in himself that which was also in Christ Jesus,"[25] and of how much honor will he be considered worthy? For the companion of great tribulation will also be the companion of unmeasured consolation.

(9) Disciple: "I know, O Lord, that the way of a man is not his, nor is it in a man to walk and direct his steps."[26] Therefore I lift up my eyes and my hands to you, most loving Redeemer, devoutly entreating you that the image and likeness of your adorable Passion may be so fruitfully printed in me, your servant, that its healing effect may always work in me, to the praise and glory of your blessed name.

(10) For the rest, you see how all my soul is set "in the excess of my mind,"[27] and still remains waiting, watching you as you suffer, and longing to hear of the end of so doleful a passion, longing, too, to know if your suffering flesh may feel some alleviation of such a sorrow, as your divine nature flows in.

(11) Wisdom: Pay great heed to the answer to this question, which rightly ought to move your whole heart to compassion. In that hour, when I was bearing the fearful torments of death,

24. Gregory the Great, *Sermon 30 on the Gospels*, quoted in the Dominican Breviary for Pentecost Sunday.

25. Phil 2.5.   26. Jer 10.23.

27. Ps 30.23.

my soul found perfect delight in the Word; and yet my divinity permitted my flesh to do and to suffer what was proper to it;[28] and since my lower powers were being drained away, my capacity for suffering was greatly increased.

(12) See now the glory of the whole earth, hung up upon the cross, and with miseries beyond measure pressing in on him, I was hanging on the gallows, nailed immovably to the wood of the cross, desolate and deprived of every human help. But even my heavenly Father seemed in some way to have left me, since he did not help me, whom he would have helped, by showing "the greatness of his works."[29] My bloody wounds poured out gore, my eyes "grew dim with weeping,"[30] and all my entrails were consumed in my great torment. "I roared with the groaning of my heart,"[31] and there was no one to look on me. I wept bitterly, and there was no one who would dry my tears. Sorrows and malice had overwhelmed me, and there was no one to cherish me. I was praying, and they cursed me; I kept silence, and they mocked me; I endured patiently, and they blasphemed me. And as all around "the sorrows of death had encompassed me"[32] so, I cried out to the Father, saying: "My God, my God, why have you forsaken me?"[33] And yet the will of the Son as he hung there was always conformed to the will of the Father. "I thirsted,"[34] and there was no one who would offer "a cup of cold water"[35] to my parched soul, "but they slaked my thirst with vinegar mixed with gall."[36] Yet though my soul might be greatly afflicted for the anguish of my thirst, far more burningly did it thirst for man's salvation. And when "all things which had been written concerning me"[37] had been completed, "I was made obedient to death,[38]

28. This is the teaching of Thomas Aquinas (e.g. *ST* III, q. 46, a. 8, quoting John Damascene, *On the Orthodox Faith* III, ch. 15), but without the specific application, which later becomes common in the West, to Christ's divine nature increasing the capacity of his person for suffering.

29. Ecclus 17.7.   30. Jb 16.17.
31. Ps 37.9.   32. Ps 17.5.
33. Mt 27.46. Cf. Bk. I, ch. 11, n. 43, above.
34. Jn 19.28.   35. Mt 10.42.
36. From the Dominican Breviary for the Holy Week triduum, alluding to Mt 27.48 and Jn 19.29.
37. Lk 24.44.   38. Phil 2.8.

and bowing my head I gave up my spirit."[39] Nor was it enough for them to afflict me with sorrows while I still lived, but even when I was dead they sought to give me pain. For they pierced "my side with the point of a cruel lance,"[40] and from it "there came out blood and water,"[41] which suffused all my dead body. And so the life of the world was extinguished for the world, and with his precious blood he ransomed the human race, and "with his loving blood he washed away the crimes of long-time sinners."[42]

(13) Disciple: "O, truly great and inestimable love of charity!"[43] O, greatest and immeasurable sorrow of your most holy Passion, by which you, the Creator of the world, have redeemed us wretched ones! Would that I could now repay fitting praises to you. Would that I could be adorned with the prerogatives of all men now on earth or still to come or who have been and departed, that I might use them in serving you. "O, who will give me Solomon's wisdom,"[44] Samson's strength, Absolom's beauty, and the riches and glory and strength of all the princes of this world, so that I might offer all this, and much more than this, freely in the service of my Savior, "for an odor of sweetness"?[45] But, alas, what can "a dead dog"[46] do, or what thanks can a deaf mute utter?

(14) Wisdom: "If you speak with the tongues of men and of angels,"[47] if you were gifted to perform all men's good works, if you shone with the purity of all consecrated virgins, if you surpassed confessors and teachers, if you bore the banner of the martyrs, if you had the power of all created beings, you could not make worthy recompense to such a Redeemer, or repay the least drop of the blood that was shed for love of you.

(15) Disciple: "What therefore shall I repay to the Lord for all the things that he has given to me?"[48] O my God, teach, I beg, your servant how at least by your grace he may please you,

39. Jn 19.30.
40. Jn 19.30, and the Passiontide hymn, *Vexilla regis.*
41. Jn 19.34.   42. From the Easter Eve *Exultet.*
43. Ibid.   44. Cant 8.1.
45. Eph 5.2.   46. 2 Kgs 9.8.
47. 1 Cor 13.1.   48. Ps 115.12.

he who is deficient through his weakness and the pettiness of his works.

(16) Wisdom: You should always have the memory of my Passion in your heart, and offer to it all the tribulations and adversities that you suffer, and so far as that is possible, you should clothe yourself in its likeness. Then, when I take away from you, through my secret dispensation, your inward consolation, and leave you desolate, you should follow the example of my true crucifixion, not seeking consolation somewhere else, but waiting patiently and looking up to "the Father who is in heaven," forsaking yourself, and "casting all your thought on him."[49] Then there can be no doubt that, the greater the anguish of your outward self and the dereliction of your inward self, if this be united with God's will, the more you will be like to the Crucified One and accepted by that Father who is to be loved in all things. For this is truly adversity's central point, at which the best tried warriors placed in the vanguard of Christ are most strictly tested. "Do not go after your lusts,"[50] but beat them down in manly fashion; then you will drink "the gall of bitterness"[51] with your beloved. You should thirst for the salvation of all men, you should show devoted obedience to your superiors, you should direct all your works to produce the perfection of virtues and their due consummation. Then you should entrust to the mercy of God all misfortunes and every sorrow, and so bear yourself freely in everything you do, like a man who is preparing to pass from this world. You ought also to be seeking an abiding refuge in the wound of my side, like "a dove in the clefts of the rock,"[52] for in that place you will always find most copious forgiveness for your sins, the fullness of graces, and a safe shelter from every evil that threatens you.

(17) Disciple: Still I make one little petition, concerning your sweetest Passion, and it had to do with something that you touched on briefly in passing: how, that is, did your most

---

49. From the Dominican Missal for the first Friday in Lent.
50. Ecclus 18.30.   51. Acts 8.23.
52. Cant 2.14.

venerated mother, your most faithful begetter, bear herself, when she stood beside the cross and saw before her very eyes her beloved Son hung up there?

(18) Wisdom: For this, go to her, with my leave, and inquire carefully from her own lips what you want to know.

CHAPTER 16

A Special Commendation of the Blessed Virgin
and of Her Sorrow, Which is Beyond Price,
Which She Suffered in the Passion of Her Son

"HERE STOOD BY the cross of Jesus his mother."[1]
When in springtime the sun begins to climb to the
heights of heaven, and to pour on the lands the fecund shining of its rays, see how all nourishing plants, which
had been locked in winter's ice, begin to come alive again,
and every beast and bird, which had taken refuge in lairs and
caves and various hiding places, begins to breathe again, at
the dawning of so much light, and to regain its strength, and
to show the gladness of its heart in joyful songs and cries. And
the race of men, "the old and the younger,"[2] grow happy at
the coming of spring, and the whole surface of the earth is
clothed in beauty, and shouts for joy and renders thanks. Ah,
every heart that loves God with a pure intention, consider now
how the same thing has happened to us, when "she clothed
with the sun,"[3] a fruitful virgin, the Queen of heaven, forecho-
sen as the sun, enters the confines of our hearts, and recollection of her is poured, bright and cloudless, into our minds.
For always whatever is hard is melted before the immensity of
such a light, and all arid places are watered in the dew of
heavenly grace. The darkness is put to flight, a new light rises,
and all our joy's great causes are heaped up for us.

(2) Therefore to you, our hope, our joy and the gladness
of our heart, we miserable sinners call out in the voice of salu-
tation, and with all love we greet you, mother of grace, from
the depths of our heart, with weeping, with tears, with devoted

1. Jn 19.25.   2. Ps 148.12.
3. Apoc 12.1.

and loving abasement. Youths sing with joy to the organ's sound, and every heart grows glad at these happy notes, and I too burn with the fire of a divine love, for I am moved by your sweetest memory, and I long to praise you, who are lauded by "the whole world and its fullness,[4] the heavens of the heavens[5] and all their powers."[6]

(3) For the goodness of every creature, compared with your honor, is like the wan shining of the moon by night to the immense brightness of the sun. For divine Wisdom has adorned you so excellently with its grace, and has invested you so variously with its goodness, so that its incomprehensible wisdom, shining again in you, makes it more desirable to us because you reflect it. When in my mind I consider the illustrious men who from the beginning have praised you, my mind falters in amazement, and I have no spirit left. But when I come back to myself, I consider these things in my mind, and I say: "Ah, I salute you, loving Virgin, ornament of virgins. Whatever any tongue could say of your fame, whatever any pen had power to write, whatever any heart could think, if all these were together summed up and gathered into one handful of violets, but multiplied a hundredfold, to an infinite degree, that I proffer with a devout heart, with gold to adorn it, with sweet savor and pungent perfume, for your praising and glorifying, blessed Virgin, now and in eternity."

(4) When I look upon you, I seem to myself to be looking upon the heavens, glittering in their starry splendor, I think that I am inhabiting a paradise of pleasure, I forget myself in your greatness, I am amazed at the immensity of your glory, and with all my strength I cry aloud: "'O the depth of the riches of the wisdom and of the knowledge of God!'[7] With what a joyful heart did you exult, when for the joy of this world you shaped this noble creature in such perfect beauty!" O virginal eyes, shining with such brightness, O rosy cheeks, O locks shining with golden splendor. Most happy your lips, deified as they were showered by your Son with kisses. And even

4. Ps 49.12.
6. Ps 32.6.

5. Ps 148.4.
7. Rom 11.33.

though it be that everything in you was formed most prudently by the compass of divine Wisdom and most fittingly adorned, still to us wretched ones "your breasts from which you gave the Lord, the King, to suck"[8] taste more singularly sweet, for from them does life proceed, does sweetness emanate, which gives healing to every sick man.

(5) And so is she happy, that woman who pronounced words about this matter as true as they were joyful, calling out in the crowd and saying to the Savior: "Blessed is the womb that bore you, and the breasts which you sucked."[9] O, "blessed are the breasts which gave milk to Christ the Lord."[10] For it is over your plenteousness and your richest fecundity that the dwellers in heaven and on earth rejoice, and they are restored by your sweet fruits. They are like "two young twin roes, which feed among the lilies, till the day breaks and the shadows retreat."[11]

(6) See how the Founder of the universe adorned the celestial bodies with stars, the earth at its beginnings with beasts and birds, the woods with verdant foliage, the meadows with smiling flowers;[12] but far above all these, blessed Virgin, he made your body lovely with its most holy breasts. These are "the two olive trees,"[13] fair and richly bearing, giving the draft of grace, of milk and of honey to the beings of heaven and earth. Apples of snowy whiteness, made fruitful by the Holy Spirit, and gathered and tasted upon "the tree which is in the midst of paradise,"[14] they bestow the fruit of immortality. These are the golden "pomegranates,"[15] "the bowls and the lilies,"[16] making beautiful the temple of the true Solomon. The "pungent mandragora,"[17] planted in the garden of delights,

8. From the Dominican Breviary, from the response after the prayer *Sancrosanctae* to the Blessed Virgin Mary at the end of divine office.

9. Lk 11.27.

10. From the Dominican Breviary: the response to *Sacrosanctae*.

11. Cant 4.5–6.

12. This follows Bonaventure, *Soliloquy*, ch. 1, as do Eckbert of Schönau, *Meditations* ch. 2, and pseudo-Anselm, *Meditation XIII*, "Of Christ"; but none of the three makes this comparison with Mary.

13. Zac 4.3.   14. Gn 3.3.

15. Cant 4.13.   16. Ex 25.31.

17. Cant 7.13.

"the grapes of the vineyards of Engaddi"[18] bring joy to the hearts of wretched men, and drive their sadness away. For "your breasts are better than wine, smelling sweet of the best ointments."[19] For "in wine there is luxury"[20] and earthly delight, but in these golden phials there is the total extinguishing of the poison of concupiscence, and a delight that is heavenly and supernatural. Anyone who has tasted knows how swiftly and completely every carnal pleasure has vanished, once he has tasted the milk of your graces. Virulent serpents, terrified, fled from the fragrance of those ointments from above, and they could not endure the presence of such purity. Then "hearts which were filled rejoiced,"[21] fully satisfied with this unwonted gift. For the tongue fell silent but "the spirit rejoiced"[22] in the Lord. The eyes wept, pouring out sweet tears, but the mouth strove to retain yet longer this sweetest flavor and divinest drink, and to taste it again and again in loving recollection. Men's whole souls cried out together, saying: "For your breasts are better than wine, smelling sweet of the finest unguents." If anyone understands, let him understand.

(7) O mother most to be venerated, if we except the immense goodness of him whom you bore, who is Eternal Wisdom, for everything that you have is from him from whom every good thing comes,[23] yet there is something that the wretched soul seems to find more sweetly and gently for itself, when it takes refuge at your breasts "full of grace"[24] and sweetness, than when it tastes of that spiritual wine which Eternal Wisdom provides. For there perfect sweetness is tasted, but here a certain mixture of bitterness is sensed; and Eternal Wisdom fastens to the staff of consolation the rod of severe chastising. See, blessed mother, you could remark how often Wisdom soothed me by the sweetness of his words, as with a gentle draft of milk, and then afterwards struck fear into me

18. Cant 1.13.   19. Cant 1.1–2.
20. Eph 5.18.
21. From the hymn *Impleta gaudent viscera*, used in the Dominican Pentecost office.
22. Lk 1.47.   23. Cf. Jos 23.15.
24. Lk 1.28.

by its austerity, pouring into the drink as it were a sharp wine. Here are your "breasts of consolation,"[25] there Wisdom deals out the blows of a severe chastising. And when I have rejoiced to possess him as my dearest spouse, suddenly amazed to remember his divinity, I have entreated him as my Judge. And when from time to time I have asked him for milk, he has rejected me, and he has shown me a sour severity, as if to "a child that is weaned from its mother."[26]

(8) But what is there to say of you? Truly, "from the sole of your foot to the crown of your head,"[27] there is in you no trace of bitterness or austerity, but all that is in you is the purest sweetness, possessing incomparable gentleness, surpassing the fragrance and costliness of all perfumes and balms. You are all that is lovely and delightful, with nothing in you that is hard or severe. You are benign of countenance, serene of appearance, honeyed of words, "gentle and seemly,"[28] fecund in goodness, "full of grace." For in you is "all grace of the way and of the truth, in you is all hope of life and of virtue."[29] "Wine with milk" is sucked from Eternal Wisdom, but from you is received "the honeycomb with the honey," the purest sweetness. For what are these, your sweetest breasts? Truly, they are the bosom most kind in which you receive all sinners, and when sinners are received, you faithfully reconcile them with your Son.

(9) Oh precious treasure of the wretched! See, when by sinning we lose our great King, when we offend against the angels, when "we become burdensome even to ourselves,"[30] we do not know at all what we should do. There is only one course open to wretches, that we lift up our eyes, our heart and our body to you, seeking for counsel, begging for help. O exultation of my heart, sole hope and joy of my life, you know how often in bitterness of spirit, in disquiet of heart, with tearstained face, when I had offended God and thought that I should become a son of hell, I had been hemmed in on

25. Is 66.11.
27. Is 1.6.
29. Ecclus 24.25.

26. Ps 130.2.
28. Cant 6.3.
30. Jb 7.20.

every side by my enemies, and then I lifted my eyes to you, most loving Virgin, and with your help, blessed Virgin, I escaped every peril. Some may rejoice in their innocence, others may be glad of their plentiful merits, let others exult in God's mercy shown to them without intermediaries; but you, my mother, you are the only hope and solace of my life. When I completely despair of God and of myself, thinking of you, recalling you, my spirit comes alive again, as if out of the deepest darkness. You are my glorying, my well-being, my honor and my life. But whence, O my hope, is this given to me? Indeed, it is because you have many dear sons whom their innocence will be able to save, whose own good works will intercede for them, who can say with the just man: "My heart has never reproved me in all my life."[31] But O, the unmeasured sorrow and grief of my heart! Sweetest mother, and our mother, mother especially of us, I say, who are miserable sinners, you know that all my life is nothing but reproach. Ah, look on me, your sick man. "I am not worthy to be called your son,"[32] but make me to be like one of your miserable sufferers. Remember, loving mother, that mothers are accustomed to cherish their ailing children with greater care, to sympathize more with them, and to give them a more constant attention. "To you is the poor man left; you will be a helper to the orphan."[33] My wounds are known to you, loving mother. Do you visit your sick, raise up the dead, and give your solace to the mourning. Let them come to the light of Wisdom, those who have lived "in righteousness and holiness."[34] Alas for me, for I am a wretched sinner, all bedewed with my tears; but I flee to your shelter, not daring to show myself naked and beggared in the presence of so much light, but with you, my mother, I take refuge.

(10) You are my hope, my tower, and you I have set up as the goal of all my health. If, God forbid, he, the angry Judge, should wish to damn your servant as guilty of sin, let him do this only with your most loving hands. But if by his grace he

31. Jb 27.6.   32. Lk 15.19.
33. Ps 9.14.   34. Lk 1.75.

will decree that I am to be saved, let him deign to send me salvation by your means. I never want to be separated from you, not alive or dead, not in prosperity or in adversity. Even if, which God forbid, I shall wish to forget him, should I become an outcast madman, truly I shall never forget you, I shall never leave you. In my mouth your memory grows "sweeter than honey and the honeycomb," my countenance rejoices in you, my heart grows joyful, and then my whole strength exults. Nor is this unmerited, for how often I am filled "from the breasts of your consolation" you know, loving one who have brought to me, a miserable sinner, such saving remedies. "Turn then, our advocate, your eyes of mercy towards us,"[35] rise up, rise up, O loving one, propitious one, and reconcile us to your only Son whom we have so often offended, for you are the advocate of the guilty. Therefore go closer to him, and ask on our behalf, we beg you, for that Son so gracious, to you so beloved, will not be able to deny you anything.

(11) O everlasting Wisdom of the Father, see how I bring now before you as my protection her, your sweetest mother, presenting her to you and hiding behind her back, "not daring to raise my eyes"[36] to the face of your glory, but asking to be heard through her. Honor her, I beg, venerate her. How could you fittingly spurn such a mother? Even if she were to appear a thousand times in a day, she will not be turned away. Hear me, hear me, Lord, because of your goodness, and because of the singular honor of your dear mother. For just as I show you as my advocate to the heavenly Father who begot you, so I show her, your dear mother, as my patroness, to you, so that when she appears, so great, so welcome and acceptable to you, she may make good "my imperfect being."[37]

(12) So now, O brightest Wisdom, consider your glorious mother. Look into the eyes of this sweetest mother, intervening before you for us, on whom she looked so mildly as she bore you in her motherly bosom, see her cheeks, flushed "with rosy color," which she pressed to your tender face in her ma-

---

35. From the *Salve regina*.   36. Lk 18.13.
37. Ps 138.16.

ternal love. Ah, how happy are her lips, with which she kissed again and again your blessed mouth, your shining eyes, your most comely limbs, mingling sometimes her tender kisses with her words. Look on these hands which tended you, these sweetest and most happy "breasts which gave you suck." O most loving sweetness, it is not right that you should see and remember these things, and should then refuse anything to such a mother, who gave birth to you, the Lord of heaven, fed you, cherished you and brought you to manhood. Remember, I beg, all the care and the nurture that you received from her in your infant years, when she nursed you in her bosom as a tender babe, and you turned your laughing little eyes on the mother who smiled at you, and with your most tender arms embraced her, beaming on you, and loved her most dearly and before all others. And remember all the sorrows that she bore in her mother's heart, moved by her loving compassion as she stood beneath the cross.

(13) For "there stood by the cross of Jesus his mother." O, words full of compassion! For how much, O my heart, ought they to move you in all your depths, the sorrows and afflictions of so loving a Savior hanging upon the cross, and yet decreeing, for us alone, that we who were once enfolded in the darkness of our sins have now been led back again to the light, with the help of the Mother of God. It is fitting to suffer with such a mother standing by the cross, bearing in her heart to the full the boundless sorrow of her suffering Son, and in some way, more special and more particular, to endure with her all that our innermost hearts could feel. It is indeed just that we, who in our miseries are constantly consoled by her, should also suffer with her in her sorrows. And even if we may not suffer with her as we should, at least, by calling to mind her dolor, let us stir up in faith, so far as we can, our heart's devotion. The depths of the grief of that loving mother we do not know, but let us seek from afar, by surmising them, from the sorrows that we have been shown. So let every lover ask himself how much he would be made to mourn, if he were to see whatever it is, so lovable, which he loves so deeply, given over to a shameful death, and with what vehement compassion

he would be moved, even though a heart that does not love should find in itself nothing like this. Let a loving mind turn these things over, and from this he will well believe all that can be said of the sorrow of her who loved and mourned, more than all mortal men, when she saw her dear one condemned to the vilest death.

(14) O Mary, what was in your heart, when you stood by the cross and saw, hung up like that, "Jesus, the blessed fruit of your womb"? Truly, reason insists, experience proves, and the power of love confirms that you mourned greatly. You mourned greatly, because you loved greatly. If then no more than the memory of your Son's Passion has brought such great compassion to some of the devout that it has almost killed them, what did the reality of that most cruel Passion do to her who had born him, the Savior of the world who suffered then? If the memory of this burns so in a sinner's heart, how much must it have raged in the mind of the most holy mother? Blessed Virgin, we know that the more that anyone who has made trial of love has love, fervent love, for his beloved, and the more that the beloved's presence brings him honor and delight and benefit, the more does his sadness increase when the beloved is taken away. But truly and without any doubting, I believe that the glad presence of your beloved one surpassed beyond compare in every joy the presence of all mortal men.

(15) But let that mother now recall to us that if she held her Son in such great love, she could find in him the cause of her joy, as also of her sorrow. Let her now come forward in our midst, and tell us in her own words, "absent indeed in body, but present in spirit,"[38] and say: "He who had deigned in his grace to elect me, his humble serving maid, to be his mother, he had pressed my heart to him in a most burning love, so that nowhere except from him and in him could my spirit receive such total joy, such total sorrow. For in him I had possessed all things, and his love was for me full possession of the whole world. Where Jesus was, there was my soul, and I lived in him more than in myself. To look upon him, 'fairer

38. 1 Cor 5.3.

than the sons of men,' was the delight of my heart; it was a
gentle sweetness to gaze on his divinity. To think of him
brought joy to me, it was my sweetest solace to speak of him,
and to hear the words from his mouth was to me the sweetest
music. He was the mirror of my heart, and the vision on which
my eyes gazed. For his presence, which I desired, gave to me
every heavenly and every earthly good that he possessed.

(16) "So when I saw him, my only-begotten Son, the precious treasure of my heart, as I looked up to him, hung up on
a cross among thieves with such contempt, and oppressed with
the sorrows of death, ah, how unbearable was this sight to me,
O, how lamentable and tormenting it was for me to look on
this! My soul was crucified with sorrow, my mother's heart was
pierced, and all my bones perished with my Son's death. All
my strength failed, my senses left me, and vast disaster overcame me. I lifted up my tear-dimmed eyes, I saw my dear one
hung up there, nor could I bring him any comfort. I turned
my eyes from the cross, and with immeasurable sorrow I saw
those who had carried my treasure off by force, and were so
cruelly afflicting and tormenting him. O, how was my soul
oppressed within me, with what great sorrow was it crucified!
I had no heart, for he had taken it away[39] and kept it, crucified
with his. I had cried aloud and wailed so much that I had little
voice left with which to speak. I failed for sorrow, I sank down
for grief. But when at last I came a little to myself, I broke out
into 'these words and others like them': O joy and exultation
of my spirit, 'light of my eyes,'[40] once I would look on you with
the rejoicing and exultation of my heart, yet now only with
immense sadness and grief. Alas, alas, how dolefully do I see
you now hanging. O, one half of my soul, O, single consolation
of my life! Take with you, I beg, your most afflicted mother,
for I greatly long to die, I can no longer live without you. Do
not abandon me, my sweetest Son, but take me with you. "O,
who will grant me that I might die for you?"[41] O, the incomparable sorrows of a mother bereft, the dereliction of a parent

39. Cf. Ez 11.19.   40. Ps 37.11.
41. Cant 8.1; 2 Kgs 18.33.

left alone! For now I see him die, in whom is all my life and my health."

(17) As the most sorrowful mother uttered these words of affliction, "and others like them," her Son in some fashion forgot his own sorrow, and most sweetly consoled his mother. "Dying and departing, he took his leave of me, and commended me to the disciple whom he so singularly loved. When my mother's heart heard the voice of my Son speaking, it began to burn with the greatest of sorrows, and 'the sword of affliction pierced'[42] the soul of his most faithful mother. In the longing of my heart I lifted up my hands, seeking to touch my beloved, if perhaps in that way I could better reconcile sorrow with love. But when I might have no other solace, I greedily kissed the hot blood dropping from my Son's wounds upon the earth, so that his mother's face grew bloody with the gore of her slaughtered child.

(18) "O, if you had seen in that lamentable hour the wretchedness of a mother, suffering with her Son the sorrow of the Son as he mourned with his mother! You could not have heard or looked on that without your heart being wounded with compassion for the mother mourning for her dying Son, the Son sweetly consoling his desolate mother. So at length, when the Son had breathed his last, when he was taken down from the cross, O how lovingly did I lift up his arms as they hung down, and clasp my dead Son to my mother's bosom, embrace him in my mother's love, bedew with tears his dead face, and with many kisses his fresh wounds. This was a pitiable thing, that I saw there the life of my heart, and he was dead. I looked at him again and again, 'and there was no voice or sense.'[43] I spoke to him, and he made no reply to me. 'I called aloud with the groaning of my heart.'[44] For there were those standing there who wished to take away from me my dear dead treasure, and to bury him; and then I wept and mourned and uttered lamentable cries. My heart was breaking with sorrow, as they sought to prise my dear Son loose, clutched in his mother's

42. Lk 2.35.					43. 4 Kgs 4.31.
44. Ps 37.9.

arms. I pressed my tearstained face to his, I took his face in my hands time and again, I looked into it repeatedly, and I groaned, for 'I was full of bitterness.'[45] No one could see this and not suffer with a mother suffering so. At last, after my Son was buried, I was led away in the greatest of grief. But at his Resurrection, when I saw him so glorious, I received full consolation, and so the cause of my sorrow changed into the cause of my spiritual joy." These are all the Virgin's words.

(19) Yet now the force of our compassion, and the vehemence and plenty of the many tears with which from the depths of our hearts we sorrow with you, O loving Virgin, forces us, who could not hear these things without groaning and weeping, to interrupt your words. O, how stony is the heart that does not feel with you in its very depths, how coldly dry are the eyes that can see you weeping so, and have no tears to shed, how icy the breast that does not groan for these things! O, if only all our bones might perish together with you! Blessed your arms, in which I see him who is so loved now reclining, blessed your rosy smiling mother's cheeks, blooming with glowing hue, blessed indeed above all your mother's breast, which found room for so much sorrow, and upon which my heart's eyes now see my king reposing. O, "couch of gold,"[46] elect before every throne of ivory, every golden chair, preserved until this very hour, that you might hold "the Author of life"[47] who is deprived of life.

(20) But what shall I say? See, most loving mother, how, my mind filled with grief, I come before you to entreat and adjure you in the Lord's name that you will grant me that, meditating, I may see your dearest treasure, my King and my Lord, who suffered and died for me, in the form in which you held him to your bosom beneath the wood of the cross, pallid and bruised all over, that the same compassion and sorrow that was then granted, bodily and in that place, to you as his mother may be allowed to me, at least spiritually and in recollection, as is fitting to a wretched sinner. Give me my Savior. Show me

---

45. Lam 1.20.   46. Cant 3.10.
47. Acts 3.15.

him whom I love, for I can no longer wait. Take now, my soul, him whom you love from her whom you love, and show to him the signs of your dearest love and compassion.

(21) O my dear one, "my salvation"[48] and "my helper,"[49] my love and the glorying of my soul, see now how I turn to you, with a most burning love, withdrawn from all things, with all the powers of my soul one single power, see how I gaze earnestly at you with all my mind and soul, see how you are regarded with the greatest kindness that ever a lover could show to his beloved. See, my dear one, my heart is a resting place for you alone to recline in, it is shut to this world, it can be opened only when you speak, longing to receive you when you come gently in. I open my arms wide to you with all my longings, like a rose which is closed to the chill of the night but hastens to open to the sun's radiant splendor. My soul warms with a perfect love, it opens its longing arms to embrace the whole of you, it hastens rejoicing towards you, and as its tears flow down it falls into your spiritual embrace.

(22) Ah, my whole health as now I receive you with a desire that burns so ardently, as I enfold you in my soul's arms and am made one with you in a most fervent love, with reverence and praise and thanks, I entreat you that out of the depths of your mercy you will not permit this your precious death to have been died in vain for me, but that you will take me to your grace, and unite me with you so mightily that neither good fortune nor bad can ever separate me from you. See how my eyes are fixed upon your pallid face, all my soul is set free for your love, I kiss your bloody wounds again and again, and all my strength and powers feed on the fruits of this dolorous Passion. But now I have "sat down under his shadow whom I have long desired, and his fruit is sweet to my palate."[50] And so this should be. For there are some who rejoice in their purity of life, others rely on their many merits, or rejoice in their countless spiritual exercises. But what should I do? Truly, all my hope and all my consolation depend upon your Passion,

48. Ps 61.8.   49. Ps 17.3.
50. Cant 2.3.

upon your great and precious merits, and on the most kindly love of your mother, as you alone know, who have had regard for my beggared state. And so for me to recall the Passion of my Lord is to store it up lovingly, in my heart's home, and with my words and my deeds to seek for it as I ask for the help of grace, and to extol it with every praise and worship.

(23) "O King of kings and Lord of lords,"[51] whom with faith's sight my soul now most lovingly embraces, mortified so and afflicted with miseries, grant me that my soul may merit to look on you forever, glorious and sublime and seated above the stars of heaven at the Father's right hand.

(24) But you too, blessed Virgin, most loving mother, who stood beside the cross of your Son, and received the wounds of his sorrow in your soul with all your senses, and were sprinkled red with his blood, and alone ministered to him with perfect faithfulness until his death, and were taken away from your Son's tomb with great sorrow, I call to your mind once again all the wounds of your compassion, because they are a glory to you alone, loving Virgin. And as I now receive you, O mother to be venerated, with devout love into my heart's embrace, and weeping with you the tears of compassion, lead you back through the gate of the city that was once Jerusalem to your house, following the example of those who once enacted these things, so, O mother of grace, in my last hour of agony, may my soul and the souls of all the disciples of Eternal Wisdom be received by you, as they pass out of this body's lodging, and be led with joy to that city which is the heavenly Jerusalem. Amen.

Here ends the first book.

51. Apoc 19.16.

BOOK II

HERE BEGINS THE SECOND BOOK.

CHAPTER 1

Of the Marvelous Variety of Teachings
and of Disciples

HERE WAS a certain avid disciple of Wisdom who "sought out the wisdom of all the ancients, and enquired into the sayings of renowned men. He longed to know the subtleties of parables, and sought out the hidden meaning of proverbs, he gave his heart to watch early for the Lord who made him,"[1] entreating that he would not permit him to pass from this life before he might come to know true, sublime philosophy. Meanwhile, as he proceeded from one branch of study to another, seeking eagerly everywhere for what he thirsted for, and finding nowhere what he sought, but only its image, on one occasion it seemed to him that he saw what looked like a golden sphere, amazingly vast in extent and beautifully adorned with gems, in which there lived countless masters and students of all the arts and sciences. But in this sphere two separate mansions had been built, and either of them had its own teachers and disciples.

(2) The first, which was also the lower, which was that of the liberal arts and the applied sciences, contained a great multitude of all kinds of philosophers. There the astrologers played about with their astrolabes, the physicists examined with subtlety natural phenomena, the geometricians were busy measuring, musicians were devising harmonies for voices, and every faculty was discussing the subjects belonging to it. The medical men talked about their medicine, the mechanics about mechanical matters.[2] But they all seemed to have as it were "a veil over their faces,"[3] and as they labored

1. Ecclus 39.1–6.
2. Horace, *Epistles* 2.1: "medical men undertake medical work, mechanics mechanical matters."
3. 2 Cor 3.13.

with most burning zeal, they refreshed themselves from a sweet-tasting goblet, which, however, did not fully quench their thirst, but made them dry and always thirstier still. And when this Disciple had remained in these schools for a little while, this goblet of which he had tasted began to produce a nausea in him.

(3) For this reason he withdrew, and went up to the second mansion. It was very lovely, and adorned with a wonderful variety of pictures. And as he stood outside its door he could see written above: "This is the school of theological truth, and here is the mistress, Eternal Wisdom, who is teaching what is truth, and the end, which is eternal felicity." When he read this, he hastened to enter the academy, longing with all his heart to be one of its pupils, for he hoped through it to attain his desired end.

(4) There were in this school three divisions of students and teachers.[4] Some sat near the door on the ground, listlessly staring out to the street. The honeyed words proceeding from Wisdom's mouth were turned in theirs to a bitter liquid, of which they drank till they were drunk, and looked to be swollen with wind, so that at once they became puffed up with pride, and strutted around like kings, soliciting for all kinds of headships and degrees and asking for promotions, and "dealing in great matters and in wonderful things, which were above them."[5] All they were interested in was speculation about what can be known, and they were utterly cold to true love. From their mouths there came what seemed like the finest flour,[6] and "they wove fine linen."[7] Their voice was like "sounding brass or a tinkling cymbal,"[8] dinning at men's ears,

4. Hugh of St. Victor in his *Pursuit of Learning* V, ch. 10, distinguishes between three types of students of Sacred Scripture: those who study to obtain a professional qualification, those moved merely by intellectual curiosity, and those who seek support for the Faith.

5. Ps 130.1.

6. Suso may be recalling Is 47.1–2: "O virgin daughter of Babylon . . . take a millstone and grind flour." Gregory the Great writes that the "daughter of Babylon" here typifies "an unfruitful human mind" (*Morals* VII, ch. 16), and medieval exegetes commonly drew a general moral application from Isaias's castigation of the Egyptians' luxuriousness, symbolized by their "fine linen."

7. Is 19.9.   8. 1 Cor 13.1.

but hardly reaching their hearts at all. Before their eyes there were demons disporting themselves, dancing like black Ethiopians,[9] and offering them always "the chairs of honor."[10] To some they showed gold and silver and vast possessions. Some they clothed in long and gaily-colored robes, and put fine hoods on their heads, and sent them off along the path of ambition. They walked around with frowning faces and "staring eyes,"[11] shaking their heads and lifting warning fingers, as if they had surpassed all men in wisdom, mouthing to declame their own pride, and so they studied wisdom and lived unwisely, and they were cunningly deceived by their enemies. All of these men longed and strove for one thing, to climb and to show off. For they toiled at their studies for one reason alone, so that at the end they might be more free to obtain the bodily ease they desired, and have every licence to do as they pleased without opposition. For who would dare to provoke a roaring lion?

(5) What the Disciple found in this mansion amazed him, and made him want to laugh. For there was what seemed like a silver ball that had fallen among them from the sky, rolling around, which by its beauty and costliness made all of them gaze on it in love and longing, for it promised glory and honor to those who could possess it. And when one outstanding teacher had it in his hand, and through this his fame resounded through the whole world, and his teachings shone brighter than all others, like a rose without thorn and a cloudless sun,[12] many, seeing this and envying it, tried in every way they might to snatch the ball from his hand. Now they threw sharp darts[13] at him, and now hard stones, but it did not help them, for they were inflicting astonishing hurts on themselves, and wounding themselves with their own darts. When this ball

9. Demons were commonly described, and depicted, as negroes, by the Desert Fathers and thereafter.

10. Ecclus 7.4.   11. Jb 15.12.

12. Numerous manuscripts here have a note observing that this refers to Thomas Aquinas; he was evidently the first to be given the appellation used here, *doctor egregius*, and he is sometimes depicted with a sun (though more commonly a star) as his attribute.

13. Cf. Ps 119.4.

bounced round among them, those who were present were at pains, not indeed to grasp it for themselves, but rather to do all they could to knock it out of each other's hands, and steal it away and advertise that someone else did not have it. They offered no explanations of what it was, but they wrapped it up in their own implications. And there were among them, it is shameful to say, astonishing arguments and uproars and contradictions about this ball, and in the minds of many who were listening this produced great boredom and distaste. For they derived no benefit from these things, but complained that they were at some sporting event or stupid show. And some of them mocked the others, and they wore themselves out with wordy warfare,[14] and attacked each other and sparred like fighting bantams.

(6) And when the Disciple asked from the bystanders what all this spectacle was about, someone replied that this silver ball was supposed to signify the truth of Sacred Scripture, lucid and clear-sounding and incorruptible. And he added: "Some present-day scholars spend more pains in attacking it than seeking it, for some of them do not seem to be working to acquire it, but trying with all their might to prove that someone else does not possess that truth at all, and by this they try to advance themselves and put down someone else. And so they manufacture refutations, rejoinders and astonishing newfangled opinions, which do more to surprise those who hear them than to give them anything useful. For the truth which they should have unfolded for their listeners they wrap up in what they are driving at and their unheard-of language, and for the sake of empty display for the most part they hide the truth out of sight."

(7) Furthermore, there were those among them who were in a great hurry to teach what they had never learned, not by study or by meditation.[15] What they taught was based not on their way of life or on what they had assiduously practiced, but

14. "wordy warfare": *pugnae verborum*: 1 Tm 6.4.
15. Gregory the Great, *Pastoral Care* I, ch. 2: "They are in a great hurry to teach what they have not learned by study or by meditation."

only on what they asserted. For they spurned the writings of
the holy fathers, which in times past, when religious life was
strong and devotion flourished, were in constant use, such as
The Conferences of the Fathers and other such seeds of devotion,
in which are contained its foundations and its spiritual science
and the sum of all perfection, to draw man to compunction
and self-knowledge and the restoration of his lost devotion
and godly fervor, which they spurned, and turned to what had
been written to serve ambition or greed. And if they ever did
look at the old books, it was not so that they might gain fresh
graces of devotion, but so that they might better achieve some
end on which they were already determined. They were full
of empty desires, chiefly for their own advantage or profit,
and they were looking for human rewards, and so, alas, they
had no hope in themselves, no neighbors whom they loved
more than themselves, for they thought that they were better
than the very fathers, and so they paid no heed to the study
of devotion. They allowed the books that contained this kind
of purest devotion to rot away in disuse; their only study was
in turning over volumes of sermons, assessing the value of any
that could perhaps fill their own purses, and so these miserable creatures under "an appearance of godliness"[16] neglected
their own souls. And yet, like some useless fig tree,[17] which has
indeed many leaves but lacks fruit, they gave little benefit to
the people. They were men of many leaves, their words, but
they remained sterile in the fruit of devotion.

(8) Furthermore, some from the front rank of these pupils,
when the promotions that they had desired had come their
way, then dressed themselves up like hypocrites in a seemli-
ness of living and of moral conduct, suitable for men to see,
as if they were some "worldly sanctuary,"[18] "but denying its
power."[19] For they were seeking their own peace, and pretend-
ing to seek that peace in the salvation of souls, but what they

16. 2 Tm 3.5.
17. Bede in a sermon (still accepted as genuine) on Mk 11.13–17 says
that the fig tree was cursed, not for bearing no fruit out of season, but as a
"figure" of those putting the Temple to evil uses.
18. Heb 9.1.   19. 2 Tm 3.5.

did was most sluggish and careless. They attracted to themselves like-minded friends, and promoted their interests more
than was just, for they dared to hope with their support to
establish their rule for ever. Blinded with self-love, they did
not perceive the worm devouring the vitals of their spiritual
life; their only concern was how they could simulate to the
outside world and to their subjects a semblance of decent living, just sufficient for salvation, but yet conceal their inward
lack of the life-giving Spirit. They destroyed some of the idols
set along the roadside, yet "they did not take away the high
places."[20] For if there were perhaps something to be corrected,
from which they feared danger, or if they feared even unpopu-
larity, but could not easily pretend not to see it and pass by,
they would refuse themselves to take action, but would leave it
to deputies, and they entrusted matters, which they like giants
could have destroyed with one finger, to be carried out by a
set of pigmies. But they, when they saw how things beyond
their strength were laid on them, passed by, and did either
nothing or less than they should have done.

(9) It is true that these superiors, when they saw such glaring
shortcomings in their subjects, wanted to put such matters
right, but without themselves making any effort; and so they
multiplied the regulations, doubled the number of directions,
and "laid heavy and insupportable burdens on their shoulders, but would not move them with a finger of their own."[21]
This made their subjects more case-hardened and grudging,
and in return they attributed their faults to their superiors'
neglect. For the superiors were not those who "first passed
over"[22] to lay low the enemy, to fight foremost in the vanguard;
but they were the ones who filched for themselves whatever
might bring honor or profit or worldy ease. They did not consider that it is practically impossible for men who have lost
their fervor to be reformed by words alone, but rather by good
works and living examples. If they had forsworn arriving at
their subjects' houses in such pomp, and putting them to

20. 3 Kgs 22.44.   21. Mt 23.4.
22. 1 Mc 5.43.

wasteful expense, those who wanted to put others to rights, if
they had conducted themselves simply and humbly and fru-
gally, and had shown by their words and example that they
were first applying themselves to everything that they wanted
to impose on others, they would indeed have achieved much.
But since their whole effort was for them to say a lot and do
little, it was as if they had grasped a snake by its slippery tail,
and it was not only that they were not succeeding, but they
saw themselves daily going from bad to worse. And all these
men were enrolled in the first division of students in the second house.

(10) Yet those who were in the second division seemed to
remain in their proper place, and the third division were
seated beside their master, and as they drank "the water of
wholesome Wisdom"[23] from his mouth, they grew so drunk
that they forgot themselves and everything else, and with heart
and mind they turned their eyes and their faces on high, and,
in some way immersed and absorbed in the depths of divine
speculation and sweetness, they were carried off to the contemplation of divine things. They shone in this world like a
starry sky, they leapt upwards like a torch's flames, themselves
burning and enkindling their neighbors till they blazed in
God's love. And such men were found most serviceable as
superiors and directors, for they were wonderfully furnished
with divine grace and human industry.

(11) So when the Disciple had most carefully pondered
these things, he was filled with greatest wonder what this might
be, and especially how it happened that out of the same truth
such distortions could be produced in different disciples. And
then he recognized a voice that seemed to say to him: "The
three divisions that you have seen are three ways of studying
and teaching Sacred Scripture. The first way is carnal, which
those men practice in whom the letter abounds without the
spirit. The more knowledge of letters they acquire, the more
are they swollen with pride, and they are known as harmful to
themselves and to others, for they are seeking, not to praise

23. Ecclus 15.3.

God or to edify themselves and others, but to gain promotion. The second way is animal, and it is seen in those who are seeking, "with a single eye,"[24] it is true, to find in academic exercises those things which are necessary to salvation, yet they utterly neglect to perform the works of supererogation and "to be zealous for the better gifts."[25] But the third way is spiritual, and it is followed by those who exert themselves with all the love of their hearts and with all their might to attain the things that belong to perfection, taking care and pains that their love may be as full of divine Wisdom as their intellect is full of knowledge, and so they advance in perception of the truth and also in love of the highest good. They "taste and see how sweet the Lord is,"[26] they direct themselves and others through Sacred Scripture to the due end, and no less are they led inwardly "by the spirit of God."[27]

(12) So the Disciple, passing all others by, longed to make his dwelling with them, and to devote himself entirely to the study of that true and highest philosophy.

24. Mt 6.22.   25. 1 Cor 12.31.
26. Ps 33.9.   27. Rom 8.14.

CHAPTER 2

Of the Knowledge Most Profitable to a Mortal Man, Which Is to Know How to Die.

INCE ALL MEN by nature seem to wish to know,[1] O highest and Eternal Wisdom, and since you, the universal leader and Author of nature, "in whom are hidden all the treasures of wisdom and knowledge,"[2] to whom our words are addressed, are "the Maker of all things," possessing all knowledge, "overseeing all things,"[3] I beg this of you with my heart's avid desire, that you will open to me all the treasure of your wisdom "and the knowledge of holy things,"[4] and that you will instruct me in these great things, and that you will make these most subtle and profound matters which must now be discussed the center of your teaching.

(2) Wisdom replied: "My son, 'do not wish to know exalted things, but fear.'[5] Listen to me, and I shall teach you what is useful. 'I shall give you the gift you should choose.'[6] My teaching will itself be your life. Therefore I shall teach you these things in proper order, starting from that saving discipline that comes from 'the fear of the Lord, which is the beginning of wisdom':[7] first, how a man should die, then how he should live; afterwards how you should receive me sacramentally, and finally how you ought always to praise me with a pure mind."

(3) To this the Disciple said: "My Lord, this is what I have always wished for, and have sought in all my prayers. O, if only I knew these most useful arts, to die happily, that is, and to live well, to receive you lovingly and to praise you devoutly, what more should I want to ask for? But I beg you to tell me

1. Aristotle, *Metaphysics* A, ch. 1, several times quoted by Thomas Aquinas.
2. Col 2.3.
3. Wis 7.21, 23.
4. Prv 9.10.
5. Rom 11.20.
6. Cf. Prv 4.2; Wis 3.14.
7. Ps 110.10.

what profit there is in this teaching about how to die, since death is looked on not as an acquisition but a deprivation."

(4) Wisdom answered: "'It is a great advantage in every way.'[8] This knowledge is most useful and is to be preferred to all the arts, the knowledge, that is, of dying. For it is common to all men to know themselves to be mortal, since 'there is no man who may live forever, or who may have hope of this.'[9] Yet you will find very few indeed who seem to know how to die, for this is God's greatest gift of all. For to know how to die is to have one's heart prepared, and one's soul always directed on high, so that whenever death may come, it will find the heart ready, and will unhesitatingly accept the soul, as if it were someone awaiting the coming of his dear friend. But, alas, among some religious, just as with foolish men of the world, you will find very many who have such a horror of their death that they scarcely wish to be reminded of it. They do not want to leave this world, because they have not yet learned how to die. They spend much of their time talking nonsense and jesting and making filthy remarks, and in other such utterly empty matters, and then when death suddenly comes upon them, because it finds them ill-prepared, it wrests the wretched soul from the body and leads it off to hell, just as, time and again, it would have put its halter on you and have wanted to lead you off with it, if the Lord's merciful hand had not intervened. So now leave empty matters to empty men, and listen to my teaching, which 'will bring you more profit than finest gold,'[10] more than the books of all the philosophers. And so that this teaching of mine may move you more powerfully and remain always fixed in your heart, I shall expound the mystery of this teaching to you in an illustration that you can understand, which will be of great profit to you for the beginnings of salvation, and for laying a firm foundation for all virtues. So consider this similitude of a dying man, who as he is dying is talking to you."

(5) When the Disciple heard these words, he began to with-

8. Rom 3.2.   9. Eccl 9.4.
10. Ecclus 29.14; Bar 3.30.

draw his thoughts from external matters and to give great inward attention to the similitude suggested to him. There appeared before his eyes the likeness of a most handsome young man, who had been warned by death that he was very soon to depart for the next world, and who had made no preparations for his soul's salvation, who cried out with unhappy words like these: "'The mournfulness of death has surrounded me; the sorrows of hell have encompassed me.'[11] Alas for me, eternal God, for what was I born into this world? 'Why did I not die at once in the womb?'[12] See, my life began with weeping and sorrow, and now my end and my departure come with wretched lamentations and grief. 'O death, how bitter is your remembrance'[13] to a joyous heart trained up in delights. Your presence is horrible to anyone who is in his youth and is 'valiant and strong'[14] and is enjoying good fortune. O, how little could I believe that I should have to die so soon! But now, O wretched death, you have rushed out upon me as though from an ambush. You have seized upon me and bound me with a thousand cords, and you are dragging me along with you in iron fetters, as they are accustomed to drag a condemned man to the torments of death. Now for sorrow 'I have beaten my hands together,'[15] and I groan aloud, wanting to escape death, but there is no place for me to flee. I look around me on all the snares laid for me, and there is no one to counsel and help me. 'It is determined,'[16] it cannot be changed. I hear death's horrible voice, resounding and saying: 'You are "the son of death."'[17] Not your wealth or your intelligence or your kinsmen or your friends will have the power to free you from my hand. 'The end has come, the end has come.'[18] It has been decreed, and it must be fulfilled. O my God, must I die now? Cannot this sentence be changed? Must I depart from this

11. Ps 17.5–6. 12. Jb 3.11.
13. Ecclus 41.1. 14. 1 Kgs 9.1.
15. Nm 24.10. On this as a ritual gesture of lament, see Edmund Colledge and J. C. Marler, "'Mystical' Pictures in the Suso 'Exemplar,'" AFP 54 (1984): 312–21, and Plate 1.
16. 2 Kgs 19.29. 17. 1 Kgs 20.31.
18. Ez 7.2.

world so soon? O, enormous cruelty of death, O, lamentable humiliation so pitiless! Spare me, I beg, spare my youth, spare me who am not yet of ripe age. Do not act so cruelly nor drag me down, all unprepared, out of the light of this world."

(6) The Disciple, hearing these things, turned to him and said: "My friend, what you say seems to me to be undisciplined. You do not know that the judgment of death is impartial. It makes no exception of persons, it spares no one, but it imparts itself alike to everyone. It has no pity on youth or age. It does not know who are noble, and it is not in awe of the mighty. It destroys the rich man, as it does the poor. Indeed, many are carried off from our midst before they have reached their full complement of years. Do you suppose that death ought to spare you alone, and that it would not dare to set foot inside your abode of clay? 'The prophets too are dead.'"[19]

(7) So in answer this likeness of death said: "Truly, you are 'a troublesome comforter.'[20] My words are not spoken in imprudence, but rather they are to be considered like those of unwise men who have lived impious lives to their very death, committing acts worthy of death, and yet not fearing death as it drew near. They are blind and like 'senseless beasts,'[21] making no provision for their last end and for what will come after death. I am not weeping for death's judgment but for the harms that come from an unprepared death. I do not lament that I am departing from here, but I bewail and mourn the harms of the days that have passed uselessly and without any profit. How have I lived?[22] 'I have erred from the way of truth, and the light of justice has not shone on me, and the sun of understanding has not risen for me. I was wearied in the way of iniquity and destruction, and I have walked along hard paths, but the way of the Lord I have not known. Alas, what has pride profited me, or what advantage has the boasting of

19. Jn 8.53.
20. Jb 16.2.
21. Ps 48.13.
22. Cf. Eckbert of Schönau (ob. 1184), *Soliloquy* (often spuriously attributed to Anselm), 10: "God of my life, how uselessly they have been eaten up, how fruitlessly they have passed, the days you gave me in which to do your will, which I have not done!"

riches brought me? All those things have passed away like a fleeting shadow, and like a messenger swiftly running ahead, and like a ship that passes through the waves, the track of which cannot be found when it has gone by, nor the path of its keel in the waters. Or as when a bird flies through the air, no mark of its passage can be found, but only the sound of its wings, beating the light air and parting it by the force of its flight; she moved her wings, and has flown on, and no mark is found afterwards of its way. Or as when an arrow is shot at a target, the divided air at once comes together again, so that its passage is not known. So I too, being born, at once ceased to be, and I have been able to show no mark of virtue, but I am consumed in my own wickedness.[23] For my hope is as dust that is blown away with the wind, and as a thin froth that is dispersed by the storm, and as smoke that is scattered abroad by the wind, and as the remembrance of a guest of one day who passes by.[24] Therefore my word is now in bitterness, and my words are full of sorrow.[25] Therefore is my heart sorrowful, therefore have my eyes become dim.[26] Who will grant me to be with the days of old,[27] when I was clothed in a robe of strength and beauty, and had many years before me, that I might have foreknown the evils that have rushed upon me in this hour? I paid no heed to how immensely precious time was, but 'I gave up the ship to the winds,'[28] and loosing the bridle upon my concupiscence, I passed my days in vanity. I had no reward for their preciousness, but 'I thought myself born free like a wild ass's colt.'[29] But now, 'as fish are taken with the hook, and as birds are caught with the snare, so am I taken in an evil time, which has suddenly come upon me.'[30] The time passes by, and now it is gone. It cannot be called back by anyone among men. There was never an hour so short in which I could not have gained spiritual wealth, in its value incomparably more than all the riches of the world.

(8) "Alas for me, wretched man! It is for this that my eyes

23. Wis 5.6–13.
25. Jb 23.2, 6.3.
27. Jb 29.2; Mi 7.14.
29. Jb 11.12.

24. Wis 5.15.
26. Lam 5.17.
28. Acts 27.15.
30. Eccl 9.12.

now drip tears of sorrow, 'and my eyelids run down with waters,'[31] because I cannot call back what has gone. O my God, why was I so neglectful? Why did I delay? For what reason did I pretend? Why did I spend so many days that were given to me out of grace in the longest drawn out and most foolish talk, and doing so, neglect myself so much? O, groanings of my heart, not to be described! Why did I apply myself to vanity, and why did I not learn all my life long to die? Ah, all you who are here and see my misery, still rejoicing in the flower of your youth, still having the time you need, look at me, consider my miseries, and in my danger avoid your harm. Spend the flower of your youth with God, occupy your time with holy deeds, lest, doing as I did, you suffer as I suffer. Ah, welcome days of youth, how I have lost you! O eternal God, I complain to you of the wretchedness I am suffering. My wanton young days hated words of reproach; I did not want to submit to my teachers, I failed to lend my ears to those who lovingly admonished me. 'I hated instruction, and my heart did not consent to reproof.'[32] Ah, my God, now have I fallen into a deep ditch, I have run into death's trap. It would have been better for me if I had never been born, or if I had perished in my mother's womb, than that I should have spent so uselessly the time given to me for penitence, and that I squandered it in pride!"

(9) So the Disciple replied and said: "See, 'we all die, and like waters that return no more we fall down into the earth; neither does God want a soul to perish, but he calls it back, intending that he who is cast off should not perish altogether.'[33] Therefore hear my voice, and do penance for your past deeds, and 'return to the Lord your God,[34] for he is gracious and merciful,'[35] and if your end is good, that will be enough for salvation."

(10) The young man of this similitude replied: "What are these words which you are saying? Must I do penance? Must I turn from my sins? Do you not see how closely death is pressing

31. Jer 9.18.   32. Prv 5.12.
33. 2 Kgs 14.14.   34. Os 14.2.
35. Jl 2.13.

on me? See how utterly terrified I am by the fear and horror of death—I am bound in its chains, and such cares oppress my mind that I can hardly see what I should do. But just as the partridge is somehow rendered senseless in the anguish of death when the hawk seizes it in its talons to rend it, so all my senses have left me, and I can think of nothing but how I may evade the moment of death, which yet I am unable to evade. 'The sentence of death'[36] threatens me, and bitter separation wounds me. 'Will bitter death separate'[37] me now?

(11) "O, happy is penance and conversion made in due time, for it is safe. For if a man betakes himself to penance at the last moment, this will be doubtful and uncertain, for he will not know whether he is truly repenting or merely feigning. Alas for me, for I put off so long reforming my life, because I delayed so long my salvation! O neglect, too long prolonged, of my emending, how have you passed me by! Good resolutions but never a beginning, good will but never translated into action, fair promises but never fulfilled, these have destroyed me. Tomorrow, tomorrow, how long a rope you twined, and dragged me with it into the pit of death, while I put off till tomorrow.[38] 'You have deceived me, and I am deceived.'[39] Does not this misery exceed every misery of the world? Is not my heart more afflicted by it, as it deserves, is not my soul wounded to death? See how all my days have passed by; thirty of my years have gone, they are lost, they have perished in wretchedness. They have passed in such carelessness that I do not know if ever I spent one of all these days in doing God's will, in the exercise of all the virtues, as praiseworthily and perfectly as perhaps I could and I should have done, or if I ever once showed myself to my Maker as his pleasing, welcome, trusted servant, as my station in life demanded. Alas, for my sorrow! For this is the cause that my innermost heart is wounded.

36. Tb 2.8.
37. 1 Kgs 15.32; "separatio . . . separat" is *conduplicatio.*
38. Cf. Augustine, e.g. Sermon 82: "This is what has killed many, who say: 'Tomorrow, tomorrow, and suddenly the gate is shut.'"
39. Jgs 11.35.

(12) "Ah, eternal God, with what shame shall I stand before you and all the saints to be judged, when I am made to give an account of what I have done and failed to do. What shall I have to say? 'For my tribulation is very near,'[40] when I shall pass out of this world. Listen carefully to me now, I implore. See, at this moment I should find more joy in some short little prayer, such as the Hail Mary, which I said devoutly, than over 'thousands of gold and silver pieces.'[41] O my God, how many good things have I neglected! What evils have come to me, because I did not foresee, when I might well have foreseen. How many hours that never will return have I lost; doing so much that was useless, so little that came to anything, how many and how precious good things did I neglect! I involved myself in unnecessary affairs, and I failed to do things that were needed. I looked to others for more help than I required or was good for me, and I did not look after myself. I put myself into their hands, and I failed to help myself as much as I could.

(13) "Truly I know now that a careful guard upon my heart and all my senses and on the purity of my mind would have brought me to the great joys of heaven far better; now that I have neglected this and let it be corrupted by my inordinate affections these last thirty years, no one else with his penitential acts could so well obtain for me God's rewards. Listen, listen, all you who have any share in my miseries. Because, as you see, time was short, I went to all my friends, I asked each one of them in whom I had any hope, begging them to give me some poor little alms out of the abundance of their spiritual riches and good deeds, to supply my want and emend my faults; and I was refused. They repulsed me, saying: 'Perhaps there will not be enough for us and for you.'[42] Ah, most loving God, most gentle 'Father of mercies,'[43] look on these things and have pity on your suffering child. Alas, how much good could I have done in so much time with my bodily strength, and I did not do it. What unmeasured spiritual riches and

40. Ps 21.12.   41. Ps 118.72.
42. Mt 25.9.   43. 2 Cor 1.3.

heavenly treasures could I have amassed, and I neglected this. O my God, how gladly and willingly would I now do the very smallest works of satisfaction, 'desiring to be filled with the crumbs that fall from the table of his masters, and no one gave to him.'[44] O all you, suffer with me and 'have mercy on me,'[45] and so long as your strength will last and time will help you, 'gather into the heavenly barn'[46] the treasures of heaven,[47] 'so that when you are in want they may receive you into everlasting dwellings,'[48] and that when such an hour will come upon you, you will not be left empty, as you see me empty and wanting every good thing."

(14) But the Disciple said to him in reply: "Dear friend, I see that your sorrow is overwhelming, and so I sympathize with you from my heart, entreating you by the almighty God that you will advise me, in case I should incur the like peril, an unprepared and sudden death."

(15) To this the man in the similitude replied: "The best advice, the greatest prudence and the most forethought consists in this, that you dispose yourself by true contrition and pure and complete confession while you are healthy and strong, and by worthy satisfaction, and shun all the poisons and hindrances to your eternal salvation, and never cease at all times to behave as if you have to leave this world on this very day, or tomorrow, or at the latest within the week. In your heart think as if your soul were already in purgatory, and had received ten years of suffering 'in a furnace of blazing fire'[49] for its sins, and that this one year had been granted to you in which to help yourself. So look often at your soul, burning within fiery spheres, and listen to its wretched voice, calling to you and saying: 'O dearest of all my friends, rescue me, your unhappy soul. Remember a prisoner, have pity on me, and give me help in my desolation. Do not allow me to be afflicted longer in this gloomy dungeon, for I am abandoned by this world. There is no one to show himself loyal, no one to stretch out his hand to this pauper. They all 'seek the things that are

44. Lk 16.21.
46. Mt 13.30.
48. Lk 16.9.

45. Jb 19.21.
47. Cf. Mt 13.44, etc.
49. Dn 3.11.

their own,'[50] and they leave me desolate to the avenging flames."

(16) To these words the Disciple replied: "This teaching would indeed be most useful, if anyone could acquire it, as you have done, by experience. But even though your words may seem very moving and pointed, they will still be of little profit to many. 'They turn away their faces, lest they see the end,'[51] 'they have eyes and do not see, they have ears and do not hear,'[52] they think that they still have a long life, and because they have no fear of unprepared death, so the poor wretches scorn to foresee the harm that it will bring. When the messenger of death, grave sickness, comes, the ailing man's friends and companions gather, to come visit him. They foretell everything for him that is good, they will by no means admit that death is here, that there is anything to be feared or any danger that threatens; they say that it is some discharge that will cease, or some passing disorder of the constitution, or an infirmity of limbs or nerves that will soon be over. So these friends of his body make themselves his soul's enemies, and they neglect the poor man, for his sickness grows worse from moment to moment, and yet the sufferer keeps on hoping to improve, till in the end, worn out, suddenly he dies, and breathes out his unhappy spirit without having gained the fruits of salvation. This is what they are doing who listen to you, yet rely on what seems to be human prudence and reject your words, and pay no heed at all to your counsel, which could save them."

(17) In answer the image of death replied: "So when they will be caught in death's trap, 'when suddenly calamity will fall, and destruction as a tempest will be at hand, when tribulation and distress will come upon them,'[53] they will cry out and they will not be heard, 'because they have despised wisdom,'[54] and have disdained to listen to my counsel. And just as there are now very few to be found to feel compunction for my words and reform their lives, so one will find almost no one, the

50. Phil 2.21.
51. "Hebrews" Ps 9.11.
52. Ps 113.5–6.
53. Prv 1.27.
54. Prv 1.30.

times are truly so ill, spiritual fervor is so waning and there is so much malice abroad in this world that grows old, who is so perfectly prepared for death that he lives with a heart so withdrawn and devoted, longs with all his might to die and to have eternal life and 'to be with Christ';[55] but overtaken by bitter death, he is found ill-prepared, just as I was overtaken. And so it is not so much that they leave this world as that they are somehow violently carried off, so that those may think that they have fared well who do not die like beasts deprived of all reason. And if you want to know the cause of this danger, so great and so common, it is the inordinate desire for honors, the excessive concern for the body, the love of the world and the overanxious searching for private possessions; these things blind the hearts of many in the crowds, and lead to such perils.

(18) "But if you are among the few in wanting to be saved from this danger of unprepared death, listen to my advice, and often keep before your eyes this my sorrowful image which you are looking at; constantly call it to mind, and at once you will know that my teaching will be most profitable to you. For you will profit by it, not only because you need not fear to die, but still more because you will look forward to death, fearful to all living men, as the end of your toil and the beginning of eternal happiness, and you will accept it as your heart's desire. Only do this: remember me well every day, think carefully of my words, and write them in your heart. Consider the sorrows and terrors that you have seen in me, and think of those that will come to you in the next world. 'Remember how I was judged, for so too will you be. Yesterday for me, and for you today.'[56] Look on me, and remember the night that will end your days.

(19) "O Arsenius, how blessed you are, for you always had this hour before your eyes.[57] 'Blessed is he whom his lord will

55. Phil 1.23.   56. Ecclus 38.23.
57. Cf. the Greek anthology, *Sayings of the Fathers* (probably c. A.D. 500, early translated into Latin): "Abbot Theophilus the archbishop, when he was about to die, said: 'Blessed are you, abbot Arsenius, for you always had this hour in mind.'"

find watching when he comes and knocks at the door.'[58] Happy the man whom this hour finds well prepared, for he will depart in happiness, however great the bitterness of death which he may suffer. 'Whatever the death that may seize him, he will be at rest.'[59] He will be purged and prepared for the vision of God's glory, he will be guarded by the holy angels and conducted by the citizens of heaven, and he will be received by the celestial court. The passing of his spirit will be his happy entrance into his eternal native land.

(20) "But alas for me, wretched man that I am, where do you suppose that my spirit will be tonight? Who will receive my miserable soul? Where will it find shelter, where will it pass the night? Or who will they be who will receive it in that unknown country? O, how desolate my soul will be, O, how forsaken and abject, more so than any other soul! Or who is he who will faithfully stand by it, and who will want to give it true help? Therefore I suffer for myself, and with my bitter words I pour out 'tears like a torrent.'[60] But what profit is there for me now in weeping, and piling bitterest words one upon another? It is finished, it cannot be changed. The enemy 'has blocked up my paths, he has lain in wait for me like a lion in secret places,[61] he has filled me with bitterness and made me drunk,[62] men have led my life down into the pool of death.'[63]

(21) "O my God, now I make an end to my words, for I have not the strength to lament longer. See, the hour is coming that will take me away from this earth. Alas for me, now I see and feel that I have no power to live longer, and that death is at hand. How my feeble hands begin to stiffen, my face grows pale, my vision dims and my eyes start to sink and wander. O, wretch that I am! Death with its cruelest bites encircles me, seeking to suffocate my feeble heart. O, anguish and deathly oppression of my heart! Feel how my pulse begins to fluctuate, my breath to fail and to come in gasps. No longer do I see the light of this world, and now I begin to see in my mind's eye,

---

58. Lk 12.36.
60. Lam 2.18.
62. Lam 3.15.
59. Wis 4.7.
61. Lam 3.9–10.
63. From the Dominican Breviary's office for Palm Sunday.

as if I were meditating, what the next world will be like. O my God, what a wretched sight! See how I am surrounded with savage beasts, with spectral demons' faces, with countless black Ethiopians, lurking and lying in wait for my unhappy soul as it hovers on the point of its departure to the next world, if perhaps it may be delivered to them to torment.

(22) "O strictest of judges, how dire are your judgments, how heavily, as you judge my wretched soul, do you weigh those sins which most men do not even care about because they seem so petty. This is the sweat of death, suffusing my limbs and attesting that nature is conquered and now expires. O, terrible sight of the just Judge, already present in my fears, soon himself to appear to me! Farewell now, my companions and dearest friends, for now I am to leave you. I turn my mind's eye towards purgatory, to which I am now to be led off, and from which I shall not be released until I have 'paid the uttermost farthing.'[64]

(23) "From there with the eye of my heart I see misery and sorrow, pain and manifold affliction. Alas for me, wretched as I am, among the other torments earned in that place I see mounting flames of fire, and some miserable souls being lapped in them and plunged back again, running to and fro in the midst of that white-hot fire like sparks spitting flame, as when the whole of some great house were set on fire, and among the flames and the smoke there were sparks everywhere rising and falling; and they wail and cry aloud, tormented with suffering, each of them saying: 'Have pity on me, have pity on me, at least you, my friends.'[65] Where is now the help of my friends? Where are the fair promises of my kinsmen and the others for whose sake, in our inordinate love for them, we have neglected ourselves, and have heaped this torment upon us? Alas, why did we do so? We toiled, wanting to please them, and we have been ill repaid. We burn and we scorch, but we have received no help from them. Alas, why did we not provide for our own salvation? For the least affliction which we suffer in this purgatory exceeds every torment of that mortal

64. Mt 5.26.   65. Jb 19.21.

world. A single hour of this which we endure is reckoned to have in its cruel punishments a hundred years of the miseries of that passing world. But more than every other kind of torment, the absence of that divine and most joyous countenance wounds us most.' Now that I am in my last agony, I leave these things to you as my memorial, and, having said them, I expire in agony."

(24) At this vision the Disciple greatly mourned, and for fear "all his bones trembled."[66] So turning with tears to the Lord he said: "What has become of Eternal Wisdom now? Have you abandoned me, your servant, Lord? You wished to teach me wisdom, and now I have been brought down to death. O my God, how the presence of death which I see holds me captive! This image of death has so overcome the whole of me that I scarcely know whether what I have seen be fact or appearance. O 'Lord of lords, merciful'[67] and terrible, I give you thanks, and I promise that I shall amend. For I am utterly filled with terror. Nor in the whole of my life have I seen so plainly the perils of unprepared death as in this time. Truly I believe that this terrifying vision will always be of help to my soul. Now I know most certainly that 'we have not here a lasting city,'[68] and therefore I want to exert all my strength to insure the future state of my soul, when it cannot be changed.

(25) "I intend to learn how to die, I do not want to put off my penitence, in no way do I wish to delay my conversion. I plan to emend my life, with no turning back. I am so terrified when I merely recall what is past, so what is to be done about the present? Take away, take away from me now the luxuries of banqueting, costly array, and the sluggishness that holds me back. See how much I am wounded, how much afflicted, how much tormented by my least faults; and what is to be done about the greatest? It is hard for me to endure my small hurts; alas for me, how shall I suffer such immeasurable sorrows? O, if I were to die so, or if I were already dead, how much fuel for burning would that fire find in me, because of the multitude of

66. Jer 23.9.   67. Ex 34.6.
68. Heb 13.14.

my sins and my unfulfilled satisfactions. Now I know what I must do; I shall not allow my dear soul to perish so, but in this fleeting and shortest time I shall provide for it, by the labors I endure and the virtues I exercise, so that in that last hour it will find not torment but rest.

(26) "'O holy and merciful Savior, do not deliver me to so bitter a death.'[69] See me prostrate before you, praying with tears that you will punish me here at your will, 'lest you in your anger reserve my evil deeds for the end';[70] for in that terrifying place there is such misery and affliction that no one is able to recount it. O, how foolish I have been until now, since I cared so little about unprepared death and the vast torments of purgatory, and how great a wisdom it is to have these things more often before our eyes. But now with your fatherly warning I open my eyes and fear purgatory's torments very greatly."

(27) And Wisdom replied and said: "My son, remember these things at all times, while you are still young and healthy and strong, and can still amend your life. But when in fact you come to that hour, and can help yourself in no other way, nothing will remain except to commit yourself to the mercy of God alone, and to put my Passion between you and my judgment, lest, filled with more fear than need be of my justice, you lose your hope. Now that fear has so completely terrified you, become of calmer spirit,[71] know that 'the fear of the Lord is the beginning of wisdom.'[72] 'Search the Scriptures,'[73] and you will find that the recollection of death brings many good things to a man. The wise man says: 'If a man live many years and rejoice in them all, he must remember the shadowy time and the many days, for when they will come, things that are past will be accused of vanity.'[74] So 'remember your Creator in the days of your youth, before the time of affliction comes, and the years draw near of which you will say: They do

---

69. From the Dominican Breviary for the office of the fourth week in Lent.

70. From the Dominican Breviary for the office of the Wednesday of the third week after Trinity.

71. Cf. "The Life of St. Pachomius" in *The Lives of the Fathers*, where Christ says to St. Pachomius: "Indeed, be of calmer spirit, and let your heart be strengthened."

72. Ps 110.10.   73. Jn 7.52.

74. Eccl 11.8.

not please me; before the dust return into its earth whence it was, and the spirit return to God who gave it.'[75]

(28) "But you, 'bless the God of heaven'[76] with all your heart, and be thankful, for it is given to very few to hear so with the heart's ear how unstable is this present time, how treacherous death is, which threatens at every hour, how lasting will be the happiness of our future home. Lift up your eyes, look around you carefully, and see how many there are with blinded minds 'who shut their eyes lest they see the end, make their ears deaf lest they hear and be converted and healed';[77] and their destruction will not delay. And consider them, an innumerable crowd,[78] who have already been cut off by an unprepared death and have been lost. Number if you can that vast multitude. See how many they are, who once shared the days of your life with you, who have now gone, and have been taken from the earth. How great a number of your brethren and companions and others known to you have departed before you, in so few years, whilst you are still young, who in so short a time have fallen asleep and have left you behind them. Look on them, speak with them, and count yourself an old man who has departed with them. Ask them all, enquire from one and another, and they will teach you. With weeping and sighs they will answer you and say: 'O, how happy the man who makes provision for these last things, who will beware of sin, who does not neglect your advice, who at all times prepares himself for this hour.' So put away everything which could make you hesitate, and 'set your house in order.'[79] Make ready for the way 'of all flesh,'[80] for the hour of death, because you do not know for certain at what hour that will come, or how near it is. See, 'it stands at the doors.'[81] And as a traveler stands at the harbor and looks for a fast ship leaving for distant parts, lest he be left behind, so let all your life and your actions be directed to gaining a blessed departure, and to arriving at the place of immortality and everlasting happiness."

75. Eccl 12.1, 7.   76. Tb 12.6.
77. Is 6.10.
78. Künzle, p. 32, thinks that "an innumerable crowd" is a further reference to the great plague of 1328.
79. Is 38.1.   80. Gn 6.13.
81. Mt 24.33.

CHAPTER 3

A Concise Form for Spiritual Living

 REMEMBER THAT I read, "in the days of my vanity"[1] in which "I labored in vain[2] under the sun,"[3] in the teachings of the wise men of this world, who are commonly called "philosophers," that the end is contained in things that can be performed, as beginnings are contained in what can be contemplated.[4] When, therefore, highest Wisdom so much desired by my heart, you will give me as my beginning your art of dying blessedly, it is fitting to your goodness that you will add it now to your teachings on how to live well, and this concisely and briefly; for scholars today delight in brevity. For "of making many books there is no end,"[5] and from the beginning of the world "many have passed over, and knowledge was manifold."[6] The world is full of different teachings. There are a thousand ways of living, "one this way, another that."[7] There are so many books about vices and virtues, treating them with authority, there are so many booklets dealing with most subtle questions and various propositions, that this short life would end before one had managed to look them all through, let alone studied them. Who could number all the works on logic, the natural sciences, history, moral philosophy and divinity, all the treatises, the commentaries, old and new, handbooks of elements, anthologies, individual treatises and summas, with which the whole surface of the earth is overwhelmed as with an encroaching flood? One could well dis-

1. Eccl 7.16.   2. Jb 9.29.
3. Eccl 1.3.
4. This seems to allude to Aristotle's *Physics* II, ch. 9, or, more probably, to some Latin gloss on the passage.
5. Eccl 12.12.   6. Dn 12.4.
7. From the Dominican Breviary for the feast of St. Augustine.

pense with going through the whole of this for any disciple who is fatigued and weak. So therefore I ask that I may be given out of it all the briefest formula of perfection, something put into four words, such as is suitable for the rudiments of spiritual warfare.

(2) Wisdom replies: In that choir of the saints who shone out like morning stars in the night of this world, and glittered with knowledge's great light like constellations, you will find some who gave out a sweeter savor, not only in virtue's practice, but also in its theory. From their example and from what they handed down, you will find the most perfect lessons in the spiritual life. So, because I want to come down to the level of your untutored experience, I shall give you, as briefly as possible, some elements of spiritual living to serve as a kind of memorandum, which you will always be able to consult, and which you can translate into actions.

(3) So, if you want to obtain that perfection of all spiritual life which everyone desires, if you want to work hard to acquire it, you must withdraw yourself from all harmful company and friendships, from all the people who frustrate your intention, in a word, from all mortal men, so far as that is compatible with the vows of your religious profession, always preserving the humble and prompt obedience that you owe to your superiors; and you may seize every opportunity to seek out somewhere to be at peace and gather contemplation's silent secrets, shunning this life's shipwrecks and fleeing from the uproars of this noisy world.

(4) At all times your chief study should be for purity of heart, so that constantly your fleshly senses should be as it were shut out, and you should turn inward to yourself, and you should keep the doors of your heart carefully bolted, so far as you can, against sensory forms and earthly imaginings. For purity of heart exerts first claim, among all spiritual exercises, as it were as the final intention and the payment of every labor that any deserving soldier of Christ has ever received in this life.

(5) Do all that you can to set your affections free from all these things, which could hinder your affections' freedom, in all circumstances finding the possibility to join and fasten that

affection to what it should cling to, in accordance with the law of Moses, which said: "Let each man stay at home, and let no one go out of the door of his house on the Sabbath day, and let the people keep the Sabbath."[8] For to be at home is to draw together again all the strayings of the heart and the affections into one true and completely single good, and to keep them collected. And to keep the Sabbath is to preserve the heart from carnal loves that stain the soul, and to hold the soul free from all worldly cares that can distract it, and to rest sweetly in the heart's peace, as in a haven of silence, in the love and enjoyment of the Creator.

(6) For above all other matters, this should ever be your principal endeavor, always to lift your spirit high up in the contemplation of divine things, so that the mind may always cling to what is of God and is God, that it may forsake the frail things of earth and may always pass to those of heaven. Whatever is different from such things, however great it may seem, such as bodily afflictions, fastings, vigils and such kinds of exercise of virtues, are to be judged as it were secondary and inferior, and expedient only as they serve the heart's purity. This is why so few attain to true perfection, because the many do not spend their time and efforts on means that are beneficial, they neglect the proper remedies, and they put them off. But if you want to travel along the right path to the end that you propose, you must above all else aspire to perpetual purity of heart and peace of mind, and always keep your heart lifted up to the Lord.

(7) Disciple: Who in this frail body can be always applying himself to this science of the spirit?[9]

(8) Wisdom: No mortal man can constantly hold fast to such contemplation, and that is why I have said this, so that you may know where you ought to have your mind's intention fixed, and towards what goal[10] you should always be recalling

8. Ex 16.29–30.

9. This resembles Germanus's question to abbot Theodorus in Cassian's *Conversations* VI, ch. 13: "Can our minds continually remain in one state and always persist in the same quality?"

10. This alludes to Augustine of Dacia's verses; cf. Bk. I, ch. 9, note 61, above.

your soul's gaze, over which, if it may obtain it, the mind will rejoice, as it will sorrow and sigh when it is distracted, as often as it finds itself barred from its goal. And if you perhaps want to meet me with complaints that you cannot always remain so long standing in one place, you must know that God's power can do more than man can think, and that acts often repeated commonly produce habits that resemble them.[11] So it often happens that something to which a man in the first place has perhaps forced himself with a certain violence and difficulty is later done easily, and, in the end, with great delight, provided that he does not give up what he has started.

(9) "My son, hear the instruction of your father";[12] listen carefully to my words, "and write them in your heart as if in a book."[13] "Do not be envious"[14] of the multitude who have turned back again after "the desires of their heart,"[15] in whom devotion has grown tepid, "love has grown cold"[16] and deficient, humble obedience has been overthrown, who want "to please men,"[17] who seek after honors, who "serve their own belly,"[18] who exceed all bounds as they "love bribes and run after rewards,"[19] and who will receive what they are seeking as the payment of their labors in this world, and in the next will remain empty. But pay heed to those fairest flowers, the most holy fathers, how incomparably they burn in their thirst for holiness; hasten to imitate their resolution with a like zeal and application, as you have already resolved to do. "Whether you are eating or drinking, or whatever else you are doing,"[20] let these words of a loving father always be resounding in your ears, admonishing you and saying: "My son, return to your inmost heart, and withdraw yourself from everything, so far as that is possible." Always guard your mind's eye in purity and tranquillity, keeping your understanding free from the

11. This is Aristotle's teaching on "habituation," *Ethics* II, ch. 1, several times quoted by Thomas Aquinas.
12. Prv 1.8.
13. From the Dominican Breviary's office for the fourth Sunday in Lent.
14. Ps 36.1.   15. Ps. 80.13.
16. Mt 24.12.   17. Gal 1.10.
18. Rom 16.18.   19. Is 1.23.
20. 1 Cor 10.31.

appearances of base things. Release the affections of your will from care about earthly matters, clinging always with fervent love to the highest good, and keep your memory always trained upwards, directing itself towards what is highest by contemplation of the things of God, so that your whole soul, drawn into God with all its potentialities and powers, becomes "one spirit with him"[21] in whom the highest perfection of living is seen to consist.

(10) So accept this short teaching which I have given to you as the form for your life, for in it there is the very highest sum of all perfection, and if you will labor diligently at it and take care to carry it faithfully into effect, you will be blessed, and you will in some fashion begin your life of eternal blessedness in this frail body.

(11) This, my son, is the way of salvation that your dear Arsenius,[22] guided by an angel, followed, and commanded his disciples to follow. "Flee, and be silent, and be at rest"; these, he said, "are the first steps to salvation." And this is the purest teaching, which divine Wisdom revealed to a certain disciple of his whom you know, when Wisdom told him plainly of his state of soul.

(12) For when this Disciple, who had till then found merely human knowledge so beguiling, proposed to continue in its pursuit, many foolishnesses began to spring up as it were behind his back, and he started to aspire in unworthy fashion after worldly honors and promotions. But when his turn came, and he should have been raised up to the honors that he desired and for which he had labored for so long, he began to ponder in himself whether this would be good for him or pleasing to God. So on one occasion after matins he prostrated himself in prayer, and asked the Lord with great devotion to be pleased to reveal what he ought to do. At length, rising from prayer and sitting on the step, he saw in a vision a handsome young man coming towards him, who took him by the hand and led him to a certain church in which a little cell

---

21. Augustine's *Rule*, alluding to Acts 4.32.
22. *The Lives of the Fathers*, Bk. III.

had been built, which one man inhabited in solitude, living the life of an anchorite; he was very old and white-haired, with a flowing beard, and divine grace shone out in him. And beside this old man's cell there appeared a ladder, reared upward, and the young man we have spoken of seemed to be amusing himself by climbing up and down on it. So this young man called to the friar: "Come and hear the lesson that I want to read to you." The friar gladly ran up, and he first wanted to look at the book from which he was to hear this lesson. And he saw in the young man's hand a very ancient tome, very small, which he judged by its appearance to be of no value, and for which no one cared, because it was outmoded. So the young man began to read these words: "For a spiritual man, the fount and source of all good things is for him always to remain in his cell."[23] These words, coming from the young man's lips and read out of the old book, resounded so sweetly in the friar's ears and so softened his heart that it seemed to him that he was loosed from all ties but the love of heaven, and that whoever should read this, its efficacy would plainly show that these were heavenly words. So when the friar approached the young man, to ask him to repeat these words to him, at once his request was fulfilled, and he read the same words as before, saying: "For a spiritual man, the fount and source of all good things is for him always to remain in his cell." Then the friar was so uplifted in spirit that he said: "O, how precious and useful is this healing teaching!" And then he asked who it might be out of so many wise men who had produced this saying so full of meaning. "That great philosopher Arsenius," the young man answered. The friar asked him to read him more out of the same book. But when he began again, these were the words which he read: "On the other hand, the fount and source of all evils is when those who should preach the gospel talk uselessly."[24] The friar heard this saying with a certain perturbation of heart and tried to argue

23. This seems to adapt Cassian's *Conversations* VI, ch. 15: "Therefore one must hold fast to remaining constantly in one's cell."

24. Cassian, *Conversations* XVI, ch. 9, has much to say about garrulous men who try to pass for spiritual teachers.

against it, taking as an example the discourse of the holy Apostles, who solely to preach the gospel traveled throughout the world, for he did not then perceive that his example was not applicable to the case under discussion, and that these words were not meant to apply any more to preachers of the gospel than to all the rest of those who are seeking to please God. For it is plain to see that for anyone it will be the beginning of all evils if he wants to place no restraint on useless talking. But to this the young man answered nothing, but he said, with all gentleness: "You should know, friar, that that philosopher greatly detested useless talk." And when this had been said, the vision vanished.

(13) So this friar of whom we have told so much, feeling that heavenly consolation had been poured into him, began to turn over in his mind the things that he had seen and heard, and to enquire with much surprise who this philosopher Arsenius could be. For at that time he was still devoting much study to secular philosophy, and reading its authorities, but he was not yet paying much attention to spiritual philosophy and to those who wrote of it. So he said to himself: "You see how many philosophers' books you have read, and how many philosophers you have heard quoted, and in no philosophical discussion have you heard this Arsenius's name so much as mentioned." At length he reflected, and he began to think: "Perhaps this is the Arsenius, the most famous philosopher of Christian doctrine, a celebrated anchorite whom many years ago you heard quoted, even though it has now passed from your memory. And it was perhaps to show this that you saw that old man living in his narrow cell, and that young man holding the old book in his hand and reading out these words, to make you understand by this the lives of the holy fathers and their conferences, contained in the book that many now neglect as old and discarded, although experience can see with complete certainty that in it are the core of all perfection and the true knowledge of Christian philosophy." So rising at early light, this friar asked their librarian for *The Lives of the Fathers*, wanting to know for certain if this were so, and whether he could find this Arsenius somewhere in the *Lives*, because

he could not now remember any of his sayings. So, when he had opened the book, suddenly the name "Arsenius" caught his eye, and he found exactly the same statement among his sayings as the young man had read out of the ancient volume. When he had found enough information there, he decided to stay where he was, and he abandoned his classes, which he thought could be better conducted by others, taking no part in them himself, as if he were mentally disturbed, and he elected to model himself on the teachings of this philosopher.

(14) Disciple: Your words might be taken out of some heavenly bookcase, I find them so utterly compelling, and with their sweet gentleness they so increase the fervor of my devotion, making plain to me as I listen the smoothest path to a more perfect life, and taking away every difficulty.

CHAPTER 4

How Christ Should Be Devoutly Received in the Sacrament of the Eucharist

ECAUSE YOUR profitable teaching and the sweetness to my taste of your words have moved me, O highest and Eternal Wisdom, to hasten with fervent desire to the school of virtues and to study there with zeal, where I find more and more how I ought to die and to live, still I confess that as I take part in its regular exercises, I fail through my own weakness; and therefore I take refuge with your omnipotence, and I ask you, to what remedies should I have recourse in adversity, if you will deign in your love to show me this?

(2) Wisdom: The Church's seven sacraments are the seven remedies[1] by which man is somehow reborn as a spiritual creature, he is cherished and nourished, and with grace as the means, he is brought up to the highest grade of perfection. And yet, among them, by some way still more excellent, the ray of divine love and a certain flood of heavenly grace, setting devout souls joyfully on fire and sweetly inebriating them, are known to emanate more especially from the eucharistic sacrament. For just as dry wood provides good material for making earthly fire, and makes its flames mount on high and shoot out in every direction, so truly this sacrament, kindling the heat of the spirit, offers and promotes our great nourishment by feeding the fire of divine love, when it is devoutly received. For among all the signs of love, there is none that so overpowers all the lover's mind as the beloved's longed-for presence, which is put before everything else. So at the Last Supper I offered myself sacramentally to my beloved disciples, and I delegated to them and to all the ministers of this sacrifice by

1. Thomas Aquinas teaches this; e.g. *ST* III, q. 63, a. 6, c.

the power of my words this immense ability, that they may have me present bodily, who am known to be everywhere through the presence of my divinity.

(3) Disciple: "I beseech you, my Lord, let your servant speak a word in your ears, and do not be angry with your servant, for you are my Lord,"[2] and I am your servant. If I have understood well, you have said that you are in this sacrament, not figuratively, but really, not in intention, but bodily; and I humbly ask to be taught if this be so, because this would give me much reason for loving you fervently.

(4) Wisdom: Most certainly and truly and without any doubting, I am contained in this sacrament, God and man, with my body and my soul, my flesh and my blood, just as I came out of my mother's womb and hung upon the cross and sit at my Father's right hand.

(5) Disciple: Do not, I ask, be angry, my Lord, if I speak. What I am saying is not rooted in unbelief, but comes from my great astonishment. For it seems utterly miraculous, if I may lawfully say this, how the lovely body of my Lord, with all its proper dimensions and utter perfection, may be contained under the minute forms of the sacramental species, bearing no relationship whatever to its proportions.

(6) Wisdom: No tongue has the power to explain how my body may be contained in the sacrament, no sense can perceive it, no human reason can apprehend it, but only faith is equal to knowing it. For this is an operation only of the divine power, and it is immense; and you must therefore believe it faithfully, and beware of presumptuous investigation. Yet because I want to help your devout simplicity, I shall reply to your artless words, more to stir up your devotion than to show something that is known to God alone. My way will be to proceed from what is by its own nature known, though it is not known to you, to things that surpass the knowledge of all mortal men. So tell me now, you who know nothing of optical science, how can the eye's little pupil take in the sky's entire hemisphere, or in what way can a broken mirror receive a

2. Gn 44.18.

perfect image in each of its fragments,[3] when these are un-
equal and disproportionate? And though in this elementary
example there may be more dissimilarity than similarity, just
as any natural event may produce effects unlike, and not at all
like what was intended, still one can accept without incongru-
ity from this that if nature can work in such marvelous ways,
why cannot the power of nature's Creator stretch out to work
far greater marvels? So, if it is seen to be possible that the
Creator of the universe spoke, and that "all things were made"[4]
from nothing,[5] why does this transmutation seem so impossible? And whether this act of transubstantiation be either
greater or less than the act of creation, or equal to it, there is
nothing irrational in believing that he who could produce the
world out of nothing in no way limited his power to that one
act. But as "he has done all things, whatever he wished,"[6] so
"no word shall be impossible with God,[7] for his power is at
hand when he wills."[8] So why are you astonished at one thing,
and not astonished at all the rest? What is more, you believe
that divine Wisdom fed five thousand men with five loaves of
bread, so I ask you, what kind of matter was it that then was
obedient to his omnipotence?

(7) Disciple: I am so simple that I do not know how to answer
these questions, except by proclaiming that God's works are
wonderful.

(8) Wisdom: But I shall add this question, suited to your
simplicity. Tell me if you believe that you have a soul, or that
there are invisible beings that exist?[9]

(9) Disciple: I do not believe that I have a soul, because I
know it,[10] since I have knowledge of this matter from motion
and sense and from the other definitions we have inherited

3. Künzle observes that the example of the broken mirror is first found
in Alan of Lille's *Against the Heretics*, c. 1180.

4. Ps 32.9; Jn 1.3.   5. 2 Mc 7.28.
6. Ps 113B.3.   7. Lk 1.37.
8. Wis 12.18.

9. Cf. Gregory the Great, *Homily 2 on the Gospels:* "No one sees his soul,
and yet no one doubts that he has a soul which he does not see."

10. Cf. *ST* II-IIae, q.1, a.5: "It is impossible that the same thing be an object
of knowledge and of belief for the same person."

from the secular philosopher who wrote about the soul.[11] So reason dictates that many beings exist in the natural order that could not be captured by any sense; and it may be that there are more of God's works unseen than those that sight can comprehend, which any diligent enquirer can easily find out from the perfect order in which all things are arranged.

(10) Wisdom: Apply what we have been saying to what you are asking about. You can see that the intellect of any man who is blessed exceeds the intellect of someone who is wise, far more that a wise man's intellect exceeds that of a simpleton; and yet experience teaches us that many uneducated people consider things to be impossible that experts can prove with complete certainty, as appears especially in geometry and astronomy. So, in what we are discussing, though it may be that the matter surpasses the knowledge of the wayfaring man, well known to be intellectually blind to nature's most evident facts, yet those who enjoy the knowledge of the blessed perceive these things perfectly in God. Listen to the Church's preacher as he says: "There is a man whose eyes take no sleep day or night; and I understood that man can find no reason in all the works of God that are done under the sun. The more he will labor in seeking, the less will he find; even though the wise man will say that he knows, he will not be able to find it."[12] And one of the pagan philosophers produced the best proofs of this for you, for when he had made the most learned enquiries about the number of the moving heavenly bodies and had failed to find what he was seeking, he said: "Let us leave these things to better minds."[13] How many truths do you reckon that nature's most profound investigators, the subtlest hunters after reasoning and the acutest adducers of syllogistic complexities, really enjoy possession of through scientific deductions? Very few indeed. This is adequately proved by the differences of opinion and the opposing reasonings about the same conclusion, yet sometimes a conclusion is so common and so easy that even its accidental qualities can be submitted to the

11. This is Aristotle.   12. Eccl 8.16–17.
13. Aristotle, *Metaphysics* 12, ch. 8.

senses, so that it can be seen and felt that it is so. And if this is true of matters belonging to the natural order and "the things that are before us," when it comes to "the things that are in heaven," which cannot be seen but surpass all nature, "who will search them out?"[14] "If I have said earthly things to you," God's Wisdom says, " and you do not believe, how will you believe if I shall say heavenly things to you?"[15] Such doubts and false conceptions about things that are of faith sometimes arise because man imagines and judges about what is divine as though it were human, and about the supernatural as if it existed naturally, but this must not be done, and it is most to be guarded against in what we are considering. For the body of the Lord is not present in the sacrament in the same way as a body is in a place, with dimensions commensurate with the place, but the Lord's body is present in some special way.

(11) And if you ask what this way may be, I say that it is such as is appropriate to this sacrament, and your imagination cannot come to know this. So you must "bring into captivity your understanding," as if it were blinded, "into the obedience of Christ,"[16] and you must keep before your eyes how much that infinite power to whose command all material things are obedient can do. But "he calls those things that are not, just as those that are,"[17] even though man cannot see this, for the defective vision of his intellectual eye. You have a common example[18] to prove this well: a boy born and always brought up in a prison, who would consider the many facts someone wanted to tell him about the course of the stars and the disposition of the heavens as miraculous. Therefore, it was very necessary for divine Wisdom to stoop to human ignorance, and to give all these matters, as exceeding human powers, to men for them to believe in, and the faithful, clinging to this as to infallible truth, are relying on a solid foundation, having a greater certainty from that than if they were to rely on any intellectual understanding, their own or someone else's, of a thing that has been known and weighed up.

14. Wis 9.16.   15. Jn 3.12.
16. 2 Cor 10.5.   17. Rom 4.17.
18. It is found in Gregory the Great's *Dialogues* I, ch. 1.

(12) Disciple: Indeed, your arguments are so evident that they add to my faith in this sacrament, and set my weak spirit free from the poisonous bewilderments and timid notions that attack it. For from this I perceive that an intellect that is seeking the impossible and wanting to scrutinize the inscrutible is stupid, trying to know about the wonderful works that are God's alone, and yet lacking knowledge of the workings of nature. What more do I need to know or find out? I know and I believe most firmly that you are the highest and infinite power, who "can do all things,"[19] the highest and eternal Wisdom, who know and see all things, the most simple and unchangeable truth, who cannot deceive or be deceived. And so you are the goal of my faith, the anchor of my hope, now and in eternity, for I know that "blessed is the man who trusts in you."[20] And for this my whole heart now rejoices, for what I have been seeking I have found, what I wanted I have obtained, what for so long I have desired now I have gained.

(13) "Why are you sad, my soul, and·why do you trouble me?"[21] You have been seeking Jesus, and you have found Jesus. Until now you have often complained that your beloved was absent, and when you saw someone else rejoicing in the presence of a loved one, you would envy him and mourn because you could nowhere find him whom you loved. You used to say: O, cruel departure of my beloved, whose memory alone feeds me. He writes letters, he sends messengers, yet he withholds his presence, and with an eye that I cannot see he looks on everything as he looks on me. But alas, this is not enough for a lover. "In my bed by night I seek him, but I do not find him."[22] I look around me at table, but I do not see him. I long to have "a fruitful vine on the sides of my house,"[23] and I am cheated. So I say that I have a beloved one and I lack a beloved one, because I do not find him with me. "A cloud took him out of sight,[24] and he sits at the right hand of the Father.[25] He walks about the poles of heaven, and does not consider our

19. Wis 7.27.
21. Ps 41.6.
23. Ps 127.3.
25. Mk 16.19.

20. Ps 83.13.
22. Cant 3.1.
24. Acts 1.9.

affairs."[26] O, if only I might have a beloved who could be with me, in whose presence I might rejoice and at times receive consolation for my troubles!

(14) But now my healing, which I no longer hoped for, "has been seen to arise,"[27] the voice of mourning is changed to one of rejoicing, and the love with which I sought him has become the love with which I give thanks. Then I lamented his absence, now I have seen his presence; and him whom I believed to be far off I have now found close beside me. And therefore "rejoice with me,"[28] all you "who love the Lord,"[29] because I have found my beloved, not only as he is in his divinity, ruling over all, but also as he is in his humanity, sacramentally present. "I have found him,"[30] not where he had turned aside,"[31] but where before he did not so clearly appear to me. I have found him, not where he was not before, but because he has given me the light of his presence through some new ray of his teaching, he has revealed what was secret, what was hidden he has drawn out into the light, and what before I knew only in writing he has now taught me by a certain spiritual and life-giving grace. It will be strange, from now on, if I can force myself to come out of church, if I do not stay day and night where I have my Lord present, not only spiritually but bodily too, not only as God but also as my dear brother and friend.

(15) O, how grateful I once should have been, if I had been worthy to receive only a single drop of that most precious blood from my beloved's open wounds into my mouth. I should have counted myself happy if I had been able to take the least falling of that most precious liquid from his breast. But now I begin to ponder most deeply how I have received not merely one drop or two flowing from his hands or feet or breast, for I have rather received the whole of his blood, and his body has been joined to my body. O, joy and immense exultation of my heart, for this ineffable grace that my beloved has given to me! Is this not the greatest and first of gifts, to be

26. Jb 22.14.   27. Est 8.16.
28. Lk 15.9.   29. Ps 96.10.
30. Cant 3.4.   31. Cant 5.17.

extolled with fitting praises, to which not even the nature of angels might dare to aspire? And therefore, would that all my skills and all my might and all my inwardness could be set free for your praises, that I might be able, with what ability I possess, to respond to your love.

(16) Your presence sets all my love violently on fire, but your majesty strikes fear in me. Reason counsels me to show respect to such a guest, love compels me to embrace so beloved a spouse with ardor. For truly you are my Lord and my God,[32] but you are also my brother, and, if I dare say so, my beloved Spouse. Ah, how much good do I possess in you, who are one single and most simple good. For I do not have in you this or that particular good, but the highest good, in which all good things are contained as in the fount from which they flow. O, how fitting that the presence of this good should move me to love, and even though it be plainly not possible for him to be seen here in the sacrament as he is in his native land, still a fervent love, based on a foundation of faith, should be so built upon God that the presence of this sacrament in the heart conquer every worldly love. And so this sacrament is fittingly called the sacrament of love. For what is there more of love than this, what more loving than this close union of the lover with his beloved?

(17) Now be consoled, my soul, for what you were seeking you have found. Receive Christ, present to you, truly with you, as "Simeon, that just and devout man"[33] received him at the Presentation. For this is what you have asked for in your prayers for long, and now you have obtained what you wished and beyond your wishes. For though it is true that he was visible to Simeon when he received him, but is invisible to you, still you have not received him any less truly. For as my bodily eye cannot now see your humanity present in the sacrament, neither could that man Simeon, carrying you in his arms, see your divinity, except with the eyes of faith, just as I see you present now. But why should I care about bodily vision, since those eyes are called blessed that see, not according to the

32. Jn 20.28.   33. Lk 2.25.

flesh, as did the scribes and Pharisees, but spiritually, as the chosen disciples? For what more, O soul, do you want to know about your beloved? What more do you seek, what do you desire? Most truly and without any doubt, you have him present to you in the sacrament, though it be invisibly. But consider the divine decree. Is it not much more fitting that this mystery is enacted under a strange species than in his own form? For who might there be of such savagery that he would presume to chew him under the form of flesh and blood? So divine Wisdom has made the very best provision, "ordering all things,"[34] so that as the flesh and blood remain under the appearance of bread and wine, things that commonly serve for human refreshment, this sacrament may be received. What could be more apt, more easy, what could be found more seemly, to meet our needs and not depart from the truth? When I consider these and such other great and wonderful works of yours, so exceedingly well arranged, O Eternal Wisdom, my powers fail in astonishment, and I cry out within myself: "'O, the depths of the riches of the wisdom and of the knowledge of God,'[35] what are you in your own essence who are such and so great in the power with which you flow into created being?"

(18) So now, "my King and my God,"[36] who have deigned to choose me, "not for any merits of mine,"[37] to the office of the priesthood,[38] and to make me the minister of such mysteries, so that I may receive and offer you each day, the immaculate Lamb, I pray you to teach me how I may worthily receive you, so that it may be for your glory and the health of my soul. I know this for certain, that there was never any king, however great or glorious, received by any city with such honor and respect, there was never any dearest friend coming from afar so joyfully and affectionately greeted, there was never any well-loved husband so gladly and lovingly welcomed, so carefully tended by a faithful wife, as my soul longs today to receive you,

---

34. Wis 8.1.
36. Ps 43.5.
35. Rom 11.33.
37. From the Easter Eve *Exultet*.
38. From the Dominican Missal's prayers for the priest after Mass.

my most welcome Ruler, my sweetest friend and guest, my most beloved spouse and lover, into its dwelling and into the most secret chamber of my heart, and there to show you every reverence, to treat you with love, to offer you all the honor possible to a mere creature before its Creator.

(19) Wisdom: "When you go up to bow to the altar, look on the sacred Body and Blood of your God,"[39] with the eyes of faith, so, that is, that with utter certainty and with no hesitation "you may believe with all your heart and confess with your lips"[40] that that consecrated host is the true Son of God, born of the Virgin, who died and rose again, Judge of the living and the dead, so that you may be of the number of those who are true Jews, "not in the letter, but the spirit,"[41] not according to the flesh but "according to the promise,"[42] putting on the confession of your heart and lips like a garment, so that all your being may confess him to be the Lord, and all your bones may cry it aloud. Then with due reverence and especial honor, "running to meet your God,"[43] be filled with humble devotion and wonder that so great a lord deigns to come to so poor a servant, such nobility to a wretched little worm, so much majesty to a vile leper, and say with fear and respect: "'Lord, I am not worthy that you should come under my roof,'[44] but, confident in such love and pity, 'I come sick to the Physician of life,'[45] thirsty to the fountain of mercy, 'poor to the Lord of heaven and earth,'[46] a sheep to the Shepherd, the image to its Creator, desolate to my loving consoler and liberator."

(20) Afterwards, filled with most ardent desire, let your heart reach out and draw him within you, receive him, so glorious a spouse, and take delight in his sweetest presence. And this is what should move a loving mind more than anything

39. From the Dominican Breviary's lessons for Maundy Thursday, quoting pseudo-Chrysostom, *Sermon on the Betrayal by Judas.*
40. Rom 10.10.   41. Rom 2.29.
42. Gal 3.29.
43. From the Dominican Missal's introit for the Purification.
44. Mt 8.8.
45. From the Dominican Missal and Breviary; the prayer before communion attributed to Thomas Aquinas.
46. Ibid.

else, when, that is, it thinks that it has its own beloved present, its friend, for love of whom each day it dies to this world and forswears every earthly love. See how the foolish lovers of this world, when on any day they have so much as looked on the house where they recall that their beloved is, rejoice more all day long and are made the gladder for it. So from this consider how fittingly a man will rejoice, how greatly he will exult who has received under this visible form no vile created thing, but the Creator of all things, no earth-trodden dung, but "the Wisdom of God"[47] made man. It will be strange if on that day, when he has received his beloved Creator, a man's loving mind can be saddened by any temporal business, for without doubt he then has such great reason for rejoicing that this should properly swallow up and destroy anything that might happen to sadden him, as the ocean will with a drop of vinegar poured into it.

(21) So now, if you want to experience the sweetness you have never known from this sacrament, take care first to withdraw your soul "from secular businesses,"[48] from vices and carnal matters, so that your receiving of it may be preceded by profound contrition and full confession. And so let yourself be drawn by the devotion of the moment, rather than by lazy habit. Adorn the little hospice of your heart with most ardent affections and most holy meditations for him, as if with blushing roses and paling lilies, and prepare a bridal couch for such a bridegroom with true peace of heart. And when you feel that he is present, lay him to rest in your heart's arms by shutting out every earthly love and shutting in your heavenly spouse.

(22) Then let my devout soul make me hear his voice, singing to me "of the songs of Sion,"[49] its melody written in three parts to give the sweetest sound, composed, that is, of the perfect oblivion of earthly things, the fervent love of eternal things, and a certain beginning on the praises sung by the blessed spirits. Happy is the man who has merited to taste this

47. 1 Cor 1.24.   48. 2 Tim 2.4.
49. Ps 136.3.

in his heart, who has known these things by true experience, rather than through telling or reading. In this happy union, if we were granted from on high such a time of rest beyond all telling, we should be caught up in a certain contemplation, and find delight that we had never known in him, the highest and true good present to us, which can draw the soul up above, and for a little while make it pass over into pure contemplation of the beloved, "so that it may give thanks to the giver of all good things";[50] but it will not pour itself out in words, but it will keep secret its secret, knowing that "the sensual man does not perceive the things that are of the spirit, for it seems foolishness to him."[51] "Nor will any stranger eat of this."[52] But with deep lamentation in his heart let him break out and say: "'Truly you are a hidden God,'[53] and 'what eye has not seen nor ear heard, nor has it entered into the heart of earthly man,'[54] not only what God has reserved in the future for his elect, and not even those things that he is accustomed to give to his lovers in this life."

(23) Disciple: It is wonderful and astonishing, how blind my heart is, and I should mourn that it is so hard. I have lived for so long a time as a wretched pauper, surrounded by the greatest abundance of spiritual riches, I have been pitiable in the midst of so many delights, I remained arid among overflowing graces. Wretch that I am, a second Tantalus! I brought sweet blushing roses from the rose garden, yet I did not smell their sweet perfume. I carried "budding flowers,"[55] and I did not see their beauty. I had my eyes open, yet I was too torpid to look on so many wonderful things. The dew from heaven fell on me, but I did not feel it. Every day I was bidden to the most delectable table, and I came away from it empty and starved.

(24) O my God, I lament to you with the deepest sorrow of my heart that I strayed from you for so long, and yet you were so near to me. You were with me, and I was not with you, for

---

50. Augustine, *Rule* 6.5.   51. 1 Cor 2.14.
52. Lv 22.10.   53. Is 45.15.
54. 1 Cor 2.9.
55. From the Dominican Breviary for the office of the Assumption.

I was involving myself in worldly cares and useless vanities, and I cared little about you. O "sweet guest of the soul,"[56] how have I received you, from the beginnings of my mature years, when you first came to me, until this present time? How have I treated you, who are all beauty? Alas, wretched man that I am, how often have I received you, who are all majesty, with irreverence! How tepidly have I eaten the bread of angels, the sum of all delights! O, the insensibility of my soul! I had a balsam-flavored liquid, honeyed, delicious and most sweet, in my mouth, yet I did not taste its fragrance. O you, most joyous mirror of all the blessed, glad vision on which all the angels gaze, happiest rejoicing of good men, I have spent my wretched life so that rarely or never have I known such sweetness from your presence, nor sometimes have I had that spiritual consolation from your sweetest presence which I might have had if I had disposed myself with due reverence and devotion towards your most sacred Body and Blood. Ah, what sorrow is my wretched lot! I had involved myself so much in worldly activities and earthly loves, I so clung to them in my desires, that "to my diseased palate"[57] bodily things tasted better than spiritual, and earthly matters concerned me more than things eternal. So if I had known in advance that on the next day some dear friend would be arriving, I could have lain sleepless for joy all that night, planning carefully with all I was capable of how I could please him in every way.

(25) But, O my God, never once have I received you, face to face, you who are most revered, most loved, whom all the choirs of heaven revere, "whom earth and sea and sky worship, adore and preach,"[58] before whose face the abyss trembles, and whom every created thing obeys, with such love and desire, nor have I honored you as I could and should. Alas, wretch and fool that I am, how far short did I fall in this. O, how quickly I turned from you to other things. "I have turned

56. From the sequence, *Veni, Sancte Spiritus*, for the Mass of Pentecost Sunday.

57. *Conf.* VII, ch. 16.

58. From the hymn for matins on feasts of the Blessed Virgin Mary, *Quem terra, pontus*.

away my face so as not to see the end."[59] How quickly I drove you out, nor would I let you have a resting place in me. Often I behaved towards you as if wearied, as if you, my God, were not there. So I pretended, as if I wished in no way to see that you were present. But now I have cast aside all pretence, as though I have been roused from sleep to keep watch, and have opened my eyes, most lovingly saluting your presence with the longing of my heart and soul. For as often as I recollect that you are present, "my spirit begins to exult"[60] in my rejoicing, like someone who receives a welcome messenger coming from afar. I say nothing of the presence, so much to be venerated, of my Lord, but even what is less, the joyful presence alone of your angels, however far off that may be when I discover it, I should salute with utter love, for even if I had not seen them with my bodily eye, still what I know by faith and am taught by inward affection must make me pay honor to their presence.

(26) Yet now I know most certainly that not only the delectable host of the angels but the Lord of the angels too makes this a place to be honored. For "indeed the Lord is in this place, and I did not know it."[61] And so I greatly mourn that I have not shown much reverence for this place in my words and my deeds. For wherever I knew my Lord to be present, I should have bowed myself humbly when I could show him no other sign of respect, as Daniel, "a man of desires," did, when, settled in a strange land, he turned his face towards the city where he knew that the Lord's temple was, and prayed to his God.[62] And see, "here there is something greater than the temple."[63] Alas, how often have I stood in choir in the presence of the sacrament with so undevout and distracted a heart. I used with my wandering eyes to show my heart's lack of devotion. O, how often have I passed by this place, in which you were present, under the form of the sacrament, as a guest most dear, carelessly and hastily, not even troubling to open my lips in some greeting of devotion, so as to pay you my heart's loving respects.

59. Ps 9.11.
61. Gn 28.16.
63. Mt 12.6.

60. Lk 1.47.
62. Dn 6.10.

(27) And yet nonetheless it is you, my Lord and my God, who are my love and my heart's most precious treasure, and therefore in your presence the heart should delight, the mind applaud, the eyes sparkle with joy, the mouth jubilate, the lips bless and glorify you, and every single member and limb show signs of your love. "Can a man hold fire in his bosom, so that he will not burn,"[64] and hide this kindled fire from his dear one who is present, so that it is not made known? Whether he wishes or not, it will be revealed by its light. So see what a slothful lover you are, and, therefore, you are no lover, because you are slothful. For an attentive lover cannot be slothful; if he is a lover, he will perform great things, and if he does nothing, he is no lover. What did he do, that musician of yours, a man after your own heart, who "naked like one of the buffoons"[65] to the sound of portable instruments "danced with all his might"[66] before the ark, in which there were merely physical objects, yet possessing "a shadow of things to come,"[67] which things have now been discovered by the truth and brought to the light? For this sacrament contains "the manna, not indeed that which they ate who died in the desert, but the bread that comes down from heaven, so that whoever will eat of it will live forever."[68]

(28) And therefore "from henceforth let no man be troublesome to me,"[69] if I find wonderful words to extol these great things, for if the members of my body numbered more than the sands of the sea, and were all sweet-sounding instruments, and all my powers were triumphant voices, with all these abilities of mine I should long to praise you, the Creator of the universe. And I weep, too, and I mourn, because until now my understanding has been too blinded, my feelings too hardened for this heavenly mystery, so that I have passed by, touching only the surface, nor have I pondered what should be weighed, and I have done too little to enable me to receive such grace. But now, with my hands stretched out as it were upon the cross, and my eyes lifted up towards heaven, I ask

64. Prv 6.27.
66. 2 Kgs 6.14.
68. Jn 6.50–52.

65. 2 Kgs 6.20.
67. Heb 10.1.
69. Gal 6.17.

pardon for what I have left undone. For until today I have been in the darkness of indolence and carelessness. Yet now Wisdom's light has driven away the darkness, and has shown you to me with a love that is beyond words, has vanquished my sloth and awakened my sleeping faith.

(29) So now it remains for you who have fed me with your welcome presence, as if "with the bread of life and understanding, to give me the water of wholesome wisdom to drink,"[70] and to teach me with it, answering these questions from your servant.

(30) First, therefore, I ask: What will you give by your presence to a man receiving you devoutly in the sacrament?

(31) Wisdom: And I ask, from where does this question come? Are you a lover, or are you a hired servant? Do you think that what you are asking is befitting to a loving spirit? A devoted lover, so long as he may have the one whom he loves, does not care much about anything else. He seeks his beloved, and so that he may possess him, he feigns indifference and passes other profitable good things by. Is it love you are seeking, or the reward of love? What have I to give that is better, that is more profitable, or that is more precious than myself? He who possesses what people know that he loves, what more should this man wish for? Whoever has given his whole self to his beloved, what, I ask, has he denied his beloved? See how I give myself to you in the sacrament, I lift you up from yourself, and I change you into me. "For it is not you who will change me into you, like food for your flesh, but you will be changed into me."[71] But perhaps you have not grown perfect in love, you love not love alone, but you love some reward of love; so now I answer you with a question just as weighty. Tell me what the sun's light bestows on the air, when it shines out in all its power, obscured by no cloud, and at noontide pierces the air as it were directly from above? Or what do the glittering Pleiades or the blazing morning star offer the cloudy night? Or what indeed of beauty does the springtime calm bring to the earth bound fast in winter's ice?

70. Ecclus 15.3.   71. *Conf.* VII, ch. 10.

(32) Disciple: There can be no doubt that all these bring with them many benefits and great beauty.

(33) Wisdom: And they all seem great and splendid to you, because they are known and understood. But in truth the spiritual gifts brought in the sacrament are in their way far greater. For the smallest grace, making a man acceptable, which anyone devoutly partaking of the sacrament merits to receive, will in the future illumine the soul with a spiritual radiance greater than any ray of the sun can shine into the pure air, for spiritual gifts surpass bodily gifts beyond all compare.[72] Yet I pass over in silence some of those divine and secret shinings with which sometimes the soul is found worthy to be transfused, even in this troubled life, so much that it thinks that the depths of light have been opened to it which yet cannot be grasped by any sense, but are known only to those who receive. So such a grace will be a schooling for the illumination that is to come, greater than if all the stars of heaven were placed close around the earth, and gave light to this world with all their power. And such a grace, if it be faithfully preserved, will in the future give to the soul a spiritual loveliness and beauty greater than any physical fairness which any summer could bestow on all the growing things of the earth. And if you want to know all these things with more certainty, consider carefully the properties of this sacrament. Is not a ray of the godhead, veiled in this sacrament, but in our native land clear and plain to see, more ready to give light to a soul, united to it here by this grace and in the future by glory, than is this visible sun to illumine the sky's whole hemisphere? For it is he alone who glows out and fills the essence of blessed spirits with himself so that they are made one spirit with him. O, how great will be the glory, how immeasurable the brightness, when the whole soul, drawn out of itself, is wholly transformed into God.

(34) And my glorified body, received here in faith with the grace of the sacrament, is it not able to adorn the whole heavenly court and every elect soul with a beauty greater than the

72. Cf. *ST* I-IIae, q. 113, a. 9, ad 2: "The good of one single man's grace is greater than the good of the nature of the whole universe."

courses of the stars and the changing of the seasons could give to this physical earth? And my soul, most noble, most closely united to the Word, and contained in this sacrament, is it not, in its fashion, both formally and effectively, greater in its light-giving power than all the morning stars and the evening constellations can be? And all these qualities will in the future be given to the faithful soul through its due partaking in this sacrament, apart from the other graces and daily profits, great and unnumbered, which are renewed again and again.

(35) Disciple: I am astonished when I hear such great marvels told of this glorious sacrament. But I beg you, do not deride one doubt that I will bring forward. Since you, omnipotent God, have been pleased to adorn this venerable sacrament with such numberless and glorious spiritual effects, not only for the future, but now in the present, I ask why all this is so secret and hidden, so that it is hardly perceived by anyone, nor does its power, if I may dare to say so, seem to be clear enough to those who believe? What may happen to others I do not know, since I am no searcher of men's consciences; but I have found this about myself from time to time, when I wanted to come to the most holy body and blood of the Lord, from whom I have heard that such good things come, that I have discovered in myself such a hardness of heart and dullness of mind, as I went to the altar and returned, that I have known nothing of all the spiritual illuminings and divine charismata that proceed from this sacrament, so far as I could tell, and I have remained so destitute that I could savor nothing of its sweet taste, but have remained without fruits, as if the sacrament itself could have in it scarcely any effect. O great "counsel of the Almighty"[73]—if only a foolish and stupid servant dared to take his lord, most wise, most blameless, ordering all things for the best, to task! Why, I ask, have you kept secret so many and so great good things? Would it not be better to restore our faith in such great mysteries by plainer signs and more evident proofs?

(36) Wisdom: Do you not know that "you walk by faith and

73. Ps 106.11.

not by sight"?[74] Do you not know that what sense shows, experience tests, and faith, so far as it can, accepts? For indeed faith must be lacking where proof knows how to find room, and, consequently, the great merit of faith will be lost.[75] So, therefore, if you want to entrust the mystery of this sacrament to experience, you will have to drive out faith and faith's merits. And suppose that one of the elect does feel "fearful thoughts"[76] passing through his mind, but still does not give in? Indeed "he will be crowned, if he has fought lawfully."[77]

(37) Open, I ask you, the book of your heart, and see how it is granted to the hearts of some men to understand the mystery of this sacrament through the plainest knowledge. Even though this may not always happen, still at times by grace and special privilege they are permitted, in some way which cannot be told, to perceive this sacrament's truth. And this is done so that even if it were possible for there to be some greater and more certain knowledge than the knowledge of faith, still it is through faith's knowledge that you are granted to know and to perceive this inestimable sacrament's truest existence, so that, for a time, faith seems somehow to cease to be actual faith, and the matter seems to pass into the realm of true and perfect knowledge. It is true that what I have said is not according to the common mode of proceeding, because this knowledge surpasses all the elements and principles of all branches of knowledge. Nor will this grace always be present in those who are most dear to God, "he providing some better thing for them"[78] by the principles of faith, but only from time to time, when, that is, the soul is caught up on high and lifted to the perception of heavenly mysteries, as divine grace then deigns to make manifest "these, and things like them," that grace which "reveals deep things out of darkness,"[79] and sometimes grants the soul to transcend manifestations, which are riddles made known to the senses, lifting them up to the invisi-

---

74. 2 Cor 5.7.
75. Cf. Gregory the Great, *Homily 26 on the Gospels*: "That faith has no merit for which human reason provides proof."
76. Wis 9.14.   77. 2 Tim 2.5.
78. Heb 11.40.   79. Jb 12.22.

ble and "hidden things of the secret places"[80] of God. But when the soul is separated from such things, it will return to the customary proofs of faith, and will know almost nothing of what it saw before.

(38) Therefore, out of all this, deduce how plain it is that this sacrament is not less true because its spiritual effect is invisible or imperceptible to the senses. For God's presence exists everywhere as a light, not indeed such a light as the human eye can see, or that is diffused upon the outside world, but such at least a light as can be seen only by the divine understanding or by one who has been blessed by it, that light which in its essence is essentially light. For the more noble that spiritual substances may be, the more simple they will be,[81] for things that are least in quantity are greatest in power.

(39) Disciple: O, how few there are in this world who use diligence and pains to ponder the most precious power and profit of this sacrament! For they drift along, led by some outworn custom, following the tracks of the herd. They hasten, not to arrive but to draw back, and their haste is not from devotion's longing but from their lack of fervor for God; and so they roam forward as if dazed, and stray back again, empty and lacking grace. And they are like "beasts that do not chew the cud,"[82] which in the Old Law were rejected as unclean. For they take no care to think or to enquire who it is that they may receive, or how many good or ill things may follow from this, as they receive him well or ill. But even if this were perhaps to come to their minds, superficially and perfunctorily, as it were, at once it is exstinguished, like a little spark in a cold heart, and it is not seen again.

(40) Wisdom: There are three kinds of men who receive me sacramentally; some of them are wholly ill-disposed, such as those who are involved in crimes;[83] there are some well-

---

80. Is 45.3.
81. Cf. Thomas Aquinas, *Commentary on the Sentences* II, d. 3, q. 3, a. 2 ad 3: "By as much as something is one and simple, by so much is it more powerful and noble."
82. Lv 11.26.
83. That is, in mortal and public sins.

disposed, such as the perfect; and some are halfway between, such as those who are not devout. The first deserve death in eternity and cursing on this earth; the second deserve eternal life and spiritual blessing; the third are eating dry bread and tasteless food, and not perceiving the sweetness of the sacrament.

(41) Disciple: What if some frail man has perhaps committed some secret sins, but just as he goes to the altar he is seized with contrition for his sins, and does what he can, according to the laws of the Church? Dare this sinful man rely on your grace to go to the altar?

(42) Wisdom: If he is truly contrite, and makes use of the counsel of physicians of the spirit, then, strictly speaking, he is not a sinner. When Mary Magdalen with contrite heart fell at the Lord's feet and washed them with her tears, she had indeed a sinner's reputation, yet she was no longer a sinner, because Christ had forgiven her sins.

(43) Disciple: "Let every man abound in his own sense."[84] In the matter that we are discussing, I truly think that the divine mysteries of this sacrament surpass all power and excel all God's wonderful works in this world. For who in this world lives in such purity and innocence that he could be "a fit minister"[85] or partaker of this sacrament? Or who would dare to presume with the very one whom Peter, glorious prince of the Apostles, drove away, saying: "Depart from me, for I am a sinful man, O Lord"?[86] And so the man whose faith among Israel God's Wisdom singled out for praise said: "I am not worthy that you should enter under my roof."[87] So who, "born of woman,"[88] will be able to prepare himself with true worthiness for such mysteries?

(44) Wisdom: "There has not risen among men born of women"[89] anyone who out of his own power and the justice of his works could prepare himself sufficiently to receive me with true worthiness, even if there were one man with the natural

---

84. Rom 14.5.
85. 2 Cor 3.6.
86. Lk 5.8.
87. Mt 8.8.
88. Jb 15.14.
89. Mt 11.11.

purity of all the angels, with the cleanliness and brightness of all of them together, and with the merits of all men living on earth in austerity of life. All the divine grace of all of these reckoned up together could make no one fitting enough to receive such mysteries.

(45) Disciple: O eternal God, how terrible it is to me and to sinners like me to hear this! "Alas, alas, Lord God,"[90] if even "the heavens are not pure in your sight,"[91] and in your angels you have found wickedness,"[92] so "men of great deeds"[93] do not merit to receive you because of their own justice. Alas for me, what will become of us, constantly rolling in the slime of sin, and as it were a lame man in the mud, as we in even our few good works vacillate and "limp between two sides"?[94] We who have little or no devotion, who are not even contrite as we should be for all that we are neglecting, do we not justly tremble to come to your altar in fear, lest perhaps what should bring us to pardon bring us instead to ruin?

(46) Wisdom: Observe carefully that this sacrament of love was ordained as a remedy, and so, whenever a man has done what he can to enable him to receive grace, that is enough. God does not demand from man what will seem to man impossible. So whenever a man receiving the sacrament does what he can, divine pity will supply through grace what he cannot attain without grace. And so, all other things being equal, you should rather go to the altar trusting in divine pity than stay away from it through considering your own frailty, even though the time and place might suggest either course as commendable. Does a sick man not hurry to the doctor, does a poor man not knock on a rich man's door? Come, knock, do not hesitate. He is a physician, a most loving giver, a most generous rewarder. He with his word alone restores all things. His presence heals wounds, mends hearts. He drives away sadness, and he gives joy of heart.

(47) Who therefore will be so ill-advised and rash as to say

90. Jer 4.10.
92. Jb 4.18.
94. 3 Kgs 18.21.

91. Jb 15.15.
93. 2 Kgs 23.20.

that those who are spiritually sick ought not to come to him
who "has borne man's infirmities and himself carried their
sorrows"?[95] See how the woman who was diseased "came behind him," and, touching him, was healed;[96] the sinful woman
was made clean whilst she kissed his feet;[97] the Canaanite
woman, because she followed him and would not go back, was
heard.[98] As lepers came up to him, they were cured.[99] The
blind, the possessed, paralytics and deformed of every kind,
because they believed and came to him, obtained their health.
For "power went out from him and healed them all."[100] Even
"tax collectors and sinners,"[101] when they drew close to Jesus,
were worthy of forgiveness. Indeed he did not despise their
feasts and hospitality, he who "did not come into this world
to call the just, but sinners."[102] So we may say, with no incongru-
ity, that as his coming in the flesh was for the salvation of
sinners, so should this "saving victim"[103] be given to the faithful
to remedy their sins. For God's Wisdom himself said, at the
Last Supper, as he instituted this health-bringing sacrament:
"This is my body, which will be given up for you," and "this is
the cup which will be poured out for you for the forgiveness
of sins."[104] And therefore, when you have done what you are
capable of, come up in confidence, with no trepidation, in
faith and love, never doubting his loving kindness.

(48) Disciple: O, words so full of grace and so lovable that
even I, a wretched sinner, knowing my own wickedness, dare
to come to the Lord of majesty! Yet now I also ask you to tell
me whether it would be better to come often or more seldom
to this heavenly sacrament?

(49) Wisdom: In this matter, accept the well-known maxim of the great teacher Augustine, who says that according
to place and time, both are commendable—at times to abstain, out of respect, and nonetheless to receive, out of devo-

---

95. Is 53.4.
96. Mt 9.20–22.
97. Lk 7.37–47.
98. Mt 15.22–28.
99. Lk 17.12–14.
100. Lk 6.19.
101. Mt 9.11.
102. Mt 9.11.
103. From the hymn *Verbum supernum,* used for the feast of Corpus Christi.
104. Mt 26.26, etc.

tion.[105] And for those in whom both respect for the sacrament and devotion increase through frequent receiving, it will be profitable to receive it frequently.

(50) Disciple: But what about those who seem to remain always in the same cramped state of heart, and do not feel either that their love grows greatly or diminishes notably? Yet still they often feel so oppressed by a certain hardness of heart that they seem to have "a sky of bronze above them, and to tread on iron ground,"[106] so arid are their spirits and so hard their hearts. Though they may recite their accustomed number of psalms and prayers, and cleanse themselves in the waters of confession, they still remain hard of heart and cold in love, nor do they ever savor any taste of spiritual grace. But let me also add this, that it is pitiable and hurtful enough for men of good intention, who often complain that at times, when they receive the sacrament, grace seems to vanish more surprisingly than at others, so that they think that it somehow spurns them who are pursuing it, driving them off as they cry out after it. This seems to me to be quite astonishing, and quite as lamentable.

(51) Wisdom: Such hardness does often afflict the devout soul, and for many reasons and in many ways. The experts have said a lot about this, but let us ignore them; hold on to this one thing, that whenever you do not find by careful self-examination that you have been the cause of this but that you have done your part, and that if such hardness of spirit is still present in you it is by God's permission, for he is accustomed to afflict his elect in a thousand different ways. Do not let this break you, and do not for reason of this make any noticeable withdrawal from this saving sacrament, but know that very often God's love makes the soul safe in ways most secret and most trustworthy, when the soul relies solely on the support of faith, not propped up by any spiritual sweetness, not helped less than if it were abounding in the richness of spiritual charismata, and yet always keeping careful guard of itself, as should

105. *Epistle 54*, To Januarius, ch. 3.
106. Dt 28.23.

be. And so from time to time such graces are withdrawn to the soul's greater benefit, so that while they are withheld they may be more eagerly sought, and, when they are received, more carefully preserved, and that in this way the beloved soul may be trained in the school of humility.

(52) And yet there is one matter, very important, that you should observe with attention: this spiritual foretasting, this kind of inward sweetness, is no effect due to faith, nor is it of this present time, but it belongs to eternal blessedness; and when it is given, in the sacrament or outside it, give thanks, but when it is not given, still give thanks, and endure patiently, knowing that this is not in your power, but belongs to the highest and most benevolent of givers, who will give, not as or when you wish, but when it will please him and as he will judge it to be to his glory and your benefit. And observe too that that highest good is so copious and so infinite that the more it is perceived, the more the receiver is in some way made able to receive it.[107] So, very often, in this sacrament it happens that the more someone is seen to be suffering from inordinate fears and to be withholding from it, the less, day by day, as he holds back, is he disposed to receive it. If other things are equal, it is better to go to the altar out of love than to stay away out of fear. It is better to go every week, or even every day, with true humility and in recognition of one's imperfection, than to go once in the year presuming on one's own righteousness.

(53) Disciple: Say, I beg you, what should be the moment when anyone going to the sacrament should pay the greatest attention, wholly recollecting himself and preparing for its grace?

(54) Wisdom: That very moment when he receives the most sacred host and feeds upon it spiritually, for it is then that heaven is somehow opened, and the beloved Son is sent and united, bodily and spiritually, to a soul disposed towards

107. Gregory the Great, *Homily 36 on the Gospels*, writes of "spiritual delicacies" that "the more he who eats them longs for them, the more are they eaten by him who longs."

him, and this is why "Mass" has its name, from the Father's sending.[108]

(55) Disciple: What about those who have the greatest longing to receive you in the sacrament, and yet cannot have what they desire? They see the minister of this sacrament standing before them and receiving you. They watch, and in the longing of their hearts stretch out their arms to you, and the soul opens its mouth, wanting to receive you, yet there is no one to hear, to offer you to the hungry soul to fill it with your desired presence. You know that to see and not to taste is a great affliction to a loving soul.

(56) Wisdom: There are those who receive me sacramentally at this table and still go away fasting. And there are those who are cheated of this table and are still filled to the full of its plenty. For those men perceive the sacrament alone, these, however, the sacrament and its power.

(57) Disciple: I still have two doubts remaining on this matter. First, does the man receive more who feeds bodily and spiritually upon you, or the one who does so only spiritually—that is, as concerns the effect of the sacrament? You know the one who is the cause of my doubting, he who says: "Believe, and you have eaten."[109] Then next, how long can this venerable sacrament remain, after it has been received by a man?

(58) Wisdom: Indeed, he will have more reason for devotion and thankfulness who has received in both ways than he who has received only in one of them, for the first man will have the giver at the same time as the gift, the cause with the effect. As to your second question, you have it clearly stated in sayings of the fathers that the body of the Lord remains so long as the sacramental species remain.

(59) Disciple: This is a prayer to the sacrament: "Hail, most holy body of the Lord, contained in this sacrament. I acknowledge you with my lips, I love you with all my heart, I long for you with all that is within me. Deign, I beg, today to look on

---

108. Latin: *propter quod et missa a missione paterna appellatur;* this was a popular explanation, though it is not the etymology—still disputed—of *missa* now favored.

109. Augustine, *Tractate 25 on the Gospel of John.*

this sick soul, longing to receive you, saving victim and fount of all graces, so mercifully and graciously that it may rejoice to have found from your presence healing for body and for soul. Do not look, Lord, on my many iniquities and neglects, but on your infinite mercies. For it is you through whom the whole earth has been created and healed, through whom all plants and all things that are strong derive their strength. You are that immaculate Lamb who are today sacrificed to the eternal Father for the redemption of the whole world. O sweetest manna, a most soothing nectar, give to my mouth the honeyed taste of your saving presence. Kindle your love in me, extinguish my vices, pour into me strength, increase your graces, give me health of mind and body. 'Bow down your heavens,' I beg, 'and descend'[110] to me, so that, joined and united to you, I may be always made one spirit with you. O venerable sacrament, let all my enemies, I implore, be driven off by you, all my sins be forgiven, and all evils be shut out by your presence. Give me good intentions, amend my way of life and direct all my actions in your will. Let my understanding now be enlightened by a new light through you, sweetest Jesus, let my love be set on fire, let my hope be strengthened, so that my reformed life may always lead me to better things, and in the end may permit me a blessed death."

110. Ps 143.5.

CHAPTER 5

How Eternal Wisdom Should Be Praised with
All Our Hearts and All Our Souls,
Always and at All Times

"HEAR ME, the waters' divine offspring, and break out in buds as the roses planted by the brooks. Give out an odor sweet as frankincense. Send out flowers like the lily, give a perfume and shoot out leaves in yielding thanks, and praise the Lord with canticles, and bless him in his works. Magnify his name, and give glory to him with the sound of your lips, with canticles from your lips and with harps, and in praising him you should say: 'All the works of the Lord are exceedingly good.'[1] Blessing the Lord, exalt him as much as you can, for he is above all praise."[2]

(2) Disciple: O my beloved, "who will grant me" that my longing heart, thirsting in love for you, yearning to praise you, may have the power to put into words what it has conceived of these praises, before death, which is so close, will come, so that the fire that burns within me might break out and travel over the whole earth, and might raise your praise in every heart and make it blaze fiercely with your love? O, if only every sweet-sounding instrument of music, the harmonies of heaven and the melodies on earth, might rise from my heart and might sound out in gentle and worthy praise of you, so that they could be welcome "to the eyes of your divine majesty,"[3] and might give some new and untellable joy to the whole celestial court!

(3) But what shall I say? I know myself, Lord, to be unworthy to praise you, yet nonetheless I pray at least that other created

1. Ecclus 39.17–21.   2. Ecclus 43.33.
3. From the Dominican Missal's last private prayer after Mass.

beings, splendid in their nobility, may deign to make up what is wanting in "my imperfect being."[4] So I ask, and this comes from the desire of my whole heart, that the planets in their courses and the starry heaven, radiant with its most pellucid light, and, too, the flowering plants, lovely to see in their vernal beauty and adorned with their fair hues, and the burning desires of love in the hearts of all who yearn for you with a most fervent longing, may praise you and bless you for ever and ever. My heart melts, my Lord, only to recall your praise, my senses are dazed, my reason is astonished, my words falter, and turned inward upon myself, I sigh more deeply. For I find in myself some desire, for which I have not words and which transcends every natural faculty, to praise you, the highest good, and yet I mourn that this is not possible, and that I must leave it unspoken. For if I wish to compare you with intelligent or intellectual created things, I find beyond doubt that you infinitely surpass everything that has been created. If I consider what is good, what is sweet, what is lovely or gracious, I know for very truth that you are more, beyond all telling, in grace than are all these, and, what is far more, that you are the spirit and the essence of them all.

(4) There is one thing that I wish to say: It is from such confrontations that I find myself acted upon again and again. When sometimes creatures, beautiful and delightful to look upon and lovable, present themselves to my mind or even in my sight, suddenly these words, spoken clearly though soundlessly, come into my heart: Ah, see and think how fair he is who made me fair. Who is he, you ask? Indeed, "he who is fairest of all."[5] Then in restless meditation I wander the heavens, I walk around the earth, I look at the North Pole, I gaze into the ocean's depth. I consider this world with its delights, I wonder at the groves and the vivid greenness of their leaves. I take into view the meadows, verdant and adorned everywhere with flowers of many hues. I walk through fields, I climb mountains, "I skip over the hills,"[6] I race through the valleys, and

4. Ps 138.16.
5. Boethius, *Consolation of Philosophy* III, meter 9.
6. Cant 2.8.

when I consider all things and see each one of them, they set my heart on fire, as with some sweet harmony in which they are all blended, in the praise of the Creator.

(5) But when in peaceful meditation I consider with care how most beautifully and how best of all you, O divine Wisdom, order all created things, the good together with the bad, what is just and unjust,[7] so that in your universe you leave nothing unordered, you who so dispose all you have made in its workings, so that nature's work is considered for its efficiency to be somehow the work of intelligence, you "who with certain laws encompassed all things, and set bounds to every single thing"[8] you who "with great favor govern us,"[9] I begin to exult greatly, and I am compelled to break out in a voice of thanksgiving with these words: "All the works of the Lord are exceedingly good."[10] Then, when I begin to transcend all these things, and I see you again as the highest good, uncreated and Eternal Wisdom, the one spouse and friend of my heart, chosen before all others, I have no mind left for amazement and ecstasy, but everything that is in me fails, and in you I greatly exult. Ah, therefore, my Lord, look now on this great love of my heart, and teach me to praise you and to glorify your glorious name, for this is what I want and seek, more than all the joys of this world.

(6) Wisdom: And ought not a loving disciple of Wisdom want to praise her, his mistress, Eternal Wisdom?

(7) Disciple: O eternal God, why do you afflict the spirit of one who loves you and has not offended? What do you ask of those whom you know? Why do you so draw out the anguish of my mind? "Lord, you know all things,"[11] you know that this is what from my childhood I have always desired in the depths of my heart, and have asked for in all my prayers.

---

7. . . . .*the good together with the bad, what is just and unjust*: this repeats Augustine's teaching, in *Of the Free Will*: "Even our sins are necessary to the universal perfection which God established." Eckhart's *Counsels on Discernment* allude to Augustine on this matter; nonetheless, he was condemned for his pronouncement, in *The Book "Benedictus"*: "Since God in some way wills for me to have sinned, I should not will that I had not committed sins." See Edmund Colledge and Bernard McGinn, *Meister Eckhart* (New York, 1981), 13–14.

8. Prv 8.27–29.   9. Wis 12.18.

10. Ecclus 39.20.   11. Jn 21.17.

(8) Wisdom: Do you not know what the prophet said, that is, that "praise is becoming to upright men,"[12] and that "praise is not seemly in the mouth of a sinner"?[13]

(9) Disciple: Indeed I do, Lord. And woe is me, because therefore I have nothing that I can say. "Or what will he answer to me, since I myself have done so?"[14] "If I wished to justify myself, my own mouth would condemn me."[15] But shall I then not praise you, because I know myself to be unclean? Do not the very worms, and the foul frogs, generated out of filth and croaking in the marshes, want to praise you, their Creator, as well as they know and can? For even if they do not know how to sing sweetly, like the little lark or the nightingale, nor can they know you by reason as man does, still they do this so that they can offer matter for your praise to those who know you.

(10) O "Father of mercies,"[16] I know and I truly perceive that it would be more fitting for such a wretched sinner as I to prostrate himself before you, and to entreat with weeping and mourning for pardon for his sins, than to praise you with the mouth that he has dirtied; yet with confidence in the power of your most loving goodness and the natural sweetness that you make known to all mortal beings, I long to praise you from the depths of my heart, imploring all your inward mercy that you will not despise me, filthy worm, "dead dog"[17] and "rotten carcass,"[18] O Lord my God. For "the powers of the heavens"[19] are unable to praise you worthily, so how much less may a frail man, filth and a worm? Indeed, "you have no need of my goods,"[20] but you make your superexcelling goodness the plainer to us as you show the more mercy to our infirmities, stooping down to us and freely giving us grace only by grace of your generosity.

(11) Wisdom: "He is catching at a shadow and following after the wind"[21] who considers that he is praising me worthily. He is attempting the impossible who is striving to praise every-

12. Ps 32.1.
13. Ecclus 15.9.
14. Is 38.15.
15. Jb 9.20.
16. 2 Cor 1.3.
17. 2 Kgs 9.8.
18. Is 14.19.
19. Mt 24.29.
20. Ps 15.2.
21. Ecclus 34.2.

thing that is in me. This is however no reason for ceasing to praise, but it is fitting for you, as for all creatures, to praise your Creator, for there is nothing created that may not praise its Maker, or at the least show him as praiseworthy. And you must consider how much more sweetly in the ears of the divine majesty a holy meditation sounds than resounding words produced without feeling, and "the groaning of a heart"[22] than the mere noise of a tongue, the humility that is sincere than a trilling voice. And that you may understand what I have said better in an example from life, look at me, and see how, though the whole of my life on earth was for the glory of my Father in heaven, he was yet in some way more perfectly shown in me when, confessing him upon the cross and redeeming the human race, out of obedience I sustained "the sorrows of death."[23] There are some who praise me with their rhetorical language but anger me by their unpleasing conduct. "They honor me with their lips, but their heart is far from me."[24] And there are some who praise God while all goes well, but when things turn out badly they are loud in voicing their impatience, and their praise is unwelcome to God, because it is not pure. But the praise of those who with their whole heart, at all times, in misfortune as in prosperity, confess God, and when they are variously punished and afflicted, give him thanks, is most welcome and acceptable to him.

(12) Disciple: "I beg that your servant may speak a word"[25] to the heart of his Lord. Truly I confess that with regard to what you have said, until now I have been wanting, that I have given you more praise in prosperity than in adversity. But now I offer my whole self to your will as a sacrifice of praise, and my spirit is eager for this, so that, whatever evils or ill fortune were to come to me, I should wish to praise you no less, but rather give thanks to you in all things, and endure them all patiently for love of you. And if my death were to be more to your glory than my life, then indeed I should choose to hand over gladly my life, still in my youth so dear to me, to death;

22. Ps 37.9.
24. Is 29.13; Mt 15.8.
23. Ps 17.5.
25. Gn 44.18.

and the remaining years that I may have, if I be not forestalled by death, I want to offer in this spirit to my Lord. For I should ask with my whole heart that if "my youth, soon ended,"[26] had lasted as long as Methusala's many years, out of all that long time its every year, and every month of those years, and every week of those months, and every day of those weeks, and every hour of those days, and every minute of those hours may all together praise you in my person as devotedly and lovingly as ever any one of the number of the blessed spirits "in the splendor of the saints"[27] could praise you in all such a length of time, as if I might in my own person have accomplished all this. And might the frequent renewal of this praise in its infinity exceed any number that could be counted.

(13) What is yet more, if what were pleasing to your will and redounding to your praise were to consist—though might that never be so—in the soul, departed from the body, having to accept either the fire of purgatory or indeed the torment of hell as punishment for its misdeeds, might I never wish to praise my Lord the less, but with a ready spirit, if I could at all, might I supply all men's neglects and make amends for every irreverence shown to you since the beginning of the world. But if we suppose the impossible, that my soul were already "in hell,"[28] where no one confesses your praise, yet so that in my love I wished still to praise you, still I should wish to call out from the deepest darknesses of the infernal regions praise in a voice resounding your praise, so that my great cry might reach to the ends of hell and the whole structure of the world and the heights of the sky and the heavens, and might come even to the high throne of your splendor. What else? Do with me what may be pleasing to you, for so long as there is breath in my nostrils, I shall not cease to proclaim your praise.

(14) But even when my powers of speech will fail in the hour of death, and for weakness I can no longer proclaim my Jesus, I pray that by at least moving my eyes or pointing my

26. Wis 4.16.
27. From the first Mass of the Nativity.
28. Ps 6.6.

finger I may renew and strengthen all my loving desires, and my words and my deeds past and to come, which I should wish to offer to you in devoted service until the day of judgment, if I could live so long. What is more, my beloved one, I add this, the desire of a loving heart, that when my body will be reduced to smallest particles of dust and covered with a stone, some pleasing sound giving praise and glory to you may rise from every minutest particle, and piercing the hardest stone may rise to the heavens' heights, and may sound the proclamation of a loving praise until the day of judgment, until at the blessed resurrection my body and my soul, united with one another, may be joined to praise and glorify you eternally.

(15) Yet so long as I am still in this body's prison, I beg that I may be taught how I may come to be able to praise you "with my whole heart and my whole soul and with all my strength"[29] at all times and as it were unceasingly. Out of my great desire for this, I have often said inwardly with a burning heart: "O swiftest movement of the cause of all motion, why do you hasten so? Why do you pass so swiftly by? What is the reason for this speed? I implore you to make possible what is impossible, and to stand still a little while. Act with less haste. Let the sun not move towards its setting until for one instant, one twinkling of an eye in this brief hour, I may utter, one hundred thousand times over, praises and glory to my Lord, my beloved and the one joy of my heart, out of the very depths of all my love!" I confess that this has often happened with me: when my mind for a time has been distracted by various matters, and I have then come suddenly back to myself and have recollected, I have said: "O my beloved, a thousand years have passed by since last I had you present in my memory. So, love of all my heart, open to me your treasure, and teach me, I ask, for as long as I shall live and survive, how I may be able, so far as that is possible, always to praise you without the hindrance of any interruption."

(16) Wisdom: Whoever has God in his intention in everything that he does, and guards himself from sin, and does not

29. Dt 6.5; Lk 10.27.

abandon the exercise of virtues, never ceases to praise God continually. To answer honestly what you are asking, the sayings of the fathers which you know should indeed teach you that when the human mind has been purged of earthly vices, and restored from all the dregs of the passions,[30] and attains, so far as that is granted to human weakness, to an unshakable peace of mind and to perfect purity, such a man will come to the unbroken perseverance in my praise, which is recognized as the end and consummation of a spiritual man's whole perfection. "And when the mind will be established in such a peace, or freed from the toils of all carnal passions, and will cling with a most persistent intention of spirit to that one and highest good,"[31] he will then praise God without ceasing. For when the mind's understanding has been absorbed by this purity, if one may say this, and changed from its earthly station into a spiritual and angelic likeness, whatever it accepts, whatever it considers, whatever it does will be the most pure and sincere praise and prayer to God.

(17) Disciple: Yet it now remains for you, O most loving Wisdom, after these sweetest words, which you have produced from divine Wisdom's storehouse, to condescend to instruct me about certain doubts. And the first is, where shall I be able to find the greatest incentive and the best matter for your praise?

(18) Wisdom: In the contemplation of that highest and most divine and superexcelling majesty in which are contained from eternity, as in their fount and beginning, most simply and without difference of form, all good things.[32] Then next, in the streams of particular good things flowing out from that highest good, which are shared in different ways by created things, to a greater or less degree, as the cause of all causes deigns to communicate them to individual creatures.

(19) Disciple: I am ailing, and I have no strength to mount

---

30. Cf. Cassian, *Conversations* IX, ch. 4: "Let us take care to lead the mind, purged of all earthly vices and purged of every filth of the passions, on to its natural subtlety. . . ."

31. This is almost literally from the *Conversations* IX, ch. 6.

32. Cf. *ST* I, q. 13, a. 4, c., and *CG* II, ch. 2.

to the contemplation of those heights of divine majesty, but I leave this to the cedars of Lebanon, that is, to those who are stronger, and I shall seek a place in the depths, apt to hold me, along with the thistles. Yet on this account I shall not be silent in your praises, though I may seem in my weakness to have done no more than make this possible for stronger men. For truly we often see that among the sweetest songbirds of the grove and the warbling nightingales, there are also croaking crows, humbly serving their Creator with what little they have been given.

(20) So I too, sinner that I am, have a song for sinners ready, and as well as I can I shall praise and glorify my God with it forever, since I know no sweeter song about God to sing except this one, which is that "the Lord is sweet to all"[33] and "his mercy is over all his works."[34] O "my God, my mercy!"[35] In this the soul rejoices, the conscience is gladdened, and "all my bones"[36] are strengthened with an immense joy. My soul will sing this sweet canticle forever, with a joyful and sweet melody among the kingdom of God's birds. Whenever I turn over in my mind what once I was, from what crises I have escaped, in how many dangers you have protected me and out of what evils you have rescued me—"you have loosed my bonds,"[37] healed my festering wounds, and "you have broken the" perilous "snares,"[38] and sweetly and in a fatherly manner "you have set me free"[39]—when, I say, I muse on these benefits and others like them which you have shown to me, it is wonderful that in the loving remembrance of them all I can hold myself upright for love, so do I burn with love's most ardent fires. O my God, how long have you waited in patience for a sinner who was resisting you! How often have you given me fatherly admonishment, sometimes, it is true, sweetly, but sometimes harshly. "You went before me with blessings of sweetness"[40] when I did not know it, you hastened out like a father to meet your prodigal son, weighed down with sins and naked of graces, you did

---

33. Ps 144.9.
35. Ps 58.18.
37. Ps 115.16.
39. Ps 123.7.

34. Ps 144.9.
36. Ps 43.10.
38. Ps 115.16
40. Ps 20.4.

not turn your merciful face away from the traveler along the roads of depravity, but always and everywhere you were loving and merciful.

(21) And what is more than all this, for all these manifold graces I have always been ungrateful, but you, highest goodness, for all this you did not give up, until at last you had drawn me sweetly to you. Ah, greatest gentleness for which there are no words, how for all this can I prevent myself from praising you? I cannot, in any way. "My God, my mercy," for all these and your other innumerable benefits I ask and desire that I may utter to you such joyful praise as was that of the blessed spirits, when they rejoiced, at the first sight of your most divine majesty, to be eternally made strong in praising you when the evil ones were endlessly rejected by you. And let it be as great and as joyful as that of the holy souls, when they are loosed out of purgatory's prison and first presented before your glorious face, so that they may look into your joyful countenance, as great as will be the praise in the streets of the heavenly Jerusalem after the last day when all will rise again, when the elect, separated from the wicked, will all praise God with joyful heart and eternally glory in their salvation.

(22) Now, O sweet and loving teacher, I wish to know from you how I may convert the feelings of love that sometimes rise up in me, about which I doubt whether they come from nature or from grace, into your praise. Then, how may I turn not only good things but also what is bad, those visitations "sent by evil angels,"[41] and all things that are seen and heard and felt everywhere "into the praise of my Creator"?[42]

(23) Wisdom: I answer these three questions in your order. And first we say that it is difficult to make distinctions between those feelings of love of which you speak, because they so greatly resemble one another. And therefore all such feelings that are truly pure and sincere, such as joy and exultation, provoking in you a certain joyousness, or even, as happens from time to time, moving you to sweet tears or to such other

41. Ps 77.49.
42. Augustine, *On the Literal Sense of Genesis* IV, ch. 22.

emotions, about which "you do not know from where they come or where they go"[43]—as soon as you feel all these overwhelming sensations pervading you, you should as it were show them with devotion and offer them up to the maker of all things, in the manner of the acceptable sacrifice that "Abel offered up"[44] to God, that they may be used for his praise, who is the Creator of nature and the giver of grace; and so such graces, which are in themselves natural and not meritorious, through the end to which they are put can in some way be made supernatural, that is, meritorious.

(24) Yet as often as you hear the evil spirits' blasphemous suggestions beginning to whisper in your mind, rise up at once and say: "O God most high, it is my prayer and my wish that my soul may have the power to usurp the place and function in which this malignant spirit should have praised you to all eternity, if he had only stood fast, and that he may be brought so low that, whenever he will invade my mind against its will with these abominable thoughts, always, through all that I pray and wish for, they may become praise and thanksgiving beyond words to you in all eternity. And as often as I sustain the invasion of these evil promptings, so often I offer with love the sacrifices of praise most pleasing to you." And so, as you see, "to those who love God all things work together for good,"[45] since even such pestilential suggestions can give way to their profit.

(25) As to the last question that you have asked, this is what should be done. Whenever you see or become aware in any way of something especially remarkable, it may be a leafy grove or a meadow fair with flowers, a field heavy with seeds, a tree full of fruit or any other such thing, lift your heart and your eyes and your hands to heaven, and say out of the deep love of your heart: "O noble and loveliest Wisdom, in accordance with the fair and excellent prerogatives and gifts obtaining in this matter, may 'a thousand thousand ministrants' of the heavenly hosts salute you for me, and 'ten thousand times one

43. Jn 3.8.   44. Gn 4.4.
45. Rom 8.28.

hundred thousand standing before you'[46] glorify you, and the worldwide melody sung by all created things praise you for me, now and in eternity."

(26) Disciple: O eternal God, if praise to you in this wayfaring life is so joyful, what will it be in our native land? If to recollect it gives such delight, what will its presence be? But alas, through this wonderful and indescribable sweetness of your praise, O divine Wisdom, my heart is at once made joyous, and yet within, as it were, wounded with cruel sorrow. For when I think of myself in this vale of misery, and see myself still so far off from the perfect praises of the blessed, among my words of praising there break out tears of mourning. O, when will that longed-for day come, which "will deliver me from the body of this death"?[47] For who will not long and greatly "desire to be dissolved and to be with Christ,"[48] and to pass from this state of misery, from this field of battle "into the liberty of the glory of the children of God"?[49] It is time, Lord. "It is enough for me, take away my soul, for I am no better than my fathers."[50] See how perilous the state of this world is becoming. See how many evils begin to shoot up in every place. Woe, "woe to those who are with child and give suck in those days."[51] Happy the man who is well prepared, and who awaits an early death, yet I shall call him happier who already has passed from mortality's dwelling place and "has come in happiness to the heavenly bridal chamber."[52] But I, who am in neither one state nor the other, how shall I be consoled? O my God, what in the meantime, while such labors and anguishes oppress us, what should refresh or rejoice my soul?

(27) Wisdom: See, here is something on which for a while you may ponder, that is, this page of joyful divine praise, which, if you turn back to it often, you may use to console yourself in adversities. For spiritual joy and a readiness for divine praise is as it were a certain prelude to the celestial joys

46. Dn 7.10.
47. Rom 7.24.
48. Phil 1.23.
49. Rom 8.21.
50. 3 Kgs 19.4.
51. Mt 24.19.
52. From the Dominican Breviary's office for the feast of the Assumption.

in which all the elect with full voice and joyous heart will praise me and glorify me forever. This divine praise refreshes the mind in adversity, it lifts up the spirit, and it drives off excessive sorrow. It puts spiritual enemies to flight, it appeases God, it rejoices the angels, it sets souls free from purgatory, and it offers new joys to all the celestial court.

(28) Disciple: O, "arise, arise" now, my soul, "and utter a canticle,"[53] a canticle indeed of praise "with a voice of joy."[54] Let cymbals clash, let hearts together jubilate, let the whole firmament dance to the creator's praise. O most loving Wisdom, eternal goodness, I pray you that at every dawn, when I rise to you and open my eyes, I may also open my heart in your praise, and that from it there may then arise a great brand, of some resplendent and light-bearing star, blazing with the fire of your praise, containing in it the most intense degree of your love ever granted from above to human heart. Let it kindle within itself an ardor like that of the spirit which burns most fiercely among the highest rank of the heavenly host,[55] in you and because of you, no less like the burning of that supersubstantial and superessential and ineffable love in which you, O heavenly Father, love most fervently your only-begotten Son in the Holy Spirit. And I ask that this praise may resound in your fatherly heart as sweetly and as gently as the sweet modulation of every harp and instrument of music is wont to sound in a joyful heart, when men are still in the days of blossoming youth. And from this torch of praise let there then arise a perfumed "pillar of smoke" of your glorification, pleasing as if it were composed of all "aromatical spices, of myrrh and frankincense and of all the powders of the perfumer,"[56] lovely as the flowers of the field, blossoming in springtime in beautiful hues, as the trees stand adorned with their leafy branches and their welcome fragrances. Let the torch of this praise be

53. Jgs 5.12.   54. Ps 41.5.
55. The seraphim: cf. pseudo-Dionysius, *The Celestial Hierarchy*, ch. 7: "The seraphim have their holy name because in Hebrew it means 'knowing' or 'burning' or 'giving heat,'" which Thomas Aquinas quotes, *ST* I, q. 108, a. 5, ad 5.
56. Cant 3.6.

so full of love and delight that your eyes may turn to it in pleasure, and let the whole hall of heaven dance. And let this mount constantly and ceaselessly, with the most ardent fire and the swiftest heat of your love, up from my heart through devout meditation, through fervent words from my lips, and from all my works, by means of my holy and heavenly way of life; and may this torch of praise by its power repel every enemy, increase grace, gain me a blessed end and acquire for me the glory of eternal blessedness, so that the end of this praising on earth may be the beginning of the eternal praise in our heavenly native land. Amen.

CHAPTER 6

A Guide for Incorporating These Matters into
Sermons and Conferences

HIS MOST excellent teaching of yours, O most loving Wisdom, will also be "a treasure to be desired"[1] in the mouth of a wise man, if it be so ordered that it is not only easy to understand or pleasing to hear, but also applicable to every man's state of life. For its own perfect integrity requires that this should be so. For a zeal for souls demands that we should often have a worthy recourse to the true love that we feel when we praise you. So "a faithful and wise servant"[2] who follows the example of the apostolic Church is bound by the obligation of brotherly love to be concerned not only with himself but also with "the salvation of souls and the profit of his neighbors."[3] And therefore, now that you have shown me these proofs that this wisdom can save, I ask you to show me how I shall be able easily to turn this same teaching to the profit of my neighbors, and make it widely known. Next, give to a simple pupil a convenient and practical form and technique to do the same with any other similar material that may be vague and imprecise, that out of the honeycomb's broken cells I shall be able to draw honey, and break bread for children, and distribute it to the crowds, with the grace to make it multiply.

(2) Wisdom: You could be well and concisely informed about what you are asking from me if you would make the effort and take the pains to put into practice that most useful maxim which you once read in what one learned man had discovered, instead of throwing it to the winds. If you ask me

1. Prv 21.20.   2. Mt 25.45.
3. From the Dominican Constitutions.

what that was, it is simply what this famous man says: "A wise man's task is to set things in order."[4] What could be better than this, more useful, more excellent? For the things that are from God are well ordered,[5] and what retains its order will last. So I shall do in this matter as in everything we have discussed before and teach you what you are asking by an example, rather than through discourse; and you can observe everywhere the procedure and order I am showing to you now.

(3) So see from what we have said, that anyone wanting to strengthen not merely himself but also his neighbor, wisely and piously, with this teaching from Wisdom, as he examines it carefully, will find there something that can be of profit to them both. For some of the chapters are arranged so that they can in some way be applicable to anyone who wishes to devote himself to them with some diligence. This is true of all the chapters that treat of Christ's Passion. In them, all that need be considered is how much Christ suffered and the nature of his sufferings, and how many there were, and how every man ought to conform himself spiritually to them through meditating on these passages. For example, the chapter that you will find above,[6] where divine Wisdom begins to stir up the Disciple's fervor by explaining the Passion, ought to be arranged in this way for the people:

1. (4) Even though Christ, the Son of God, when his terrifying Passion drew close and he knew with terror that the death that was to come upon him was so near, poured bloody drops of sweat upon the earth, still freely he entrusted his will to that of his Father, and faithfully accomplished what he had begun. So every faithful soul, in all the pains of adversity and the anguishes of tribulation, however strong his natural reluctance may be, should entrust himself to the Father's will and devoutly accept what may come.

2. (5) And as Christ was arrested and bound fast, and could

---

4. Aristotle, *Metaphysics* I, ch. 2, frequently quoted by Thomas Aquinas.
5. Künzle notes that this is a common medieval argument from Romans 13.1: "Let every soul be subject to higher powers, for there is no power but from God, and those that are ordained of God."
6. Bk. I, ch. 3, above.

not go where he might wish, so a man must hold himself captive, nor must he follow the desires of his flesh and his sensual appetites, which will lead him to what will harm him.

3. (6) Then, on that same night he bore patiently all the mockeries shown to him and the shameful treatment heaped on him by wicked men, and so let a man patiently endure all the contemptuous and hurtful words and the insults and all the injuries done to him by evil and cruel men, for love of his Redeemer, suffering all this and indeed much more for his sake.

4. (7) Then when he was led to Caiphas, at the risk of death he did not forsake the truth, but with all modesty confessed that he was the Son of God, so bringing cursing and condemnation on himself. So no true servant of his ought to forsake the truth because of any earthly danger, but should hold out in constancy even to death.

5. (8) When his sweetest mother saw her Son in such anguish, she greatly mourned, and suffered with him in her whole heart, and wept most bitterly. So let a faithful friend mourn and suffer with his dear friend when he is enduring evils.

6. (9) Then when he was brought before the governor and falsely accused of wicked deeds, he showed every mildness and patience. And so it is that a true imitator of Christ will not murmur or complain or contradict when he is unjustly injured or attacked by envious men.

7. (10) Divine Wisdom was dressed up in white, and despised and mocked as if he were a fool;[7] so a spiritual man will patiently suffer all the mockeries commonly imposed on him by the empty-minded men of this world who do not have God before their eyes.

8. (11) "The King of glory"[8] is crowned with a crown of thorns, he is made sport of with a sceptre and purple to deride him, and so too when Christ's servant in this world is despised and rejected as if unworthy of any honor, and is looked down upon by the presumptious and is jeered at, let him think that

7. Lk 23.11.   8. Ps 23.7.

"a servant is not greater than his master,"[9] and do not let him count this as affliction, if things like it were suffered by the King of kings.

9. (12) After this he is stripped and flogged, and with the knotted scourges that most holy flesh and those most delicate limbs were most cruelly torn. His lovely body is livid with wounds, and crimson everywhere with his blood. So a valiant warrior should chastise his body with harsh treatment and fitting hardships, lest it should begin to disobey him and to shrink back.

10. (13) Then at length, when the sentence of death has been pronounced upon "the maker of life,"[10] carrying his cross, he is hustled outside the city to the place where he will suffer; as if he were a criminal, he who is judged unworthy to live in this world, and so let a true imitator of Jesus Christ "deny himself,"[11] and carrying his cross "outside the camp" go out with Jesus, "bearing his reproaches,[12] made like the refuse of this world,"[13] "always bearing about in his body the mortification of Jesus that the life also of Jesus be made manifest in his body."[14]

(14) And so in a way like these ten articles should all the chapters following that deal with Christ's Passion be treated, and this should also be done in the chapter already discussed,[15] that is, about the profits of worldly tribulations, out of which similar treatments can be assembled and applied as may be seen fit. And so let a preacher do with the many such discussions that resemble these and may have power to move: let him order and enumerate them for presentation to his listeners, and then, by dealing with them at greater length, make out of them a conference of his own choice that can move men's minds. But some will require more careful examination.

(15) For example, in chapter 1 above, dealing with how God draws men to him, a careful reader will find, among other

9. Jn 13.16.
10. Acts 3.15.
11. Mt 16.24.
12. Heb 13.13.
13. 1 Cor 4.13.
14. 2 Cor 4.10.
15. Bk. I, ch. 13, above.

matters, these profits in God's espousals with us: from this there will come purity of conscience, peace of mind, a good reputation, an enduring fame, the greatest riches of delight of the spirit and of divine joys, peaceful sleep because one has found a safe protector, glory and honor and eternal happiness. Whoever takes Wisdom as his friend will be adorned "with beauty of life," and will be clothed "in a robe of glory" and crowned "with a crown of joy."[16] In return for a little labor, he will enjoy great rest, and he will be blessed with true and perfect blessedness, which consists in the contemplation of the highest and truest good. And he will be full of honor and grace, peaceful and fortunate, wise and experienced, spiritual and godly, lovable and the secure possessor of all good things.

(16) Then it should be observed, in the chapter dealing with fervent penitence,[17] that these evils among others are the consequences of sin: violent remorse, mourning and weeping, sorrow and sadness and crying aloud from the heart, and misery. God is lost, and the wretched soul is separated from the highest good. It is stripped of graces, and despoiled of heavenly gifts. It is clothed in confusion, and filled with ignominy. It is deceived, abandoned and somehow deprived of all good things. It is tormented by the remorse of its own conscience, it dies a living death, and though in health, it is made sick. It forgets the name of its spouse, it offends God, it destroys itself. It dishonors its Savior, it gives joy to its enemies, it even saddens the holy angels. It is filled with shame, terror and distress. Sin creeps slyly upon a man, taking away his senses, piercing his heart and destroying him with a sweet poison. It tears out his spirit's eyes, it puts to flight the Holy Spirit, and robs the man of all his strength.

(17) A sinner is exposed defenceless to his enemies' swords, he withers inside himself and is made "burdensome to himself."[18] Seeing the good of other men, he is further confounded and overwhelmed by the loss of his own.

(18) Sin is compared with lead, with a lion, with thunder

16. Ecclus 6.31, 32.   17. Bk. I, ch. 6, above.
18. Jb 7.20.

and with wormwood. It takes away peace of heart, and it will overwhelm men with horror as they sleep. So the soul grows bitter, and in the end every created thing is turned into a torment for him. Sometimes sin persuades a man "to curse the day when he was born,"[19] and to fall into the pit of unhappy desperation.

(19) About the chapter concerning bad religious,[20] in whom the fervor of devotion is extinct, note that a tepid or frivolous religious is to be mourned over, for he is somehow more wretched than all creatures, for he lacks both God and the world. He is compared with a ruinous city, which either collapses suddenly or falls away little by little, until in the end the whole of it is lost. Again, he is compared with a sea monster for his outward and inward deformity. For a true and perfect religious ought to have these qualities: spurning all worldly things, burning with love for his Creator alone, always practicing holy meditations and good works, strengthening himself and his neighbor, trapping or wounding no one, but leading a life of blessedness in simplicity and sincerity. He "crucifies his flesh with its vices and concupiscences,"[21] he practices great exercises and customs full of devotion, he makes powerful and valiant war upon the enemy's weaknesses, and offers himself even to death for the defence of truth and righteousness.

(20) But the qualities of a bad religious are these: impudence towards his superiors, quarrelsomeness, grumbling, not wanting to endure anything, but always to live by his own will, inordinate covetousness of worldly goods, and too lax a rein on the circumstances of fleshly sin, lack of divine charity, envy of his brethren's success, overmuch chasing after honors and neglect of holy customs. They are idle in God's service, busy in the search for worldly things, and always too concerned with their body's welfare. They are prone to imitate bad examples rather than good, and to defend their own negligence by pointing out others' tepidity. They talk idly, and with "evil communications they corrupt good manners."[22]

19. Ecclus 23.19.   20. Bk. I, ch. 5, above.
21. Gal 5.24.   22. 1 Cor 15.33.

Sometimes they produce spiritual talk at the right time, but at other times they steal off to indulge in carnality, fearing, rather than God's sight, the eyes of men alone. Their hearts are full of worldly desires. Even if what good they possess be little, this is mixed with great evils.

(21) And so in this way, from all the other chapters of this book to the end, anyone studying diligently will be able to gather flowers with which he may draw his neighbor into the way of salvation and stir him to devotion. So we pass over what he should do himself, so that by this study the fruits of salvation and the reward of everlasting requital may increase for him.

CHAPTER 7

How Many of the Faithful May Be Wedded to Divine Wisdom, and How They Should Renew Themselves Constantly in Wisdom's Love Through Certain Easy Daily Exercises

"COME, CHILDREN, listen to me.[1] Come, listen, and I shall tell you, all you who fear God, what great things the Lord has done for my soul.[2] For he has done great things for me, for he is mighty and his name is holy."[3] In truth these things are notable and great and remarkable, so that every man is rightly amazed by them, "glorifying God,"[4] and saying: "For he is good, for his mercy lasts forever."[5] And if it seems that I, occupied with all these topics, am "transported in mind to God"[6] in a certain sober drunkenness, that has to be admitted. "For the love of Christ urges us on,"[7] and now "our mouth is open," yet "our heart is also enlarged."[8] So I long at once with a great desire of my heart to proclaim for your hearing this message full of joyfulness and exultation, granted for the salvation of many. "For it is good to hide the secret of a king, but honorable to reveal and confess the works of God."[9] So now "hear, all you people."[10] I come from the royal nuptials, I am drunk with the wine of heaven I have quaffed, I rejoice as master of the bridal chamber. And what is more, I bring good tidings, I bear fresh joys for all men, and so I cannot contain myself for jubilation, but I am filled full of rejoicing, and I exult in the Lord. If you ask from where this rare and seldom-known cause of joy has risen "upon our

1. Ps 33.12.
2. Ps 65.16.
3. Lk 1.49.
4. Lk 18.43.
5. Ps 105.1.
6. 2 Cor 5.13.
7. 2 Cor 5.14.
8. 2 Cor 6.11.
9. Tb 12.7.
10. 3 Kgs 22.28.

land,"[11] I tell you truly that it is because "in these paschal rejoicings,"[12] the royal nuptials of our souls, that great King and divine emperor has joined me to him, me, Eternal Wisdom, his only beloved, as his spouse, he has made a marriage bond with me, and has in some way made me his son-in-law. "O, who am I, that I should be son-in-law to the King?"[13] Who would dare to aspire to such an honor? O, how great a thing is this, that anyone so poor and lowly, so vile and unworthy, with no previous merits to commend him, should have been raised up to such dignity. Who could value the price of these dearest gifts, most deserving of every kind of thankfulness?

(2) Yet not content even with these things, the bountiful King has added rewards, has heaped up benefits, has multiplied gifts and has spread his grace far and wide. For this humble Disciple of his Wisdom, when he was given the grace to see her, was called by her with a new and mystical name, "Friar Amandus,"[14] when in the chamber of his heart, the nuptial apartment, with his most divine spouse he had asked for her "silent secrets," and had been sweetly lulled in the arms of his love, and had fallen asleep, though still his heart in its fervent love was wide awake,[15] and he had spoken with her about the salvation of others, she, that spouse, replied to him in dulcet words, which were intellectual and supernatural and unlike the nature of any human converse, and she said: "For it is from you that there will proceed that in which 'all the nations will be blessed.'"[16]

(3) In reply to these words, spoken in heavenly fashion, with great delight and yet with equal astonishment, and, most of all, in great gratitude, he turned to Wisdom and said: "O 'light of my eyes,'[17] O desire of my soul and joy of my mind, what I cannot say in words, my sweetest love, so fair and nobler than all others without compare, adorned from head to foot in most seemly fashion with every grace, see, you know it to be the state and the mark of an intense love, that anyone who

11. Cant 2.12.
12. From the Easter Eve *Exultet.*
13. 1 Kgs 18.18.
14. See Bk. I, ch. 1, note 14, above.
15. Cant 5.2.
16. Gn 22.18.
17. Ps 37.11.

loves intensely longs that what he loves be pleasing to others, too, and that it should be loved and praised by all others, though still not to his own prejudice. Such is now the present state of my loving heart, as I mingle so many ardent sighs with my words. Yet you are that one and only treasury, stored up with every good that may be desired, and overflowing, and it is your singular prerogative, as you give yourself in this, that the more anyone who loves you will 'pass you on without envy'[18] to many others, the more perfectly will he in himself possess you.

(4) "Therefore, O benign Wisdom, careful for the salvation of all men, give now some means, devise some suitable way by which this love of yours and the spiritual betrothal with you may become more widely known, or may even, in these slothful ones in whom it is now enfeebled, to some extent be renewed. For even nature, perfectly constituted by you, provides for some the necessary remedies by which their constant backsliding, which is certain to happen, since all nature is subject to the laws of time, may constantly be repaired.[19] So indeed the gifts of grace also require frequent renewal, lest they perish or decrease. O my God, since so many have known by experience how joyful it is to be betrothed to you, if they only knew how little labor on their part is needed to gain so immense a reward! It makes me burn when I think that all these good things are put within our grasp and are disregarded by so many, and that "the harvest is so great, and the workmen so few"[20] to be found.

(5) "O, with what great desire for this did that great teacher, the Apostle Paul, burn! Moved by his brotherly love, he longed 'himself to be an anathema for his brethren'[21] so that he might counsel them to such spiritual marriage. For what did he say? 'I have espoused you,' he says, 'to one husband.'[22] And that godly man Dominic, our great father, as it were some heavenly groomsman at this wedding, longed to sell himself, so that he

18. Wis 7.13.
19. "continua defectio . . . continue restaurantur": *conduplicatio*.
20. Mt 9.37.   21. Rom 9.3.
22. 2 Cor 11.2.

might wholly 'spend himself and be spent'[23] for the renewal of this divine love in souls for their salvation. And so his inseparable companion, that man of the gospel Francis, 'counted all things but as dung,'[24] so that he might draw all men to this precious love, and so that he might 'gain many lovers for Christ.'[25] And so have many others done who were dear to God since the beginning of the world, who for the sake of this exposed themselves to torments and innumerable dangers, judging that so they were making themselves so much the happier in sharing their espousal, the more companions and fellows they might draw to it.

(6) "So now, my Lord, by following with devotion in the footsteps of our fathers, I who too am wounded by the dart of this love, and pierced through and through by the zeal of my love for my brothers, 'bend the knees'[26] of my heart to you, entreating with sobbing and tears that you will not allow this spiritual marriage with you so to disappear in our days, but that you will pour some grace of renewal of it into the hearts of many men. Deal with us, Lord, not according to the poverty of our merits, but as befits your lovable and most loving goodness. For all our health depends upon your clemency. It is through that that you are kind beyond words to the wretched, that you are so loving and appeaseable with those who are so unworthy. But, that I may not detain you longer, see me, a wretched sinner, burdened with my own crimes, but confiding in your immense pity, lying prostrate before you; and I shall not rise from the earth until the word full of grace will issue from your lips, until you rise and show yourself benevolent, until you offer your consent, and permit yourself, now as in former times, to be married to man."

(7) Wisdom: But I would have been prepared at all times to fulfill what you have asked and to consent to such spiritual marriage, if only there had been those who might have wished to labor duly in such a union. But it is amazing how many

23. 2 Cor 12.15.   24. Phil 3.8.
25. From the Dominican Missal's preface for the Mass of St. Dominic; 1 Cor 9.19.
26. Eph 3.14.

there are who want to receive this betrothal gift, but do not want to work to obtain it. There are those indeed without number who would choose me as their bride, if they could achieve this happiest of unions without any effort. For who, unless he is insane, would not take an enormous weight of gold given to him for nothing, and make off with it? Since it is true that "wisdom is drawn out of secret places,"[27] anyone who will want to possess it will need to search for it, as if it were wealth with toil and care, and "dig for it as if for a hidden treasure."[28] "For it is not found in the land of those who live easily."[29] And so too it has been decreed by God's deliberations that no one will receive this most worthy bride unless first he has fought most valiantly for her in the vanguard and has endured many hardships. And whoever in these tribulations "will persevere manfully to the end"[30] in this world in her service will in the end be happily joined to her forever in her glorious kingdom. It is no wonder that we have to work for our reward. For who in this brief life obtains what he wants by wishing and not working? So they who will not stoop to suffer hardships for her love are not worthy of being wedded perfectly to her.

(8) Disciple: "Indeed, Lord; for even the whelps eat of the crumbs that fall from the table of their masters."[31] And so let this at least be done, that you may deign especially to grant participation in that perfect and divine espousal to some of your lovers, weak and frail indeed, as "your hand will provide."[32] Stoop down, I beg, to those of us who are sick and assailed by the malices of these times, and give them at least some of this grace, according to the various grades in which they might participate. For there are various grades, in the beings you have created—"or have you one blessing only, Father?"[33] Give us therefore some way that is easy and general, so that all who wish by it to worship you may either be joined to you in perfect love or else, bound "in human frailty,"[34] may

27. Jb 28.18.   28. Prv 2.4.
29. Jb 28.13.   30. Mt 10.22.
31. Mt 15.27.   32. Is 10.10.
33. Gn 27.38.
34. From the Dominican Breviary's form of general absolution for religious.

be rescued from it, or else, after they have been duly cleansed
by the fires of purgatory, they may merit to share in its blessings. In this matter, do not offer universal proofs, as you are
accustomed, but descend to single and particular cases, and
proffer what is easy and common, "as if a nurse should offer
milk, and not solid food, to her children."[35] For there are some
who are powerless and simple, who have learned these things
in a sweeter way, and have more easily been filled with them.

(9) Wisdom: Since I have stated in the gospel my promise to
be with the faithful "even to the consummation of the world,"[36]
and that I shall never under any circumstances wish to desert
Peter's little bark, however storm-tossed it may be, so through
the different ages I have destined workmen for cultivating my
vineyard, and I have bestowed on it the remedies for eternal
salvation, and what I have bestowed I have not neglected often
to renew. And, too, from the beginning I have poured myself
"into holy souls throughout nations, and I make friends of
God and prophets."[37] And still I shall show you in this present
time certain works of pity and practices of my love, which I
often use, by which this marriage of eternal salvation can be
shared, in various ways, by many men of different ranks and
states. And at the same time I shall demonstrate how my love
always has the power of being renewed, and, furthermore, to
this I shall add that those who will become devout imitators
of that Wisdom's teaching, which is founded "upon the firm
rock"[38] of Catholic and apostolic truth will be forever heirs in
Christ Jesus of that blessing which was promised through "the
seed of the faithful Abraham."[39]

(10) Therefore whoever desires to become a lovable disciple of Eternal Wisdom, whatever may be his condition or state
or sex or order or even his religious life, he should diligently
observe these matters which follow, which are so moderated
that they need not bring with them any difficulty, and everyone should be able to carry them out with no prejudice to his
profession and state of life. Then, too, divine Wisdom does not

35. 1 Thes 2.7; Heb 5.12.   36. Mt 28.20.
37. Wis 7.27.
38. From the Dominican Breviary's office for the dedication of a church.
39. Gn 22.18.

intend through these to lay down any obligation or religious profession or any sort of restriction, but only a lively reawakening of a devotion that is drowsing, in which anyone who may wish to exercise himself so will act well and praiseworthily; yet, whoever does not do so, he will not on that account sin or be wanting.

(11) So, before everything else, any disciple of Wisdom must abandon carnal love, if he has any, and choose that great and eternal divine Wisdom "for his spouse"[40] and his beloved. And if perhaps anyone were still so tied by some private love that he were to consider that to force himself suddenly to do this would be too bitter and hard, at least let him form the good intention of setting himself free from this harmful love when he feels that the proper occasion to do this with divine help has come.

(12) But those who are not bound by earthly loves, but still have until now been in other ways idle and tepid and negligent in Wisdom's love, ought as it were a second time to espouse this spiritual bride, and to renew themselves in her love with a devout plighting of their affection. We say that this ought to be done so that they may now give themselves pains in pleasing Wisdom, clinging as to their sweetest bride, with an intense and spiritual love, whom before they used to serve, with fear, as a master. Let them always think of this most divine spouse's excellence and of her pity and how blessed they are who will merit in this life to be adorned by her friendship. And this betrothal, or the renewal of a former betrothal, ought to be made so that a more fervent devotion may be awakened, not only within, in the soul, but also without, even though secretly, by some sign, say by making three prostrations in giving oneself to such a bride, offering and showing oneself to her, and asking for a betrothal gift, such as some new grace as a sign of a love and fidelity which are shared, which "neither life nor death nor any creature"[41] ought ever to violate.

(13) And since for the most part deeds achieve more than words, I shall tell you of one very noteworthy and strange

40. Wis 8.2.   41. Rom 8.38–39.

event, which achieved a great deal with regard to what we are discussing. There was a certain youth, a fervent lover, who, when he had renounced earthly loves, chose for his mistress this heavenly spouse who is divine Wisdom. Greatly longing to enfold his beloved more in the depths of his heart, he sought out a secret place, and impelled by the amazing vehemence of his love, he stripped the upper part of his body, and taking a sharp knife, he stabbed the bare flesh above his heart where he could see the vital pulse throbbing most strongly, piercing himself so forcefully that every stab was followed by a flow of blood that ran from his chest and dripped down drop by drop. And he stabbed himself so often and so mercilessly here and there that finally in this way he had cut the famous name of his spouse, which is "IHC," in great capital letters over "the extent of his heart."[42] And when for a while he had carried these recent and bleeding wounds of love, so very sweet to him, in his discolored flesh with a great fire of love, in the end, after many days, they healed, and his flesh perfectly preserved that name, letter by letter, in that place.

(14) So afterwards, when this lover of God saw any earthly lover carrying his beloved's worthless name on his worldly attire, as some are accustomed to do, he used also to see, turning in the depths of his heart to his divine spouse, and remembering the prerogatives, incomparably great, of his own love, that he too bore his love's name, "not in tables of stone" or on embroidered garments, or written in red ink or in black, "but in the fleshly tables of the heart"[43] and in letters of blood, forming a chaplet of blooming scarlet flowers; and he rejoiced to wear upon his heart what could not be effaced.

(15) As he felt the saving fruits of divine love growing so remarkable, because he was constantly admonished to recollect so great a name, and because he desired that other devout men should increase in that divine love, he persuaded them to have greater devotion to this name. Not, indeed, that they should do as he had done, and so rashly expose themselves to dangers, or in any way imitate what he had been granted, by

42. 3 Kgs 4.29.   43. 2 Cor 3.3.

a gift which was only for him to acquire by a strength that came from God. But he counseled them that they should always carry that saving name upon them, formed or written out somehow, secretly, to be sure, and concealed, either in some garment or in some other fashion, as they pleased, so as to arouse their love for God. For this was why this youth Amandus had performed this act which we have recounted, that whenever he chanced to see that name where it was known only to him and to God, he would at once recall again his first love, which would be as it were renewed in his heart.

(16) So far as the intention of this act is concerned, we read something like it about the high priest Simon, who, when he wished to renew the friendship, which seemed by then long-standing, which his brother Judas Machabeus had formerly established with the Romans, sent there "a shield of gold" as a token, and revived their old friendship.[44] And in the same way the Lord himself put "a bow in the clouds as the sign of a covenant"[45] for men. And so too the sons of Israel, when a covenant had been made with the Lord, "poured out water,"[46] and set up some visible marks, either building altars or erecting stones, so that by outward signs fallible human memory might be helped. And under the New Law, many saints in the times before ours made various representations to stir up their devotion; some used to have with them images or crosses, others carried about relics or that kind of thing, as we read, for the same reason. So let anyone who may have received the grace do what has been said for the name of Jesus, because the human spirit too easily forgets what it has undertaken, unless it is often renewed in its undertakings.

(17) And Eternal Wisdom's devout worshippers and disciples who wish to do so can daily recite the hours that are copied after this, as a little way to that Wisdom. But those who cannot read, or have other proper occupations, or, it may be, those who wish to vary these hours, may say in their place seven Our Fathers for the seven customary hours, one Our Father

44. 1 Mc 14.24.   45. Gn 9.13.
46. 1 Kgs 7.6.

for each hour. And in these hours their intention ought to be that divine Wisdom may guard their hearts and bodies, lest they be completely ensnared by this most foolish world, and, in these days, by vanities and wickednesses, but that by proceeding carefully and wisely they may be preserved from all evils and dangers.

(18) Then at table after the blessing, before they begin to eat, let them say one Our Father in spiritual almsgiving to those souls in purgatory who most have need, remembering how dangerous it would be for them to eat at no cost to themselves from the alms of their benefactors, and not to serve them faithfully by their continual intercessions, and what a work of charity it can be to help those who in no way can help themselves, and how too they would rejoice if they were in such misery, to receive one little drop, or a "crumb which falls from the table of their masters" as some refreshment.

(19) And so that this exercise of piety may be made more pleasing and persuasive for devout minds, they should know that there was once a pious member of an established religious order who had undertaken the old practice of reciting with others these prayers for the intentions that we have described, and she had always a great zeal to say the *De profundis*[47] for desolate souls, and there appeared to her in a vision many souls which had been sent to places of purgation, which showed by their wretched attire and their unhappy demeanor that they were entreating the help of her petitions. Yet among these souls there was one in particular that came to this religious and, weeping, implored her to allow it to be her beggar, to whom each day at table she would give an alms of one *De Profundis*. And because of this vision, she afterwards used to perform this deed of spiritual almsgiving the more fervently.

(20) Then say one Our Father to the sweetest and saving name of Eternal Wisdom, which is "Jesus," that our Lord and Savior may save all these disciples of Eternal Wisdom and holy Mother Church, and may guard them from all adversities, and

47. Ps 129, "Out of the depths I have cried to you," since ancient times recited for the repose of departed souls.

may defend them from the snares of all their enemies. And these words may well be said in reverence for that great name, either before or after the Our Father: Blessed be the name of our Lord and God, Jesus Christ, and of his mother the glorious Virgin Mary, for all eternity and thereafter. Amen. And for this indulgences are granted. The reason for this prayer to the holy name is that this sweet Jesus, who in these last days, alas, has been banished and put out from the hearts of many who should have a burning devotion to him, and has been driven out to their condemnation, because they are without number, those who "seek the things that are their own, and not the things that are Jesus Christ's,"[48] should, I say, have his name, flowing with honey, in some way brought again to life and instilled and renewed in the hearts of the faithful, in this exercise of piety which I have described be performed. And divine Wisdom herself has appeared in visions to some, complaining in mournful voice of how Jesus has been driven from the hearts of those who once loved him.

(21) Then on the first day laid down by the Church for the reading of Wisdom's books,[49] that is, the first Sunday in the month of August, and before the vigil of the Nativity, when the antiphon *O Sapientia*[50] begins the antiphons of the days following, until that glorious night when Eternal Wisdom, to be born of the Father, deigned to enter into this world, let some special commemoration of Wisdom be made in our private prayers, either with an antiphon or collect or the Our Father. And if anyone were to celebrate a private votive Mass of Eternal Wisdom at times when he might have a free intention, Wisdom would welcome it.

(22) Then for Wisdom's disciples and lovers there are three

---

48. Phil 2.21.

49. In the breviaries of Suso's time, the reading of the "sapiential books," Proverbs, Ecclesiastes, Wisdom and Eclesiasticus, began on the first Sunday in August.

50. "O Wisdom, who proceeded from the mouth of the most high, reaching from one end of the universe to the other, mightily and sweetly ordering all things, come to teach us the way of prudence," the first of the "O antiphons," sung before and after the *Magnificat* at Vespers on December 17–23.

other days in the year that they ought specially to observe, so
that on each of the three they perform some special service
for this spiritual spouse. The first day is the feast of the Circumcision of the Lord,[51] for on this day the year begins, and according to the ancient custom of some territories it is on this day
that those who are joined in close ties of friendship give one
another gifts and wishes for a good year. And so let every devout disciple and lover of Wisdom visit his one dearest divine
spouse on this day, to reawaken his sleeping soul to the love
of God, and, in place of gifts, faithfully entreat for himself and
all his fellow disciples and for holy Mother Church a good
year, making some special prayer, or even, if this is suitable,
offering or commissioning a lighted candle in honor of that
Wisdom who is everlasting Light, at the altar or before the
crucifix, as a sign that in these unstable times a faithful disciple
recognizes and wants all his well-being to come from his divine
spouse alone, and that only her love should burn and give
light in his heart. And let him ask that if perhaps at any time
his love for her is extinguished, it may mercifully be rekindled,
and may for the future never go out.

(23) The second day is Quinquagesima Sunday,[52] which day
is called by many "Carnival";[53] and it is everywhere observed
by the stupid lovers of this world with celebrations and is spent
in the emptiest follies, and friends and companions are accustomed to meet and amuse one another with worldly games
and trifles. Therefore as a sign that the most divine spouse
should be her disciple's all in all, source of his joy and solace
and love, in this world and in the next, let him, to exercise the
devotion of his tepid heart, do as we have said before.

(24) And the third is the first day of the month of May,
when spring's serenity, welcome and desirable to all, begins
to show its beauty in the earth's vegetation. It is then the custom, and especially in the Swabian districts of Germany, that
youths go out by night to the woods and cut down lovely

51. January 1, the ancient Roman date, observed in parts of medieval
Europe, for reckoning the beginning of the year.
52. That is, the Sunday before Ash Wednesday.
53. *carnis privium,* "taking flesh meat away."

branches of green leaves, and put them, embellished with flowers, outside the doors where girls live who, they think, love them, as a sign of their love and fidelity. So, therefore, that a holy devotion may be produced from a bad beginning, let the services that they uselessly pay to human beings be devoutly rendered by Wisdom's servants to the Creator of all things; let them follow what they know the Church does on the first day of August, and with the greater zeal, since there is no doubt that this most divine friend exceeds all mortals in grace. So let them offer on that day to their dearest spouse some light to incite their devotion, or let them say some devout prayer to commend themselves with greater love to her.

(25) For that mother of the high King should be honored by Eternal Wisdom's disciples with all the love of their hearts, she who wishes to take them to herself as the special sons of her own Son, and to care for them with a mother's love. So every devoted disciple of Wisdom should honor her each day with the Hail Mary nine times repeated. Let him say one on bent knees first thing in the morning when he rises from his bed, devoutly offering into the hands of the Queen of Heaven every good work that he must perform during that day, asking that when so venerable and dear a mother presents them to her Son, the high King, they may be welcome and accepted in reverence for such a mediatress, though perhaps they might be petty and mean and little welcomed if they were to be given directly by a sinner's hands. And let him do so at night, after all his prayers have been said, immediately before he goes to bed. That he may sleep the more safely, let him ask from her that whatever he may have fallen short in during that day may be made good through her, that whatever has been ill done may be lovingly forgiven through her, and that what was well done may be through her preserved and accepted.

(26) Then let them say seven Hail Marys to the sweetest heart of the Mother of God, to the most loving refuge of all sinners, that she, that gentlest resting place of Eternal Wisdom, the most overflowing treasury of all "the mercies of the Lord,"[54] may mercifully open it and incline towards all the

54. Is 63.7.

disciples of this Wisdom, her Son, when their spirits will take their last departure, and that she may then deign lovingly to defend them and escort them to the mansions in the sky.

(27) Then, finally, let those who are priests say a Mass once a year on the weekday immediately following All Souls Day for those who are dead who have a share in their prayers, and for their dear friends, and let those who are not priests either offer a Mass or say a hundred Our Fathers; and to these prayers let them devoutly add this entreaty, that our God and Lord through his Eternal Wisdom may mercifully come to the help of his Church, so long in tribulation, and bring it into peace and tranquillity.

(28) So, to recapitulate more briefly what has been said, you should know that the lovers or worshipers of Eternal Wisdom ought to flee, as we have told, carnal or worldly love, which is the occasion of many evils, and to accept Eternal Wisdom as their spiritual bride, or, if they have already contracted that marriage, renew it with a fresh kindling of love; and, to stir up their greater devotion, they should make three prostrations in a secret place of prayer when first every day they offer themselves to this. Then they may do what follows: that is, each day they may say seven Our Fathers for the seven hours of Wisdom, one Our Father for each hour. Then at table before they begin to eat, let them say one Our Father as a spiritual alms to those souls in the greatest need in purgatory. Let them say one Our Father to the sweetest name of Jesus against every evil and misfortune of mind and body, prefacing or adding these words: Blessed be the name of our Lord and God, Jesus Christ, and of the glorious Virgin Mary his mother, for all eternity and thereafter; and that will make in all nine Our Fathers. And those who have the grace may carry secretly on their person the name of Jesus for an increase and sign of divine love. But those who are able to read ought for greater devotion to say the sequence of prayers to Wisdom and to intersperse them with seven Our Fathers, as has already been said. Then let them say one Hail Mary to the blessed Virgin when they first rise, that she may present to God all the good deeds they perform in that day; and in the evening, after all their prayers, one Hail Mary, when, that is, they are preparing

for bed, that she may reconcile them with God for the evils committed by them. Then seven Hail Marys to her most merciful heart, that she may be a helper to all their fellow disciples in the hour of death; and so too this will make nine Hail Marys. Then on the first Sunday in August, when the sapiential books begin to be read, and before the Nativity of the Lord, when the solemn antiphons, *O Sapientia* and the others, begin to be sung, they ought to make some prayer or recollection of Wisdom at their choice. Then on the feast of the Circumcision and on Quinquagesima Sunday and on the first day of May, they ought to make some special observance, saying a prayer or offering a lighted candle or commissioning one, those who can do so. And then on the first weekday after All Souls Day they should celebrate or offer Mass for all the dead disciples of Eternal Wisdom and for their dear ones, or say one hundred Our Fathers, as then will be best fitting to each man's station in life.

(29) But if there be some so weak or infirm or committed to their lawful occupations that for a time they are hindered from doing what we have said, or if they be so hardhearted and wordly-minded that through their indifference they do not know how to fulfill what has been described, let them say nine Our Fathers with as many Hail Marys, and let them make the petitions we have said; and if they do with an implicit intention what others do explicitly, that will be sufficient. But if there are some who wish to change these Hail Marys for the same number of "Hail Holy Queens," and the Our Father that is said before meals for the repose of souls into the psalm *De Profundis*, they may well do this to the honor of Eternal Wisdom, who is blessed to all eternity.

(30) So that we may for a moment return to what has been discussed, it is good to consider, divine Wisdom says, that this most profitable teaching of mine, presented indeed in simple words and yet truly producing every strengthening spiritual fruit, ought to be accepted by you with special devotion. For as you perceive it and can experience it, that teaching will kindle your devotion's fervor, your worship of God will grow, your neighbor will be profitably strengthened; and, too, loving

help will be given to the souls dwelling in places of cleansing, and to no one who has given this way of devotion a fair trial can it be displeasing, unless perhaps to envious detractors or impious faultfinders whose minds are blinded and whose hearts are hardened. Therefore, when the proper procedure of love has been observed, and when you draw from it your first draft of devotion, in so doing you will provide for the health of the souls of your neighbors.

CHAPTER 8

The Manifold Fruits of the Divine Blessing
That Wisdom's Disciples Merit to Receive
Through Their Marriage to Her

"HEN THE DAWN shall bring an end,"[1] and this joyous season, with its prayers of gladness and its festivals of praise, reached its conclusion in the happy words spoken by that sweetest and divine spouse, then, O, then was the Disciple, who for a while had rested in the visions of his God, called to toilsome outward works, and urged by obedience's goad to interrupt the sleep of this most peaceful contemplation and inward sweetness. Turned altogether towards his beloved, dissolved in tears of love, falling upon her with holy kisses, his soul from the depths of his heart said farewell to her whom he loved, and repeatedly enfolding her, his spiritual bride, in his love's arms with all affection, he suffered for some half hour, and with a weeping voice he uttered sorrowful words of leave-taking, as he said: "Now indeed is my talk addressed to you, O love of my heart of hearts, to whom alone I have given the whole of myself, longing for this to be perpetuated for all ages. I give you thanks, my beloved, for these and the other innumerable benefits presented to me from your grace alone. May praise and glory be yours forever.[2]

(2) "I entreat you with all my heart's burning desire 'by the bowels of your mercies'[3] and by the power of your scarlet blood, which you poured out abundantly in your Passion for the redemption of the human race, that all those who may have determined to wed you, Eternal Wisdom, in the way that

1. From the Dominican Breviary's office for the feast of St. Cecilia.
2. From the Dominican Breviary's antiphon to the *Magnificat* on the feast of the Most Holy Trinity.
3. Ps 24.6; Col 3.12.

has been told, and who may have wished to worship you through the devout recitation of these prayers, or who may have labored to make them known to the faithful, that you may bless all of them, I say, with your saving blessing, 'my King and my God.'[4] For you are also that 'blessed fruit'[5] long ago promised to the world, and in this you are singularly privileged, that 'whoever you will bless may himself be blessed.'[6]

(3) "Therefore, my Father, bless these children, who are your lovers and your disciples, with the blessing of all the patriarchs and of every one of your elect who have been pleasing to you from the beginning, that in the end they may be gathered with joy to their happy number. May your lovable and glorious name, I pray, be invoked upon them, that it may be for them saving protection in all the different dangers of the life of this world. May your Eternal Wisdom direct them in what they must do, may the angel of peace keep them, and may health and prosperity of soul and body smile upon them.

(4) "Give them, Lord, 'a place of penitence,'[7] that through true contrition and pure confession and perfect satisfaction they may be turned before their death to you, their Creator, and may be fully reconciled to you, and, too, that by receiving your most sacred body as food for the journey they may be defended as they labor in their last agony, so that they may in no way be seized by 'sudden and unforeseen and unprepared death.'[8]

(5) "Grant them, Lord, this grace 'because of your name,'[9] so that as they now serve you through these devout offices, so in the last hour as they breathe out their life, they may be blessed by you, and by your sweetest mother, whom I call 'mother of mercy,'[10] they may be led to the glorious kingdoms where in their celestial fatherland that holy 'troop of blessed spirits'[11] may be made joyful with 'the plenteous wine of God's

---

4. Ps 43.5.   5. Lk 1.41.
6. Nm 22.6.   7. Jb 24.23.
8. From a petition in the Litany of the Saints.
9. Ps 24.11.   10. From the *Salve Regina*.
11. From the hymn *Christe, redemptor omnium*.

house,'[12] after their exile in this present wretchedness, looking upon you, 'the King of glory and the Lord of power in his beauty,'[13] Jesus Christ, our Lord, who with the Father and the Holy Spirit lives and reigns, world without end. Amen."

Here ends *Wisdom's Watch upon the Hours,* by
Friar Amandus of the Order of Preachers and of the
convent at Constance.

12. Ps 35.9.   13. Ps 23.10; Is 33.17.

INDICES

GENERAL INDEX

Numbers refer to page and note in the *Watch*.

INDEX OF SACRED SCRIPTURE

Books of the Old Testament

Books of the New Testament